ART QUILTS:
A Celebration

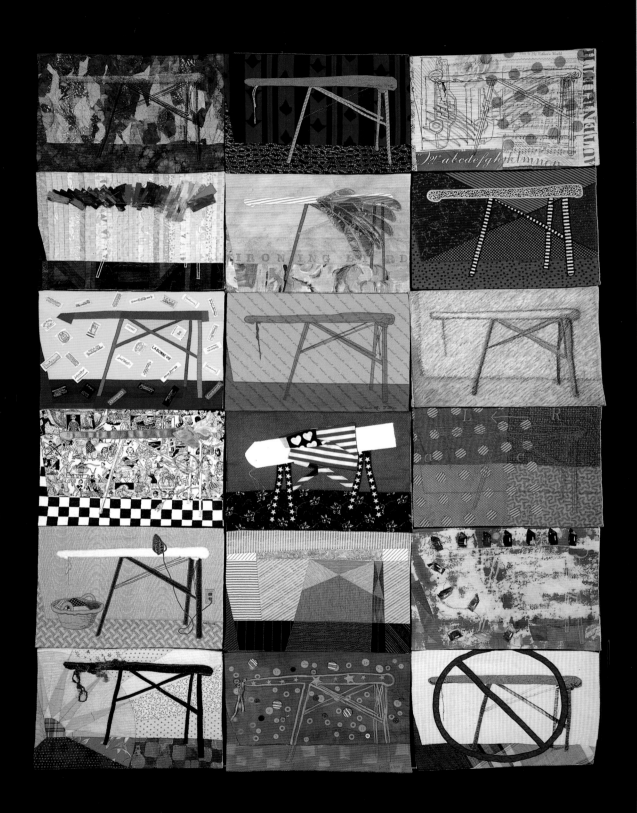

ART QUILTS:
A Celebration

400 Stunning Contemporary Designs

Introduction by Robert Shaw

LARK
BOOKS

A Division of Sterling Publishing Co., Inc.
New York

EDITORS
Nathalie Mornu, Dawn Cusick, Katherine Duncan Aimone

QUILT NATIONAL PROJECT DIRECTOR
Hilary Morrow Fletcher

ART DIRECTOR
Chris Bryant

PRINCIPAL PHOTOGRAPHER
Brian Blauser

COVER DESIGNER
Barbara Zaretsky

ASSOCIATE ART DIRECTOR
Shannon Yokeley

EDITORIAL ASSISTANCE
Delores Gosnell, Paige Gilchrist, Jeff Hamilton

EDITORIAL INTERNS
Kelly J. Johnson, Metta L. Pry

ART INTERNS
Brad Armstrong, Christopher Dollar, Bradley Norris

COVER: **Janet Steadman**, *I Love a Mystery*
BACK COVER, BACKGROUND: **Eleanor A. McCain,** *Colorstudy 2*
BACK COVER, LEFT: **Dianne Firth,** *One Hundred Stones*
BACK COVER, TOP RIGHT: **Paula Nadelstern,** *Kaleidoscopic XIII: Random Acts of Color*
BACK COVER, BOTTOM RIGHT: **Jane A. Sassaman,** *Overgrown Garden*
FRONT FLAP: **Pat Sims,** *Back Yard: The Flats— Lowest Low Water*
PAGE 2: **New Image,** *Never Done*
PAGE 3: **Paula Nadelstern,** *Kaleidoscopic XIII: Random Acts of Color*
PAGE 5: **Therese May,** *Contemplating the Nine Patch*

ADDITIONAL PHOTOGRAPHY PROVIDED BY:
Bill Bachhuber (page 244), Gene Balzer (page 430), David Belda (pages 230, 391, and 466), Karen Bell (pages 151, 284, 389, 442, and 489), David Caras (pages 173, 222, 355, and 373), Kyoung Ae Cho (page 422), D. James Dee (page 415), James Dewrance (page 454), DTT Studio (page 353), Nancy N. Erickson (page 498), Caryl Bryer Fallert (page 314), J. Kevin Fitzsimmons (page 351), Gregory Gantner (page 484), Larry Gawel (page 445), Gerhard Heidersberger (page 296), Hester and Hardaway Photographers (page 352), Roland Hueber (page 268), Image Inn (page 213), Bruno Jarret (page 425), Peter Jenion (pages 270 and 356), Luke Jordan (page 310), Eric Kievit (page 456), David Loveall Photography, Inc. (page 396), Pam Monfort (pages 183, 186 [detail], 253, 304, and 397), John Bonath @ Moondog Studios (page 369), Sam Newbury (pages 344 and 438), Geoffrey Nilsen (page 439), PRS Associates, Inc. (pages 392 and 485), Mark Gulezian/Quicksilver (pages 240, 457, and 474), Sharon Risedorph (pages 130, 191, 279, 443, and 446), Roger Sands (page 146), Ken Sanville (page 440), Anson Seale Photography (pages 216 and 336), William Taylor (page 187), Seth Tice-Lewis (pages 232 and 280), Ken Wagner (page 285), Anne Woringer (page 372), Jay Yocis (page 424), and Zohar Zaied (pages 277 and 386).

Quote on page 11 by Hilton Kramer, "Art: Quilts Find a Place at the Whitney," *New York Times*, July 3, 1971.

Library of Congress Cataloging-in-Publication Data

Art quilts : a celebration : 400 stunning contemporary designs / introduction by Robert Shaw.– 1st ed.
      p. cm.
   Compilation of quilts from the biannual Quilt National exhibitions of 1995-2003.
   Includes index.
   ISBN 1-57990-711-3 (pbk.)
   1. Art quilts–United States–History–20th century–Exhibitions. 2. Quilt National.
I. Quilt National.
NK9112.A725 2005
746.46 ' 0973 ' 07477197–dc22

2005006038

10 9 8 7 6 5 4 3 2 1

First Edition

Published by Lark Books,
A Division of Sterling Publishing Co., Inc.
387 Park Avenue South, New York, N.Y. 10016

This book is composed of the following titles,
published by Lark Books, a division of Sterling Publishing Co., Inc.:
Quilt National: Contemporary Designs in Fabric © 1995 Altamont Press
Contemporary Quilts: Quilt National, 1997 © 1997 Lark Books
Quilt National 1999: The Best in Contemporary Quilts © 1999 Lark Books
The Best Contemporary Quilts: Quilt National 2001 © 2001 Lark Books
Quilt National 2003: The Best of Contemporary Quilts © 2003 Lark Books

© 2005, Lark Books

Distributed in Canada by Sterling Publishing,
c/o Canadian Manda Group, 165 Dufferin Street
Toronto, Ontario, Canada M6K 3H6

Distributed in the U.K. by Guild of Master Craftsman Publications Ltd.,
Castle Place, 166 High Street, Lewes, East Sussex, England BN7 1XU

Tel: (+ 44) 1273 477374, Fax: (+ 44) 1273 478606, e-mail: pubs@thegmcgroup.com,
Web: www.gmcpublications.com

Distributed in Australia by Capricorn Link (Australia) Pty Ltd.,
P.O. Box 704, Windsor, NSW 2756 Australia

If you have questions or comments about this book, please contact:
Lark Books, 67 Broadway, Asheville, NC 28801 • Telephone: (828) 253-0467

Manufactured in China

ISBN 1-57990-711-3

For information about custom editions, special sales, premium and corporate purchases, please contact Sterling Special Sales Department at 800-805-5489 or specialsales@sterlingpub.com.

CONTENTS

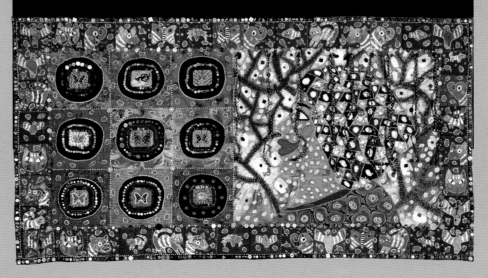

FOREWORD

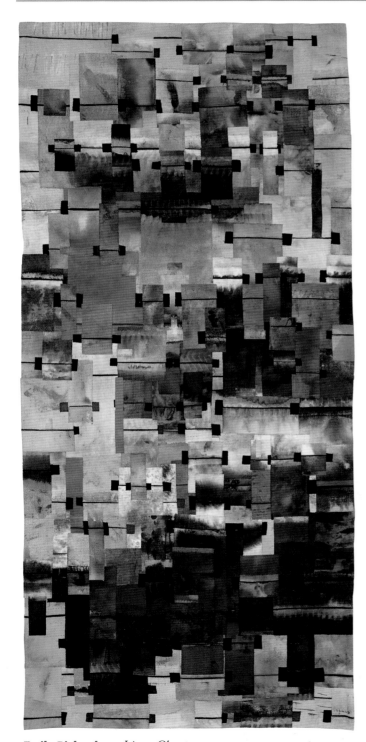

Emily Richardson, *Linen Closet*. See page 168.

It all began in 1978. Fiber artist Nancy Crow was asked to teach a quilting class at an embryonic cultural arts center in rural, southeastern Ohio. Knowing that she was one of many artists whose work was unwelcome at existing quilt shows, Nancy instead proposed an exhibition of maverick or contemporary quilts. Less than a year later, and with the help of a corps of dedicated volunteers, Quilt National made its debut in Athens, Ohio, at the Dairy Barn Cultural Arts Center. The gallery—a 64-year-old, 7,000-square-foot abandoned barn that had recently been saved from the wrecking ball—had trenches in the concrete floor, metal stanchions, bare windows, and zillions of flies!

Almost 200 artists submitted work for the jurors' consideration. Most of the 56 selected pieces featured the same materials and techniques found in classic bed covers, but the designs were unfamiliar. There were also examples of surface design techniques and use of nontraditional materials that are now common-place. Visitors to that first Quilt National were surprised, and even outraged, that the objects were called quilts. They were obviously not made for beds.

Although they were breaking sacred rules, the artists were doing exactly what had been done for generations: using available materials and techniques to create unique objects that expressed something about them-selves and their world. The pioneers of the art quilt movement may not have known what a quilt should be, but they certainly knew what a quilt could be.

Quilt National's numbers tell a story of significant growth and increasing reputation. Twenty-five years later, however, those who make and appreciate innovative quilts are like a pebble on a beach: largely invisible. Fortunately the pebble's visibility is enhanced when, after being dropped into the water, it causes a series of expanding ripples that touch countless numbers of lives.

Serious fiber artists are, of course, Quilt National's *raison d'être*. They perceive the show as an oasis of acceptance and encouragement in the vastness of the quilt world. Since it began, the number of entrants has more than tripled; almost 20 percent come from foreign countries, most notably Australia, Canada, Germany, and Japan. In recent years, jurors have had a target of 80 to 85 quilts, to allow the display of each at maximum advantage in the available space. As a result, due to the mounting number of entries, as few as seven percent of submissions get selected. Almost half of the works in recent shows are by first-time exhibitors, many of whom cite earlier Quilt National exhibitions as the impetus for their creative explorations of the medium. The artists benefit further from the fact that there are now more exhibit opportunities through other competitions that appear to follow the Quilt National model.

The broader quilting industry has also been affected by Quilt National. Exposure to exhibition pieces stimulated a demand for dozens of previously unavailable products. These serve the needs of serious artists as well as hobbyists primarily interested in making classic (and often functional) quilts that reflect their preferences and visions.

Although art quilts have yet to achieve full acceptance as fine art, more and more of them are finding their way into corporate and private collections. In the past, wonderful heritage quilts were lost because people failed to recognize the aesthetic strength of functional objects created by people who never thought of themselves as artists. I would like to think that collections of modern quilts, and the work of the art quilt movement's trailblazers, will eventually be housed in museums where they will be protected, preserved, and available to enrich the lives of future generations.

Without doubt, visitors who have neither a quilt-making history nor an expectation of ever picking up a needle are the largest group affected by Quilt National. Exhibitions at the Dairy Barn, and at dozens of venues in 31 states that host the Quilt National touring collections, have drawn a loyal and growing audience. The vast majority of visitors understand that these are quilts by structure rather than by function. They have learned to appreciate the works for what they are. They no longer criticize apples because they aren't oranges.

The art quilt is the evolutionary cousin of the classic quilted bed cover. Its emergence coincided with a resurgence of interest in quilting. Without the curiosity, courage, and confidence of the pioneers of the art quilt movement, the quilt might have become a cultural relic. Instead, both classic and innovative quilts continue to thrive as quilt makers influence and inspire one another.

While technology such as computers and the Internet have fostered significant changes in Quilt National's administrative procedures, the focus of the exhibitions remains the same—to support the innovative quilt maker and to serve as a showcase for the best work being created in the medium of layered and stitched fabric by artists from around the world.

■ *Hilary Morrow Fletcher*
QUILT NATIONAL PROJECT DIRECTOR

Contemporary Quilts:
AN INTRODUCTION *by* ROBERT SHAW

Since 1981, the Quilt National exhibit has been photographed and shared with the public through biennial publications. This compendium of five of the most recent books coproduced by Lark Books and the Dairy Barn offers a broad picture of changes, trends, and accomplishments in the world of contemporary quilts over the course of nearly a decade, 1995 to 2003.

The quilts chosen for Quilt National's exhibitions are not traditional bedcovers, but are instead intended by their creators to be hung like paintings and viewed as works of visual art. Presented flat on the page, relatively few of the works are obviously quilts; indeed, in their formats and subject matter, the majority seem to more closely resemble modern art. Many show a painterly focus on a single overall image rather than the modular approach of the traditional quilt maker. Leafing through these pages, one finds portraits, landscapes, and still-lifes, as well as completely abstract works, complex conceptual pieces, political and personal statements, and exercises in pattern and color. But although their ties with tradition may sometimes seem tenuous, these quilts grew from a long and rich historical background, and there are actually many points of connection between them and their ancestors.

Roots in Tradition

Quilts have been a part of American life for more than 200 years. Quilted bedcovers were made in Europe as early as the 1500s, and settlers from the British Isles and other European countries brought the craft of quilt making to America. However, because quality fabric was imported and expensive, quilt making remained largely a pursuit of upper class women until the American textile industry began to produce affordable cotton fabrics in the 1840s.

With the explosion of choice provided by the burgeoning mills, American women began to make quilts in earnest. Contrary to romantic myths about the frugal use of scraps, most 19th-century quilt makers chose fabric specifically for their quilts, as is the case today. And while today's quilts may look quite different from traditional work, they usually share the same basic construction structures as their ancestors.

Quilts are traditionally made from three layers of material, with a soft filling or batting sandwiched between top and backing layers, the whole joined together with hand or machine stitching. Whatever their visual content, quilts can still be divided into three basic types defined by the construction of their top layer—whole cloth, pieced, and appliqué. As its name implies, the top of a whole cloth quilt is a single piece of material. Linda R. MacDonald's *Town News* and Deborah Fell's *Painted Squares* are examples of contemporary whole cloth work. The top of a pieced quilt, such as Ruth Garrison's *Overlay 4* or Nancy Crow's *Construc-*

Jane A. Sassaman, *Seeds and Blossoms.* See page 262.

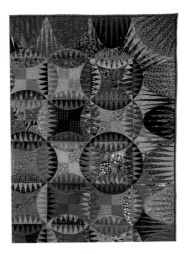

tions #17, is made by assembling and sewing together a number of pieces of fabric to create a new whole. And the top of an appliqué quilt, like Miriam Nathan-Roberts's *Spin Cycle* or Jane A. Sassaman's *Seeds and Blossoms*, is made by sewing pieces of fabric onto a whole cloth or pieced background.

Pieced works are the most familiar and iconic of American quilts. They were traditionally organized in sets of small repeating blocks, that could be worked individually and then assembled into the finished quilt. Nineteenth-century women devised hundreds of geometric patterns that were given evocative names like Log Cabin, Robbing Peter to Pay Paul, Drunkard's Path, and Bear Paw. The patterns were drawn and passed from hand to hand, and also shared in newspapers and popular ladies' magazines of the time. (Quilting magazines such as *Quilter's Newsletter Magazine* and *Better Homes and Gardens American Patchwork and Quilting* continue the latter tradition today.)

Because so many personal variations are possible on the basic themes provided by pieced patterns, many remain popular, and they continue to inspire and provide context for contemporary quilt makers. Karen K. Stone's dynamic *Indian Orange Peel*, which is based on two traditional patterns, is a prime example of how an imaginative contemporary quilt maker can pay direct homage to tradition while creating something personal and entirely new. There are also a number of post-modern Log Cabin quilts in this book—a few, including Amy Orr's *Twist Tied Log Cabin* and Jane Dunnewold's *Log Cabin for Hildegard von Bingen*, reference the pattern directly, while others like Liz Axford's *Within/Without 6* allude to it visually. John w. Lefelhocz takes an even more innovative approach to traditional work in his *Match Schticks*, a tongue-in-cheek commentary on marriage which appears to be a traditional Double Wedding Ring quilt until it is carefully examined. Up close, however, we realize that while the four-patch blocks that center the rings are made from pieces of fabric, the rings are actually constructed of matchsticks glued to bonded paper and nylon net!

CLOCKWISE FROM TOP LEFT: **Karen K. Stone,** *Indian Orange Peel* (see page 36); **Amy Orr,** *Twist Tied Log Cabin* (see page 375); **Jane Dunnewold,** *Log Cabin for Hildegard von Bingen* (see page 147); **Liz Axford,** *Within/Without 6* (see page 352). BELOW: **John w. Lefelhocz,** *Match Schticks* (see page 479).

Teresa Barkley, *Tea Will Make It Better.* See page 135.

Like studio quilts, crazy quilts broke with traditional geometric design modes. They were in effect textile collages, made up of irregularly sized pieces of fabric assembled into asymmetrical compositions. The pieces were edged and embellished with fancy embroidery stitches, and the quilts also often included such found household objects as beads, lace, silk commemorative ribbons, photographs printed on fabric, and even bits of family dresses and other clothing. All these additions helped to personalize the quilts, and many crazies can be read almost like diaries of the quilt maker and her loved ones.

A number of contemporary quilt artists, including Jane Burch Cochran, Pat Kroth, Terrie Hancock Mangat, Therese May, and the husband and wife team of Susan Shie and James Acord, have brought the crazy quilt into our times. Like their predecessors, they juxtapose seemingly unrelated techniques and objects in their quilts, and their work is often full of personal references. But they encrust the surfaces of their quilts with buttons, beads, and a host of other three-dimensional objects never imagined by Victorian quilt makers.

Whereas piecework designs are usually abstract, appliqué lends itself to a more decorative, pictorial approach. Appliqué quilts were often made for special occasions, such as a wedding, and many appliqués were reserved "for best," only to be brought out to dress a bed for company or a special family gathering. Although they could be organized in blocks like pieced quilts, some of the most interesting traditional appliqués offered a single image framed in a border. Teresa Barkley's *Tea Will Make It Better*, Erika Carter's *Perspective*, and Hiromi Hayashi's *Arabesque Plates* are examples of contemporary quilts that fit within this ongoing tradition.

The so-called crazy quilts of the late Victorian era are perhaps the most direct forerunners of today's studio quilts. Like them, crazies were intended for show, and most were not functional as bedcovers. Few crazy quilts included a batting, and many also incorporated dress silks and satins that were too fragile for daily use. They were often made in smaller sizes that would not fit a bed, but might be draped over a parlor table or sofa.

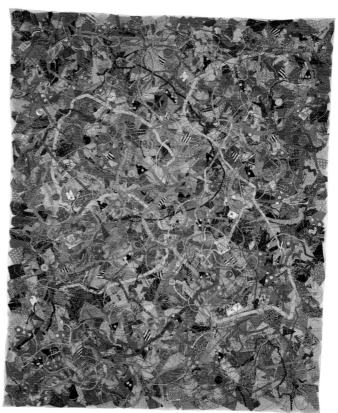

Pat Kroth, *Free For All.* See page 420.

Susan Shie and James Acord's quilts amount to a detailed ongoing journal of their lives and adventures, from their garden (*Rainbow Garden — A Green Quilt*) to their kitchen (the *Kitchen Tarot* series) and beyond. The autobiographical content of their imagery is furthered by Shie's spontaneous diary entries, which cover the quilts.

Where Shie and Acord's work is obsessively self-referential and literal, Therese May and Jane Burch Cochran prefer a more oblique approach. Cochran's *Life Line*, for example, suggests that we are what we wear; the piece depicts a country clothesline, hung with wash, that includes actual gloves and clothing. May's *Contemplating the Nine Patch* is equally allusive, with its nod to one of the most basic traditional patterns combined with the artist's trademark little creatures.

Susan Shie and James Acord, *Rainbow Garden—A Green Quilt.* See page 143.

Art Quilts Emerge

While quilts that can be considered works of art have been made throughout the course of quilt history, the involvement of academically trained artists with the medium is a relatively new phenomenon. What is now generally called the "art quilt" had its origins in the tumultuous social and cultural changes of the 1960s and '70s. During those years, quilts and other handcrafts, which had been overshadowed by machine-made products after World War II, were rediscovered by young people eager to find meaning outside the mainstream industrial culture. Pop artists like Claes Oldenburg and Robert Rauschenberg broke barriers against the use of fabric in their work (Rauschenberg's *Bed* even used a quilt as a canvas), and feminist artists like Miriam Schapiro raised consciousness about the value of what had previously been dismissed as "women's work." Feminist historians began to reveal and examine the unique stories that quilts could tell about the women who had made them, and sharp-eyed collectors, artists, and critics drew visual connections between modern art and the powerful abstract designs created by American women.

In 1971 the Whitney Museum of American Art's seminal exhibition Abstract Design in American Quilts introduced to a national audience the concept that quilts could be art. In his review in *The New York Times*, art critic Hilton Kramer summed up the exhibition's revolutionary thesis: "For a century or more preceding the self-conscious invention of pictorial abstraction in European painting, the anonymous quilt-makers of the American provinces created a remarkable succession of visual masterpieces that anticipated many of the forms that were later prized for their originality and courage."

Jonathan Holstein, who had collected the quilts with Gail van der Hoof, articulated what many artists realized as they looked at the show. In the exhibition catalog, Holstein wrote:

"Quilt makers did in effect paint with fabrics, laying on colors and textures. ...each maker had full liberty in terms of colors, arrangements, sizes of the blocks and her own variations. So no two are ever alike; each reflects the sensibilities and visual skills of its maker. Moreover, it must be emphasized that the planning of these tops was in no sense haphazard. Even the simplest show the highest degree of control for visual effect. There was at work a traditional American approach to design—vigorous, simple, reductive, 'flat'—and a bold use of color which can be traced throughout American art."

11

The Artists

Amid all these changes and revelations, a handful of adventurous, academically trained artists began making quilts, bringing art school techniques and design concepts to the traditional medium. They found that they could do things with fabric that they could not achieve with paint or other studio media, and many of them also valued the sense of connection with women of earlier times that working with quilts gave them.

Rhoda R. Cohen, *Attachments.* See page 206.

Joan Schulze speaks for many artist quilt makers when she says, "I love the idea of quilt. The layering, the fact that it can be reversible, that you can plug into this great and varied history of bed covering and with a little push you can enter a new world of walls, ceilings, or installations. It is the best of all worlds for me." Rhoda R. Cohen adds, "I started as a painter, having first studied in a variety of art disciplines such as drawing, watercolor, sculpture, color theory, and art history. But once [I was] introduced to quilt making with its reso-

nance, its intimacy, [and] its tacticity, I could not continue to paint as before. Fabric has taken the place of all other mediums for me."

A number of the artists represented in this book have been working in the quilt medium for decades. Therese May, for example, made her first quilts in the late 1960s, while she was studying painting at the University of Wisconsin. Nancy Crow, one of the founders of Quilt National, and Michael James, who is now a professor in the Department of Textiles, Clothing and Design at the University of Nebraska, have been perhaps the most prominent artists working in the quilt medium since the mid-1970s. In addition to Crow and James, Tafi Brown, Rhoda R. Cohen, Nancy Halpern (a juror in 1997), Debra Lunn, and Terrie Hancock Mangat all had quilts in the first Quilt National exhibition in 1979, and Teresa Barkley, Sylvia H. Einstein, Nancy N. Erickson, Judith Larzelere, Yvonne Porcella, and Joan Schulze are also among those who turned their talents to the quilt in that decade. Happily, all of these artists are still operating at the top of their game—most recently, in 2003, Erickson's powerful *Felis Forever (1)* took Best of Show, and James's computer-generated *A Strange Riddle* received the award for Most Innovative Use of the Medium.

As the bicentennial approached, Americans felt the urge to look back as well as forward, and interest in quilts and quilt making soared. However, as is still the case today, the vast majority of quilt makers followed traditional models. Even the pioneering quilt artists

Nancy N. Erickson,
Felis Forever (1). See page 498.

moved only slowly away from tradition. Michael James, who first realized that quilts could be art when he encountered the glowing pieced quilts of the Amish, is typical when he says, "My initial exploration of the medium revolved around the making of countless copies of traditional blocks as well as several small quilts in traditional patterns, and finally two large, traditional quilts."

But once they achieved mastery of the traditional techniques of quilt making, the early art quilt makers began pushing the envelope and incorporating their own ideas. James, for example, created a series of quilts with tricky curved seam pieces, and Nancy Crow made innovative use of strip-piecing techniques. Tafi Brown, who designed timber frame structures, printed cyanotype (blueprint) photographs of her buildings on fabric and built pieced compositions around the repeating designs, while biologist Nancy Erickson painted and appliquéd scenes based on her detailed sketches of animals. The air was full of experimentation and excitement as the new quilt artists shared their ideas with each other and taught their techniques to more traditionally oriented quilt makers willing to expand their horizons.

Nancy Crow, *January Study II,* 1979

Cotton fabric; strip pieced; 80 x 80 inches (203.2 x 203.2 cm). PHOTO BY CAROL BOBO AND JEAN ALEXANDER GREENWALD

Exhibitions and Outreach

By the end of the 1970s, a critical mass of artists had found its own voice as quilt makers and was starting to take off. But although a handful of museums organized exhibitions of nontraditional quilts in the 1970s, venues for the new quilts were few and far between. Increasingly, the work did not seem to fit within the boundaries of traditional quilt shows either. The growing community of quilt artists felt the need for a place of its own, and Quilt National was organized to provide it.

The first Quilt National was in effect an exhibition of quilt artists, by quilt artists, for quilt artists. Quilt makers Françoise Barnes and Virginia Randles worked with Nancy Crow in organizing the event, and Michael James joined Ohio University art professor Gary Schwindler and gallery owner Renee Seidel as the show's jurors.

For that inaugural show, 196 artists submitted 390 works, and 56 quilts by 43 artists were ultimately selected. The entire 1979 exhibition can be viewed online at www.quiltnational.com, and it is fascinating to compare the early quilts with recent work. In a flyer accompanying the show, Professor Schwindler described his impressions this way: "By its size and the breadth of its representation, Quilt National '79 has immediately assumed the status of a milestone in the history of American art quilting. Quilt National '79 demonstrates eloquently [that] quilting...is emerging as a vital category of the fiber arts and possesses enormous expressive potential. American quilt making is now at a stage of experimentation and development as it prepares to take its place as a major form of artistic endeavor."

As its organizers hoped, Quilt National became a regular forum for the work of quilt artists in the 1980s. Its biennial exhibitions served as a fulcrum around which the community of quilt artists grew and communicated, both with themselves and with an expanding audience. Fueled by the exposure provided by Quilt National and other exhibitions, interest in the new quilts continued to grow, and many new artists and techniques emerged. Quilt makers and other textile artists explored a host of new ways to combine and manipulate the materials they worked with; painting, photo transfer, screen printing, dyeing, embellishing, and many other surface design techniques all became accepted parts of the quilt artist's toolbox. The range of subject matter also exploded, as artists tackled political issues, psychology, personal and family relationships, and seemingly every other aspect of modern life. Ultimately, what began as a quiet American phenomenon ultimately spread around the world. Teaching artists like Nancy Crow, Michael James, Nancy Halpern, and Joan Schulze were invited to take their quilts and techniques to Canada, Europe, Australia, New Zealand, and Japan, and the art quilt movement took root wherever they traveled. Measured in numbers of participants at least, quilt making indeed became the major art form that Gary Schwindler foresaw, and with the numbers came an artistic and cultural diversity that shows no sign of abating.

Nancy Halpern, *Fitzgerald Rag,* 1995
Cottons and blends; machine pieced and hand quilted; 62 x 69 inches (157.5 x 175.3 cm).
PHOTO BY DAVID CARAS

Quilt Making Today

Quilt making of all kinds is enormously popular today;
an independent study conducted in 2003 revealed
there are nearly 20 million quilt makers in the United
States alone and that they spend more than $2 billion
annually on sewing machines, fabrics, thread, how-to
books, and other supplies. Most quilt makers remain
traditionalists. But while dedicated professional artists
represent just a tiny fraction of this vast grassroots
movement, they are taking full advantage of the myriad
choices available to modern quilt makers. In addition
to the panoply of fabrics and threads, the quilts found
in these pages also incorporate buttons, beads, oil and
acrylic paint, ink, colored pencils, fiber-reactive dyes,
gold leaf, photo transfers, and thin layers of wood, as
well as a plethora of found materials ranging from old
clothing, pot holders, dental floss (mint flavored),
candy wrappers, and pieces of string to bottle caps,
wooden spoons, sugar packets, paper clips, stamps,
iron-on stars, and burned birthday candles.

A number of quilt artists are designing fabric for the
approximately 90 manufacturers now making cloth
exclusively for use by quilt makers, and many artists
also began to create their own fabrics in the 1990s.
Hand dying has become an integral part of many
artists' work, because it in effect allows them to mix
their own palette of colors, just like a painter, rather
than having to search and choose among fabrics made
by others. Nancy Crow's *Color Blocks #41* and Susan
Webb Lee's *Red Threads* from the 1995 exhibition are
good examples of quilts made entirely from their
makers' own hand-dyed cloth.

Judith Content and Jan Myers-Newbury are among
artists who work with shibori, a traditional Japanese
method of tie-dying cloth, while others like Erika Carter
and Clare Plug use discharge bleaching techniques to
partially remove color and create unpredictable variegated surfaces. In shibori, fabric is wrapped around
poles and then immersed in dye. Because the dye
only reaches parts of the wrapped cloth, the results
are completely unpredictable. Both Content and
Myers-Newbury have learned to allow the pieces of
dyed fabric they choose to save to suggest directions
for their use. Myers-Newbury describes quilts like
The Trysting Tree, *Agape*, and *Ophelia's Dream* as "fabric
driven," and says that for her, "design has become a
process of finding relationships among fabrics."

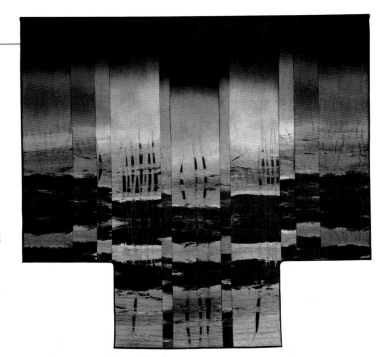

Judith Content, *Desert Pools.* See page 459.

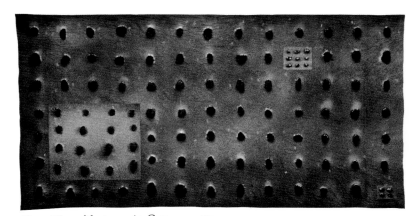

Clare Plug, *Nocturne in G.* See page 480.

Jan Myers-Newbury, *Ophelia's Dream.* See page 99.

Other artists paint their fabric. Emily Richardson, for example, paints silks, linens, and cottons with acrylic and textile paints, and layers the pieces into diaphanous compositions like *Cloud Forest* and *Full Fathom Five*. Elizabeth A. Busch also combines acrylics and textile paints but works on canvas to create bold painterly juxtapositions of color and pattern, like *Float* and *Abundance*. Other artists like Karen Perrine and Linda R. MacDonald paint pictorial images. Perrine paints with fiber-reactive Procion dye, which becomes part of the cloth rather than sitting on top of it as oil and

Karen Perrine, *Remains of the Day.* See page 37.

Linda R. MacDonald, *Wildlife Sanctuaries.* See page 467.

Emily Richardson, *Full Fathom Five.* See page 431.

Elizabeth A. Busch, *Float.* See page 56.

acrylic paint do. Her *Remains of the Day* and *Pool* are close observations of water that seem to stop time. Many of MacDonald's quilts are about living in the Pacific Northwest, which she describes as "a lush, wonderful area filled with hot political issues—logging, the spotted owl, the chain saw, tourism, 'do we want freeways?,' etc." In quilts like *Into the Tornado* and *Wildlife Sanctuaries*, she hand paints flat, cartoon-like images on whole cloth, to which she adds delicate hand stitching. Like many artists, MacDonald finds that working in the quilt medium "softens the issues" and allows more people to be open to her work than they would be to a framed painting or print.

Technology is also dramatically changing the way fabric is designed and made, and opening up a host of new possibilities for quilt artists. The use of computers is of course a double-edged sword; it can make the creative process too easy and lead to lazy results, but

Miriam Nathan-Roberts,
Cortland Street Subway Station. See page 466.

Ellen Oppenheimer, *PW Block 4.* See page 500.

it can also facilitate the imagination and control of a disciplined artist, allowing the creation of images that would not be possible by other means. For better or for worse, computer-generated fabrics are here and will be a major factor in coming years. Duncan Slade, a pioneer of dye painting who has embraced the new technology, says, "The last time something this big happened to textiles, it was called the Industrial Revolution."

For the 2003 Quilt National competition, Michael James and Miriam Nathan-Roberts entered quilts with pictorial imagery that had been designed entirely on a computer and then printed directly onto fabric. James's *A Strange Riddle* juxtaposes images, words, and patterns in a personal exploration of childhood memory and conditioning, while Nathan-Roberts's grim *Cortland Street Subway Station* imagines victims of the 9/11 attacks on the World Trade Center trapped in the station below the Towers. Both are striking works that take full advantage of the new technology.

Ellen Oppenheimer also designs on the computer, but instead of printing directly, she uses it to help her create complex linear patterns that she screen-prints on fabric. Her *PW Block 4* is made up of a grid of square blocks printed with layered patterns that cleverly play on the geometric structures of traditional piecework at the same time as they reference op art.

By no means are all the influences on contemporary quilt making high tech, however. While some artists have pursued complex, technical approaches, others have moved in the opposite direction, looking for ways to simplify their art and bring it closer to its essence. Some, led by Nancy Crow, have thrown away their templates and adopted the direct, spontaneous free cutting

Anna Williams, *LIX: Log Cabin,* 1993

Cottons and cotton/polyester blends; machine pieced and hand quilted; 76 x 64½ inches (193 x 163.8 cm).
International Quilt Study Center, University of Nebraska-Lincoln, 1997.007.1104. Courtesy of Katherine Watts

17

Introduction

Anne Woringer, *Lucarne.* See page 425.

and assembly they first observed in the work of the self-taught African-American quilt maker Anna Williams (see her work on page 17). Crow explains, "When I saw [Anna Williams's quilts] for the first time, I was dumbstruck because she hadn't used a ruler. The fact that the line actually could be...sensuous, or lyrical, just blew me out of the water... Everything she did was with scissors, so that's why the lines were crooked, because she just sort of cut the way she felt." Free cutting and hand dyeing often go hand in hand; ironically, these seemingly primitive methods can give certain artists as much control over their work as technology can. Like Nancy Crow, the French artist Anne Woringer also freely cuts her own hand-dyed fabric. Instead of cotton, however, she works with antique 19th-century French linen and hemp fabrics, which add historical resonance to her evocative faux primitive appliqué designs; *Les Mains Négatives*, for example, references cave paintings, while *Lucarne* is part of a series inspired by the weathered boards of old log cabins.

Continuity Amidst Change

As this book clearly demonstrates, contemporary quilt makers moved in an almost kaleidoscopic range of directions during the 1990s and early 2000s. The examples above represent just a few of the roads being taken by today's quilt artists. But there is also continuity amidst all the change and diversity. While each Quilt National introduces the work of new artists, one can also trace the work of established artists through these competitions.

It is particularly instructive to study the unfolding paths of artists whose work appears year after year. Erika Carter, Jan Myers-Newbury, and Jane A. Sassaman, for example, have quilts in all five exhibitions, while Rachel Brumer, Jane Burch Cochran, Linda Levin, Linda R. MacDonald, Emily Richardson, and Susan Shie and

James Acord appear in four of the five. Each has found something personal within the quilt, a distinct vein that they can mine without repetition or exhaustion.

These masters and the dozens of other outstanding artists working in the quilt medium today continue to experiment and move the art form in new directions. Like artists in any time or medium, they seek to express themselves and share their experience of the world around them through the prism of their work. Whether they tell stories, paint pictures, or combine color and pattern, the best of their quilts can capture our imaginations and touch our feelings in the same way all good art does. There is a wealth of good art in these pages, and we should all be grateful that Quilt National exists to bring it to our attention.

COLLECTING
Contemporary Quilts ^{by}ROBERT SHAW

Building a collection of contemporary quilts can be an enormously rewarding experience. Quilts are wonderful objects to live with; they are, as the pioneer quilt artist Radka Donnell has said, "good objects" that silently embrace us, and they can carry the positive primal associations of warmth and touch into any space. Like any good art, quilts can bring beauty, meaning, and pleasure to anyone willing to pay close attention. Compared with other forms of art, quilts are still relatively inexpensive, and, because contemporary quilt making is such a diverse field, there are works for every taste. One of the great advantages of collecting contemporary quilts is that you can meet artists whose work you admire and learn about their art firsthand. The early 21st century is a good time to be collecting; there are many superb artists working in the medium, and a lot of quality work is available for collectors to consider. Quilts also come in a wide variety of sizes, so you can find pieces to fit almost any space in your home or office. Many artists are now working in smaller sizes, both because collectors find them easier to display in a home, and because they are more affordable than full-sized quilts. Many artists will also create quilts on commission.

An expanse of blank wall places the focus on Velda Newman's *Hydrangea*. It hangs in the living room of owner John M. Walsh III. PHOTO BY WIT MCKAY

Informed Decisions

If you want to become a collector, the first thing to do is to educate yourself. Knowledge is power; the more you know, the better you will be able to judge what you see and make informed choices. Read everything you can find about quilts, both old and new. It is important to understand the background from which contemporary quilts grew, as well as the basic tech-

niques of the craft of quilt making. Collector and quilt maker Del Thomas advises, "Locating an experienced quilt maker who can explain the various techniques and styles will help immeasurably." John M. Walsh III, who has built one of the finest collections of art quilts in the world, goes a step further and suggests taking at least one class in quilt making. He adds, "It is not important to create a wonderful work of art. In fact you may learn even more if you have to struggle with all the steps that go into making a quilt and end up with something you would hesitate to hang on your wall."

Subscribe to magazines like *Quilter's Newsletter Magazine*, *Quilting Arts*, *FiberArts*, and *American Craft*, and join and support organizations like Studio Art Quilt Associates and Friends of Fiber Art. Learn who the major artists are and pay serious attention to their work, whether you like it at first or not. Look at quilts on the Internet. The websites for Quilt National (www.quiltnational.com) and Studio Art Quilt Associates (www.saqa.com) are great places to start. Be aware that many artists have their own websites, and both of these sites include links to dozens of them.

Most important, go to shows and exhibitions to see quilts in the flesh. You can find calendars of quilt shows and museum and gallery exhibitions in magazines and on the web. Then attend as many shows as you can. Immerse yourself in quilts of all kinds until you feel like you have some grasp of the universe. Go to both national and regional shows; as Hilary Fletcher, the director of Quilt National, notes, "the quality of a regional show will be quite different than an international juried show, but the novice collector will get an idea of some of the kinds of work that are being done,

and can make some judgments of what is most appealing." Regional shows and galleries can also be places to discover exciting new work by emerging artists.

Always remember that quilts are three-dimensional objects and that there is a vast difference between a flat photographic image on a printed page and the real thing. In person, you will discover that some pieces have real presence and that others are not at all what you expected. As Walsh warns, "There is probably no medium for which photographs can be more deceptive than quilts. Seeing quilts in shows will create the caution not to dismiss a work too quickly based on the printed image." If you are thinking about buying a quilt you have not seen "in the cloth," ask if you can live with it for a few days before making up your mind. If the seller is willing, this is a good idea whether you have seen the quilt or not. It relieves the pressure of quick decision making, and gives you time to get to know the work better and to see how it works in your home.

If you are thinking about making a serious personal and financial commitment to collecting, get expert advice. Talk with curators, gallery owners, and collectors who have seen hundreds of quilts and can offer opinions about artists and their work. Don't be afraid to ask questions, no matter how dumb they seem; you will find that most people who are passionate about quilts are happy to share their knowledge with someone who is genuinely interested. Best of all is to find someone whose knowledge and judgment you trust completely; if you are lucky enough to work with such a trusted advisor, he or she can save you a great deal of time and money. But no matter whom you are listening to, don't let yourself be talked into buying something that doesn't excite you. See as much as you can, look as hard as you can, and learn to trust your own instincts.

Buy what you love. Never buy a quilt because you think it is a good investment. If you don't love it, it won't be. No matter how much money you have to invest in quilts, stretch and buy the best you can afford. Don't be afraid to make a mistake. All real collectors do, and they learn from them. Most likely, you will never regret the pieces you buy—just the ones you loved but did not reach for because they seemed too expensive at the time. Also be aware that less is usually more, that collecting is not about accumulating

A landing in the home of John M. Walsh III benefits from displaying Denise Burge's *The Sower.*
PHOTO BY WIT MCKAY

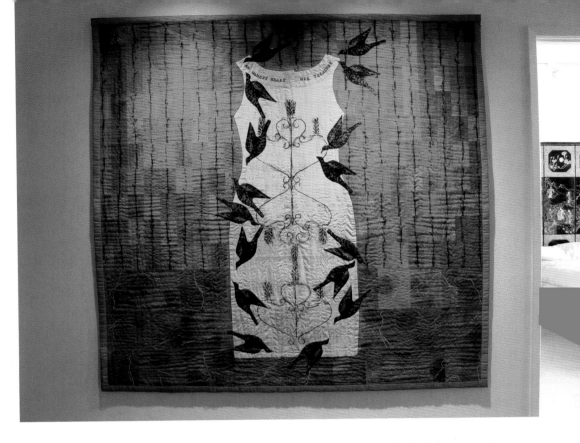

Rachel Brumer's 1999 piece, *Marker VIII*, hangs from a commercial system on a landing outside the master bedroom in the Brakensiek home. The artist incorporated favorite sayings taken from headstones into this series of quilts; this one reads "an honest heart her treasure." Because the collectors rotate the quilts throughout their living space, a number of their quilts grace this wall in turn.
PHOTO BY MARK STEPHENSON/
SUN VALLEY PICTURES

but about making disciplined choices. Go for quality, not quantity. You will find owning one quilt of real quality more rewarding than having 10 lesser pieces, and the more focused your collection, the more you will appreciate each work you own.

Set clear goals for your collection. Having a collecting focus will help you to make choices; you might want to collect quilts by artists in your geographic region, landscape quilts, geometric quilts, or quilts of a particular size, for example. Or you might take a more expansive approach and try to build a collection of key works that represent the history or state of the art of contemporary quilt making. Whatever focus you choose, your collection should reflect who you are and what

you feel strongly about. Remember that building a collection is a creative act, an expression of self as valid as the art you collect.

Also think carefully about the time and space it will take to care for what you own. As one collector put it, "I think quilts are like Jell-O—there's always room for more. The more you have, however, the greater the challenge for display and storage." Although it should give you joy, collecting is also a privilege that brings responsibilities. Objects live longer than people, and great objects can (and should) live a very long time. Collectors should look on themselves as caretakers who preserve works they love so that future generations can enjoy them as much as they do.

Protecting

Most quilts are fairly durable objects, but they do have some special needs. The ultraviolet light that is part of sunlight and most indoor lighting sources is a quilt's worst enemy. Prolonged exposure to unfiltered light bleaches and degrades textiles and can do serious, even irreversible damage. Never hang your quilts in direct sunlight, and cover lights with ultraviolet filters if you can. Believe it or not, the oil from your hands can damage quilts, and untreated wood also carries acids that can cause

damage. Ideally, you should wear white cotton gloves when handling your quilts, and, if they are to be stored in wooden chests or drawers, be sure they are wrapped in unbleached muslin or acid-free tissue. Temperature and humidity should be as constant as possible; wide fluctuations can be dangerous. Normal room temperature and 50 percent humidity are ideal. Homes in cold climates can become as dry as a desert during the winter heating season, so investing in a humidifier is a good idea.

Display

Deciding where and how to display your quilts is another way you will be able to express yourself as a collector. You are in effect your own curator, hanging your own show. Most quilt artists prepare their work for hanging, either by sewing a fabric sleeve or strip of hook-and-loop tape on the top back of the quilt. Quilts with sleeves are supported with an inserted slat or dowel, and those with hook and loop tape are attached to a mating strip stapled onto a slat. After mounting, the quilt can be hung in a variety of ways, depending on its size and weight. Some collectors use picture wire and hooks, others use chain or monofilament.

Most collectors experiment with hanging systems until they find something that works in their spaces. For example, some of the quilts in the highly respected Marbaum Collection are hung with monofilament looped over pairs of plastic mirror holders spaced 24 to 36 inches (61 to 91.4 cm) apart at the top of the wall. The anonymous collector explains that the system lets her install pieces of different widths and lengths in the same space without putting anything else into the wall.

Other collectors invest in display systems specifically made to accommodate textiles. Nancy and Warren Brakensiek, who live in a 1700-square-foot high-rise condominium, use a commercial system that operates through a series of hooks, holders, and sleeves hung from moldings at the top of the wall. This method gives a more formal gallery-like look and also allows the Brakensieks to rotate their quilts much more easily than if they were attached to the wall. Since they own 140 quilts but can only exhibit about 40 at a time, this flexibility is very important to them. As Warren says, "Logic would tell us that 40 is what we should own, but we don't."

Quilts should be rotated on and off display on a regular basis to reduce light damage and other stress. Don't leave a quilt on display for more than a year; four to six months is ideal. One collector advises, "I would encourage people who have bought a piece for a specific space in their home to be on the lookout for another piece that would be suitable for the same space. That way when one has been up long enough, there will be something else to put in its place."

A SIMPLE, INEXPENSIVE HANGING METHOD

■ The anonymous owner of the Marbaum Collection uses a hanging system of plastic mirror holders and monofilament (highlighted here in red) that gives maximum flexibility at very little cost. Available from any home improvement store, the hardware (below) is permanently screwed into the wall at a distance that approximates the width of the smallest quilt projected to hang in a given spot, about 1/4 to 1/2 inch (0.6–1.3 cm) from the ceiling to allow for hanging of tall pieces (left and bottom).

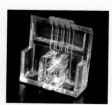

DETAIL

■ Hanging a quilt from a slat or board slipped inside the casing works better than from a dowel, because it lets the work hang flatter against wall. The slat can be cut a little shorter than the width of the piece. To protect the quilt from the acids in the wood, seal the wood with varnish or paint, and allow it to dry. Make two marks on the slat, the same distance from each other as the mirror holders and roughly centered. At each mark, wrap a scrap of fabric 2 inches (5.1 cm) wide three times around the board, and staple it on one side to keep it in place (below).

Most of the Brakensiek's collection focuses on work by artists from the Pacific Northwest. The stairway in their home displays a pair of quilts that are a challenge to hang because of their irregular shapes. On the left is *Stepping Down*, made in 1989 by Joyce Marquess Carey. Because of the angling and size of the wall, when the Brakensieks rotate this quilt off display, the space remains empty. Nancy Erickson's 1987 piece, *The Arrival*, right, is one of the largest they own. Attached to the wall with a complicated arrangement of hook-and-loop tape, it explores the impact of the human presence in the habitat of wild animals.

PHOTO BY MARK STEPHENSON/ SUN VALLEY PICTURES

■ After slipping the slat in the casing, with the staples facing away from the front of the quilt, you can still feel where the wrapped fabric scraps are. Push the slat against the upper edge of the casing, and attach a safety pin, its hinge toward the top of the quilt, through both the casing and the scrap fabric (above). This helps distribute the quilt's weight along the entire length of the board.

■ To determine the amount of monofilament needed, measure the distance between the mirror holder and where you wish the top of the quilt to rest. Multiply that by two, add the distance between the two safety pins, plus a little extra for knotting. Tie one end of the monofilament (highlighted here in red) to each hinge of the safety pins (below). The quilt is ready to hang from the mirror holders.

ALL PHOTOS BY BRIAN BLAUSER

collecting

Storage

If you can, choose a storage space off the beaten path in your home, such as a spare bedroom. Whatever storage method you use, be sure to make lists of the quilts as you put them away; these will save endless hours of searching later. If you have the space, rolling is the best way to store your quilts, because it avoids the creasing that can be created by folding. Quilts can be rolled individually or several quilts can be rolled together. Individual quilts can be rolled around the foam swimming pool floats known as "noodles," or what Del Thomas calls a "stuffie" of fabric scraps wrapped in muslin. After rolling, the quilt should be wrapped in unbleached muslin and tied shut at each end.

Groups of four to seven quilts can be rolled on carpet tubes. First, wrap the tube in heavy plastic. Then start with the largest quilt and secure each one with tied strips of muslin after rolling. After the quilts are rolled together, the outside quilt should be wrapped in muslin. Rolled tubes of quilts should ideally be supported on poles suspended between sawhorses or slotted wooden or metal racks.

If space is at a premium, you can fold your quilts for storage. Fold the quilt in thirds over crumpled strips of

When they're not on display, John M. Walsh III stores his quilts in a spare bedroom. In the photo, some of the layers are pulled back to show how the quilts are arranged flat on a bed with sheets between them. Walsh protects the top with a sheet as well.
PHOTO BY WIT MCKAY

acid-free tissue to prevent creasing. You can store your folded quilts in properly lined drawers or chests, or better yet in acid-free archival boxes, which can be stacked.

Quilts can also be stored the way they were traditionally used—flat on a bed. Flat storage is often the best idea for fragile or heavy quilts. Del Thomas, for example, keeps quilts from the Thomas Contemporary Quilt Collection that are fused, embellished, or smaller than about 36 inches (91.4 cm) on the bed in her guest room, with a sheet underneath and one covering them.

STORING WITH "STUFFIES"

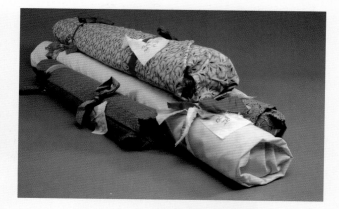

ABOVE AND RIGHT: Collector and quilt maker Del Thomas makes what she calls a "stuffie" by wrapping pre-washed fabric around a roll of batting and stitching the openings closed. It should measure about 9 inches (22.9 cm) in circumference, and be about 2 inches (5.1 cm) longer than the width of the quilt. Thomas stores a quilt, face out, rolled around the stuffie.

ABOVE AND RIGHT: To protect them, Thomas wraps the rolled-up quilts in clean pieces of fabric. She secures the ends loosely with rag ties; a label through the tie identifies the artwork within.
ALL PHOTOS BY GARY GREGG CONAUGHTON

Caretaking

As caretakers, collectors should keep careful records about their quilts. One collector jokes, "If I had known how much record keeping would be necessary, I might not have started collecting." Your records should include provenance information such as previous owners; where, when and from whom the quilt was acquired; and the purchase price, as well as current appraisal values and any information supplied by the artist or discovered in research. After you own more than a few quilts, it is also a good idea to keep records of where your quilts are—display, storage, or loan—and when they were moved there.

Insurance is also essential, whether you only intend to display your quilts in your home or loan them to museums or other venues. Be aware that insurance companies may not be familiar with quilt values and that you may need to prove their worth if you have to make a claim. So keep your sales records, and consider having your quilts appraised if you believe they have increased in value over the years. Jack Walsh also advises that insurance may not cover damage to loaned quilts and suggests that any museum loan agreement should state that "the borrower is responsible for returning the quilts in the same condition that they were in when they were borrowed." That way, he says, "If anything happens—and it does occasionally—the borrower does whatever is necessary to set things right. Plus the lender doesn't have to deal with the borrower's insurance company."

Finally, consider how you can share your passion for quilts with others. Del Thomas speaks for most collectors when she says, "I collect quilts not only for my own enjoyment, but also so that others can enjoy them. I hope to promote understanding and interest in anyone who will listen." To that end, the majority of collectors of contemporary quilts choose to loan works for exhibitions at museums and shows. Both Del Thomas and the Brakensieks also lecture frequently about their collections and the collector's perspective, and in recent years, the Brakensieks have served on the board of SAQA, funded a speaker series for the Contemporary Quiltart Association in Seattle, and initiated and funded the "Brakensiek Caught Our Eye

John M. Walsh III also exhibits some of his quilt collection at work. Terese Agnew's *Flight Pattern over Electric Company Easement Property* livens up his office.
PHOTO BY WIT MCKAY

Award" at Quilt Visions 2004 and Quilt National 2005. Ultimately, as all collectors must, the owners of the Marbaum Collection are starting to think about what will happen to their collection when they are no longer around. They are researching and talking to museum people to find a place "that will think our collection is as wonderful as we think it is," says the anonymous collector. But they are also looking ahead in other ways. "Hopefully," they say, "we'll have lots more years before this kind of decision has to be finalized. There are still lots more quilts out there for us to buy."

JEANNE LYONS BUTLER

HUNTINGTON, NEW YORK

The Writing's on The Wall

Commercial and hand-dyed cotton, silk, and synthetic fabrics; machine pieced and quilted; 56 x 60 inches (142.2 x 152.4 cm).

It's up there on the wall, sliced in half like a horizon between the sky and the ground, between reality and myth, or between preconceived attitudes and the truth. It is my hope that you are drawn in by the light and not fooled by the writing.

PETRA SOESEMANN

WOOSTER, OHIO

M
WOMEN, Chapter 1
N

Natural and synthetic fabrics;
direct hand and machine appliqué
by fusing, hand quilted; 75 x 76
inches (190.5 x 193 cm).

*Each side of this quilt is always seen through the
veil of the image on the other side. The veiling effect
is relative and can reveal or conceal, depending on
the light. An expressway image from a Chicago
map runs through a back-view self portrait to suggest an interior mapping of place, time, and female
identity. The shorthand encryption reads: "Women
veil their egos the way men mask their emotions."*

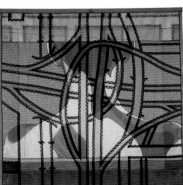

REVERSE VIEW

MELISSA HOLZINGER

ARLINGTON, WASHINGTON

Circular Thinking

Canvas that has been painted, drawn, and airbrushed with acrylic, pastels, and ink; layered, fused, and machine quilted, mounted, and framed; 32 x 40 inches (81.3 x 101.6 cm).

My current work is about reconciling my love of the quilting tradition with the spontaneity and pure joy of drawing and painting. The circle has been a recurring theme in my quilts for as long as I've been making them. Now and then I return to an old friend with new information and new experience.

DOMINIE NASH

BETHESDA, MARYLAND

Peculiar Poetry 4

Cotton and silk fabrics treated
with fiber reactive dyes, screen
printing with textile paint and
fabric crayon; machine appliquéd
and machine quilted; 43 x 43
inches (109.2 x 109.2 cm).

In the Peculiar Poetry *series, the garden, seen in different lights and
weather, is the guiding inspiration. My aim is to create a sense of
structure while juxtaposing strong and sometimes chaotic colors and
patterns. Likewise, the inherent order of each plant form is retained
as it is combined with others in a seemingly random fashion by
nature, or by a gardener with more enthusiasm than forethought.*

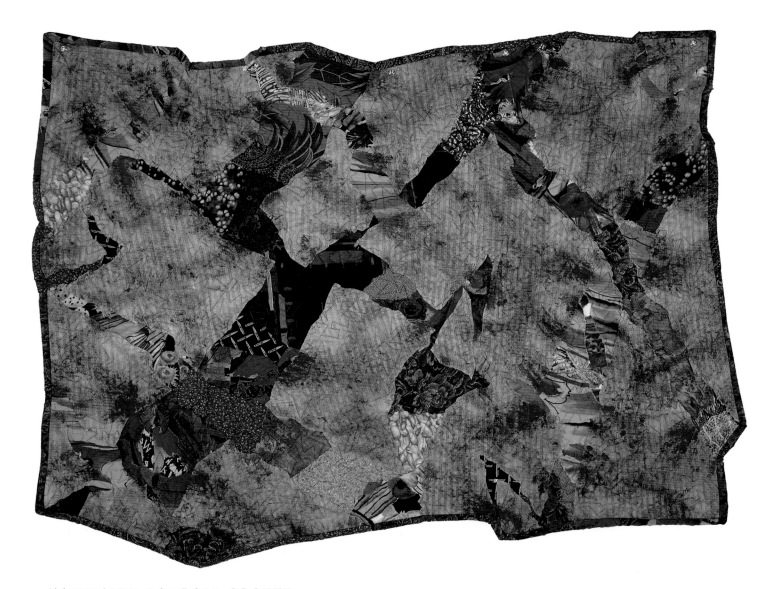

STEPHANIE RANDALL COOPER

EVERETT, WASHINGTON

Curse

Cotton, rayon, polyester, silk,
and blended fabrics hand
embellished with acrylic paint;
cut-and-paste construction,
machine quilted; 58 x 47 inches
(147.3 x 119.4 cm).

*Each piece in this series—Celebration of the Female/The Uterus
Series—is intended to expose/discuss aspects of life for women
today: physiology, emotion, culture, and transformation. The
irregular shape and style indicate the weaving of a continuing story.
Originating from my confusion, this work is largely autobiographical.
In a larger sense, the story I tell could and does represent many
other women with similar tales. The story unfolds once a month.*

JOAN SCHULZE

SUNNYVALE, CALIFORNIA

The Angel Equation

Silk and cotton fabrics, paper; appliquéd, laminated, painted, pieced, and printed; machine quilted; 57 x 56 inches (144.8 x 142.2 cm).

DOMINI MCCARTHY AWARD

I have been enamored with surfaces in most of my work—color overlaying color, peeling surfaces, edges that define and contrast. Now the final marks are getting larger, more dramatic in, perhaps, a gesture to come closer and take in all the quiet detail.

LIZ AXFORD

HOUSTON, TEXAS

Emotions & Abstractions 2

Cotton fabrics hand dyed by Fabrics to Dye For (Liz Axford and Connie Scheele); machine pieced and machine quilted; 80 x 45 inches (203.2 x 114.3 cm).

From 1917 to 1923 Frank Lloyd Wright designed a group of "Textile Block" houses built from concrete blocks cast with low-relief patterns. This inspiration came from watching Chinese weavers make rugs Wright designed for the Imperial Hotel in Tokyo. My Emotions & Abstractions series began with the block Wright designed and had custom-fabricated for the Millard House in Pasadena, California (1923). After slightly modifying the block and altering the "set" of blocks, I had a pattern I could work with. I then immersed myself in the subtle patterning and colors of my hand-dyed fabrics.

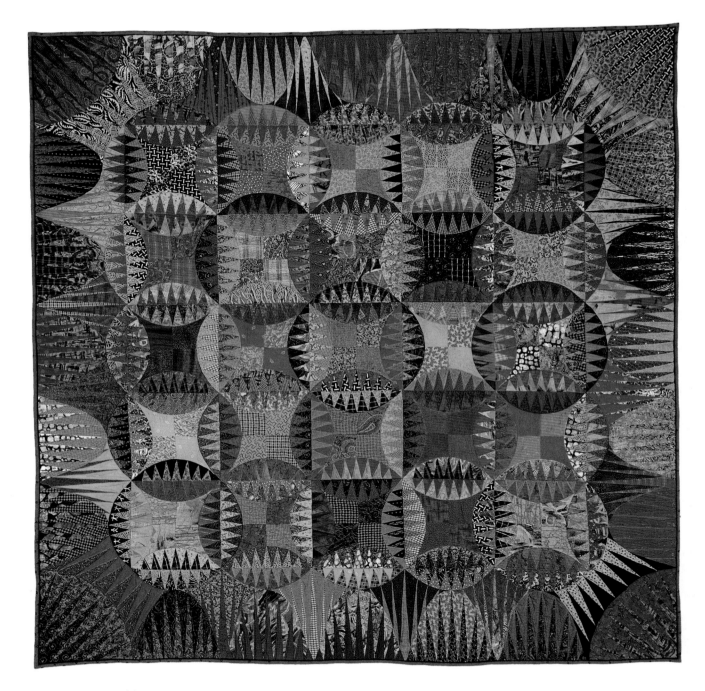

KAREN K. STONE

DALLAS, TEXAS

Indian Orange Peel

Cotton fabrics, mostly homespun, batiks, and reproduction fabrics; machine pieced onto original paper foundations and machine quilted with rayon thread; 63 x 63 inches (160 x 160 cm).

While the fabric choices in the quilt may seem to reflect the tension and complexity of my urban life, its inspiration is actually the traditional orange peel quilt and an orange Indian wedding ring quilt from the Pilgrim/Roy collection. While I've come to associate this piece with fire and gospel music (which, like quilt making, have changed little in 100 years), I think its appeal lies in the simple juxtaposition of two opposing colors.

KAREN PERRINE

TACOMA, WASHINGTON

Remains of the Day

Cotton, sateen, and nylon tulle treated with Procion dye, fabric pigments and felt marker, cotton and metallic threads; hand painted and airbrushed, hand appliquéd, hand and machine quilted; 44 x 43 inches (111.8 x 109.22 cm). From a private collection.

Every body of water I've seen in recent years has unmistakable signs of human presence—trivial garbage like candy wrappers or foam cups. In Remains of The Day, *the time is dusk, and it's a little spooky. There is no evidence of plants or water animals. I don't know if the water is pure or polluted...it is very clear but dark. The people have gone home, leaving, as always, something behind.*

ANNE SMITH

WARRINGTON, CHESIRE, ENGLAND

Catherine Wheel

Cotton blends and recycled fabrics;
machine pieced and appliquéd,
hand quilted; 52 x 53 inches
(132.1 x 134.6 cm).

*My previous work had been subdued in tone reflecting a spiritual
theme, and I wanted to make something in a lighter mood. I took
my inspiration from the annual Hull Fair, the biggest in England.
Starting with a small pastel study, I arrived at the final destination by pinning and rearranging the fabrics on a large board.*

NANCY TAYLOR

PLEASANTON, CALIFORNIA

Nine Patch

Cotton fabric that has been dyed, painted, and patterned with wax resist; machine pieced and machine quilted; 47 x 51 inches (119.4 x 129.5 cm).

Recently I have been painting, dyeing, spraying, and using wax resist to create my own designs on fabric. The actual application of the wax and the physicality of dyeing are interesting and enjoyable. The balance between the aspects that I can control and the elements of surprise that are always present in these processes is intriguing to me.

1995

BARBARA J. MORTENSON

GLENSIDE, PENNSYLVANIA

Fractured Nights

Collagraphs on black organza, layered and cut through; machine embroidered with rayon and other threads; additional layers of hand-painted fabrics; 22 x 27 inches (55.9 x 68.6 cm).

While we think of nights as seamless, sleep-filled darkness, they are often fragile times, easily fractured from within and from without.

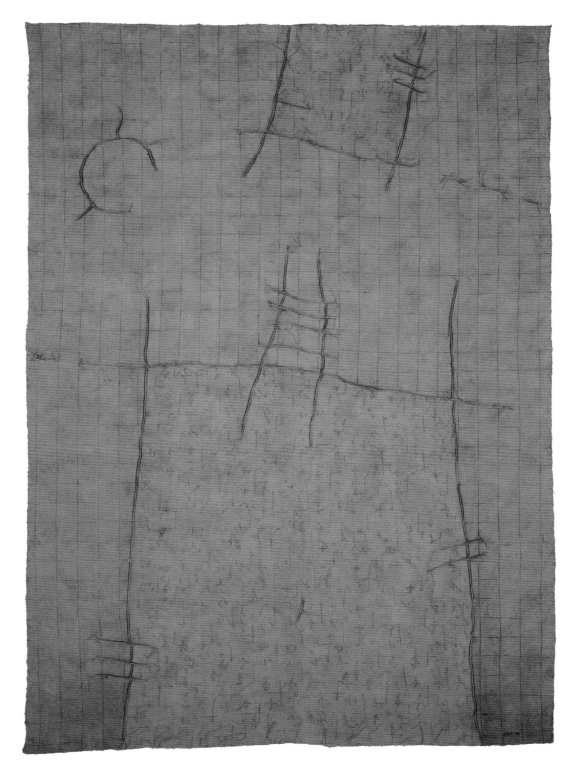

SIGI GERTSCHEN PROBST

BERN, SWITZERLAND

Ohne Titel

Mixed fiber batting, cotton, and acrylic paint; sewn, quilted, and embroidered by machine, painted; 35 x 50 inches (88.9 x 127 cm).

This is a whole-cloth quilt. It's a naked quilt. It's even a skinless quilt. It is what remains if you take away the surface of a quilt and come to the inside, where the dreams and the lifemarks are. It's a possible content, a possible meaning of a quilt.

MELODY JOHNSON

CARY, ILLINOIS

Reaching for the Light

Hand-dyed cotton fabrics, fusible web, metallic thread; machine appliquéd, machine quilted; 57 x 53 inches (144.8 x 134.6 cm).

The spirit of the time is reflected in the art of the time. Serious artists are stimulated to produce work that deals with despair, conflict, and chaos, and the breakdown of contemporary society. If one lives with a spirit of optimism, one risks being considered a Pollyanna. Nevertheless, for me, making optimistic art is my remedy for a discouraged world. Instead of reflecting negativity, I hope to reveal a way out of the darkness, a way to reach for the light.

I have been working on a series of quilts using windows as a theme—both in the literal and in the metaphorical sense. The literal choice of the window motif is probably because I come from a northern country, needing light, and seeing ruined abbeys with open sky windows. Metaphorically, windows reflect my interest in self-growth and understanding.

ELIZABETH BARTON

ATHENS, GEORGIA

Windows XIII: Aiming High

Hand-dyed and commercial cotton fabrics; machine pieced and appliquéd, machine quilted with rayon and metallic thread; 41 x 67 inches (104.1 x 170.2 cm).

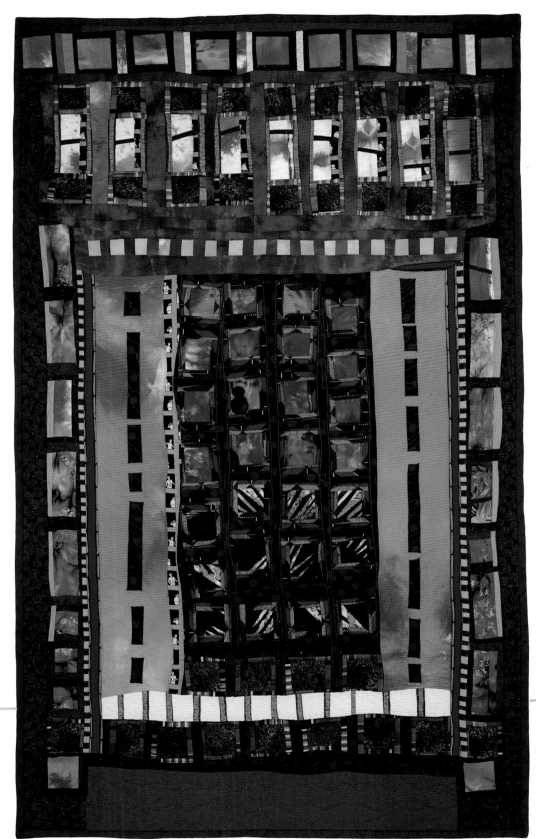

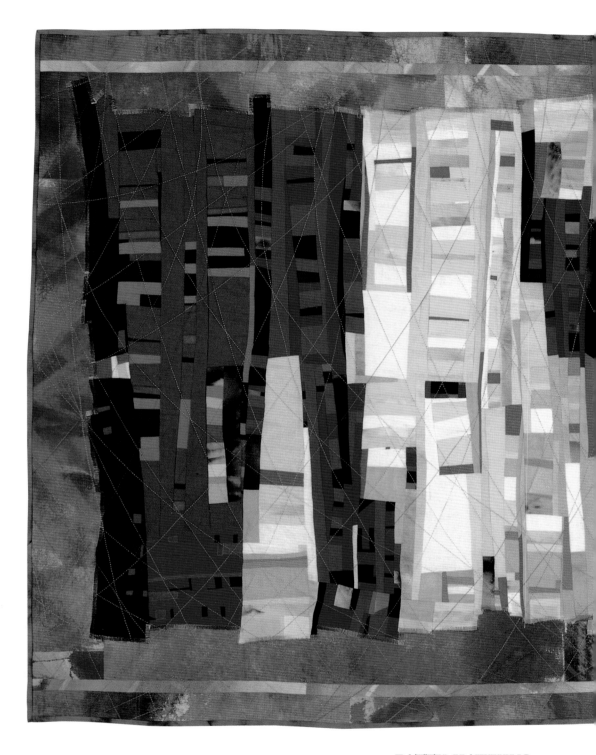

PATTY HAWKINS

ESTES PARK, COLORADO

Anasazi Dwellings: Colors Stratified

Cotton fabrics, some hand dyed by the artist, painted and chalk-marked canvas; random strip-piecing and direct machine appliquéd, machine quilted; 69 x 38 inches (175.3 x 96.5 cm).

Colorado's Anasazi cliff dwellings challenged me to depict the stonework's visual texture along with the subtle colorations and shadows of the light-colored sandstone. My hand-dyed fabrics create nuances of jewel-like areas glimpsed through an otherwise determined color field, with these "color jewels" suggesting mystique and depth. My interpretation is inspired by Monet's brush strokes and his depiction of nature's light and color by using awesome tints and hues.

SARA LONG

FORT BRAGG, CALIFORNIA

AIDS Web

Cotton fabric, canceled AIDS
stamps made into buttons, hand
pieced and hand quilted; 46 x 34
inches (116.8 x 86.4 cm).

*AIDS Web is a historical piece regarding the political and
social implications of AIDS. This is an important piece
to me because AIDS has directly affected my own life.*

JUDITH TOMLINSON TRAGER

BOULDER, COLORADO

Lunarscape

Cotton, rayon, and silk fabrics; machine pieced in crazy quilt technique, machine quilted and hand painted; 57 x 61 inches (144.8 x 154.9 cm).

My interest in space and landscape comes from growing up on the continent's western edge. At night we could see ten thousand stars curving to the far horizon. My dreams thrust me into those spaces: cold, distant, yet somehow familiar. When the astronauts landed and took their first lunar steps, I was giving birth to our son. In the cold light of the delivery room, I saw the stars in his eyes.

SUZANNE EVENSON

WORTHINGTON, OHIO

Birds in the House I

Cotton and translucent synthetic fabrics that have been embellished with beads, cloth fragments, and hand stitching; machine pieced, quilted, and appliquéd; 42 x 45 inches (106.7 x 114.3 cm).

The inspiration for this quilt is an old wives' tale told to me by my mother: a bird in the house tells of a warning. As a child, just before a fire at her farm, a bird was in her house. Years later, as I struggled with a difficult situation, a bird pecking daily on the window of my studio was a warning that my center—my creative soul—was in danger: Birds are protective spiritual entities.

WENDY C. HUHN

DEXTER, OREGON

It's a Wonderful Life

Hand-dyed and commercial cottons embellished with paint, glue transfers, and glitter; machine pieced and machine quilted; 64 x 64 inches (162.6 x 162.6 cm).

I am working on a series of quilts that explore traditional female roles and domestic objects in a whimsical way. This quilt is my way of playfully ridiculing the classical role of women as caretakers, pretending all the while that everything is perfect. Nothing is wrong and, in fact, it is a wonderful life. If only one could see beneath the smile.

ART QUILTS: *a celebration*

ALEX FUHR

OXFORD, OHIO

Spelling

Procion hand-dyed rayon challis and cotton woolsey; machine pieced and hand quilted; 83 x 81 inches (210.8 x 205.7 cm).

Spelling *refers to something elementary at which I was always horrible but at which through sheer force of will I made myself successful. So too my naive quilting skills have evolved by trial and error into a composition with which I am satisfied. I am aiming for the kind of "abstract impressionism" often found in fine ethnic textiles. This quilt can function as and is constructed as a blanket. But at the same time it is hanging on the wall as art. The image, the material, the process, and therefore the object are interdependent. They are the same thing. Its composition, both color and line, and also its structure combine to create an emotional impact.*

LINDA LEVIN

WAYLAND, MASSACHUSETTS

Composition IV

Procion dyed cotton fabrics,
flannel batting; machine
appliquéd and machine quilted;
30 x 40 inches (76.2 x 101.6 cm).

This piece is part of a series exploring space and other formal values with as much economy as I can bring to it. By removing the seduction of texture and excessive piecing, I tried to keep my focus on the formal concerns of the piece.

JANE DUNNEWOLD

SAN ANTONIO, TEXAS

Baby Quilt

Solvent transfers on silk habotai
with mattress pad, gold foil on
blanket binding, burned birthday
candles; machine quilted and
embroidered; 36 x 42 inches
(91.4 x 106.7 cm).

*I struggle regularly with the challenge of mothering. My daughter
Zenna has, without even trying, taught me more about grace,
truth, and laughter than I ever set out to learn. This quilt
expresses that bittersweet love combined with the "letting go" that
all parents face if they are doing it right. The words are borrowed
from Kalil Gibran's* The Prophet.

ANN CURTIS

BURKE, VIRGINIA

Epicenter of My Soul

Commercial and hand-dyed fabrics
by Debra Lunn and Michael Mrowka,
commercial and hand-dyed perle
cotton by Melody Johnson, Facile;
multilayered, open-centered faced
modules set into faced openings in
whole-cloth background; hand quilted;
53 x 53 inches (134.6 x 134.6 cm).

*The indomitability of the human spirit may be the most
magnificent gift God has given us. Despite hardships endured
by body and soul, we all have the capacity to rise above
difficult circumstances to become more powerful in spirit.*

1995

ERIKA CARTER

BELLEVUE, WASHINGTON

Breathe

Hand-painted cotton and silk
organza fabrics; machine
appliquéd and machine quilted;
71 x 46 inches (180.3 x 116.8 cm).

*Breathing can be seen as a metaphor for communication. When one takes a
breath, that breath is an exchange, inhale/exhale, a give and take. To be healthy,
cooperation among all parts must exist. In Breathe color is used to suggest both
the structure and movement of a breath. Within the light areas to the left and right
of the green center, brush strokes resemble the turbulence of air movement. This
becomes further activated by the mostly horizontal thin fabric lines and quilted lines
that carry parameter and center colors back and forth across the quilt's expanse*

ALISON F. WHITTEMORE

SAN ANTONIO, TEXAS

Just One Cup Before I Go

Fabric treated with Procion dyes, ink drawings, phototransfers, iron-on stars, and beads; machine appliquéd and machine quilted; 39 x 51 inches (99.1 x 129.5 cm).

This quilt is one of a series called Quiltmaker in Hell. *I began it as a healing process after my divorce and subsequent major life upheavals. The woman, a symbol of myself, stands stripped and stunned amid symbols of death and the afterlife that indicate the end of one major phase of her life.*

ELIZABETH A. BUSCH

GLENBURN, MAINE

Float

Textile inks and acrylics on canvas; painted, airbrushed, and hand quilted; 40 x 28 inches (101.6 x 71.1 cm).

Contrasts in temperature, materials and methods, and ideas and attitudes are the focus of my painted quilts. I create special ambiguities that put the viewer in different places at the same time—inside and outside, awake and dreaming. I draw upon my own everyday experiences for imagery. The last steps in the process, hand quilting and embroidery, allow me to become physically reacquainted with a piece created at arm's length on the wall, and to add another visual dimension to it.

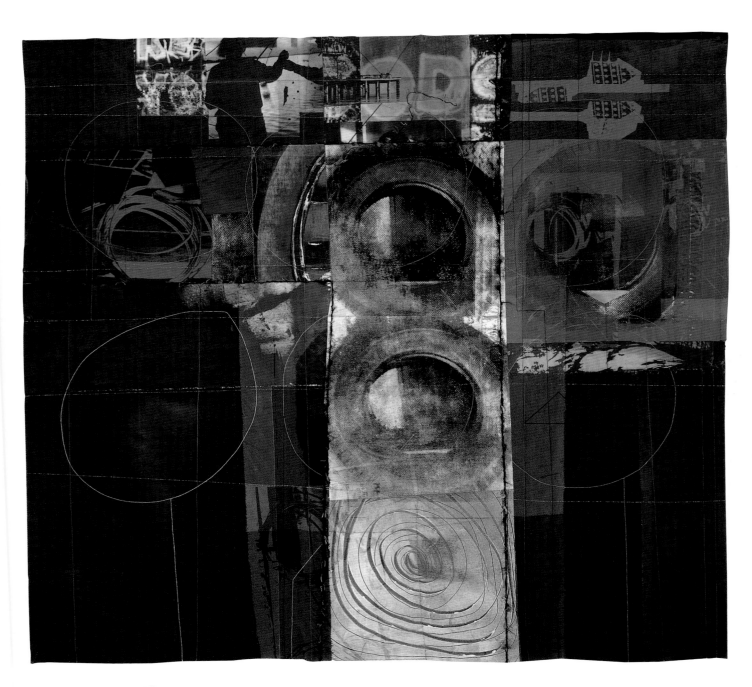

FRAN SKILES

PLANTATION, FLORIDA

Thread Bare I

Cotton duck, silk and nylon toile, fabric paint, ink, silk paint, resist, photo transfers, and yarn embellishments; silk screened, machine pieced, and machine quilted; 60 x 55 inches (152.4 x 139.7 cm).

My interest in old stuff and structures has found inspiration outside and a few steps from our rural central Florida home. It's called my husband's work shed. In my new series of quilts I use black and white photography to capture and manipulate these images. I transfer the images onto cloth using the silk-screen process.

NANCY CROW

BALTIMORE, OHIO

Color Blocks #41

Pima cottons all hand dyed by
Nancy Crow; machine pieced by
the artist, hand quilted by Marla
Hattabaugh; 51 x 41 inches
(129.5 x 104.1 cm).

Color Blocks #41 *resulted from my own improvisational process called
"floaters." I cut shapes into a background fabric directly as though I am
drawing with a pencil. As it is very difficult to make corrections, I try to be
very focused so that <u>each cut is beautiful the first time</u>. The process takes
hours of practice. The process and I become one as all the cuts are extensions
of how I see and how I feel about the shapes that develop spontaneously.
This is the most challenging way I have ever worked because it is <u>so direct</u>
with no intellectual preparation done beforehand and no templates made.*

LENORE DAVIS

NEWPORT, KENTUCKY

Montana Aspens

Cotton velveteen, poly batting, textile paint, dye, and cotton thread; monotype, and painting; hand quilted with tailor's serging stitch; 60 x 60 inches (152.4 x 152.4 cm).

By hand printing and painting each unit, my intent was to create a whole-cloth wall quilt with an image or pattern that related to traditional piecing. The process allows me to connect and build the pieces and produce a compound fabric surface with paint, color, and hand quilting.

KATY J. WIDGER

EDGEWOOD, NEW MEXICO

Pinatubo:
Fire in The Sky

Hand-dyed and painted cottons; machine pieced and machine quilted with cotton and rayon threads; 51 x 50 inches (129.5 x 127 cm).

Most of my quilts are abstract representations of my personal response to the landscape and sky of my native New Mexico. They are personal landscapes reflecting my deeply held belief that "God's eternal power and deity are clearly perceived in the things that He has created." I painted the center portion of this quilt after the Phillipine volcano Pinatubo erupted. The resulting ash in the upper atmosphere created sunsets in New Mexico that were even more spectacular than usual.

C661

JUDY BECKER

NEWTON, MASSACHUSETTS

Good and Plenty: While Waiting for My Contractor

Cotton, cotton chintz, batik, and drapery fabric; machine pieced and machine quilted; combined measurement of both pieces: 82 x 48 inches (208.3 x 121.9 cm).

My studio was packed in boxes, my life was on hold, and I was waiting for my contractor. After 18 years of deferred maintenance, we were renovating the house. I moved out for three months with a dozen fabrics, some thread, and a sewing machine. The results of those limitations are Good and Plenty *and the recognition that fewer choices often prove liberating.*

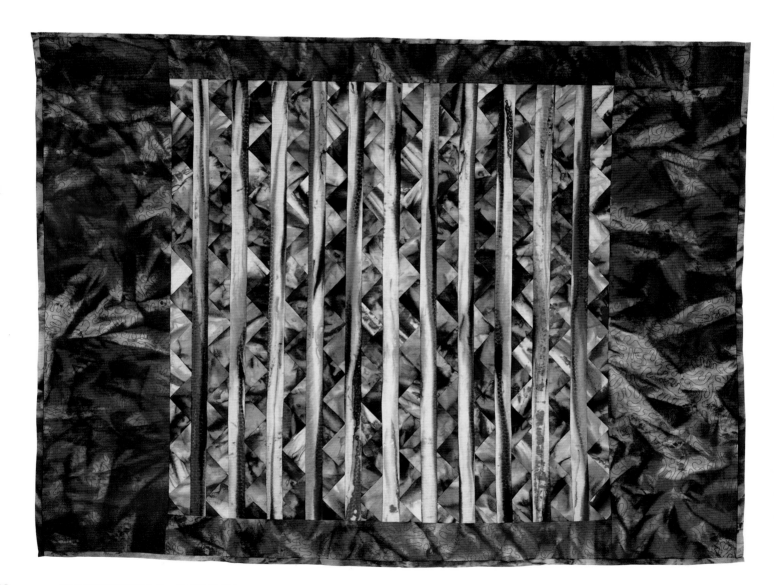

MEREDYTH L. COLBERG

FOX RIVER GROVE, ILLINOIS

Snakes and Ladders

Cotton fabrics airbrushed with
Procion fiber reactive dyes; machine pieced and machine quilted;
47 x 34 inches (119.4 x 86.4 cm).

*The journey from fabric to finish is a constant inner dialogue of questioning,
experimentation, stepping back, observing, and listening to one's instincts. There
are clues to follow along the way for the patient observer who has the ability
to play. An exciting surface design could be a springboard. A quick thumbnail
sketch might ground the energy. The creative toolbox, tapped for the skills to
verify the vision. The journey, the creative process itself, is what I love most.*

PEG BIRD

YELLOW SPRINGS, OHIO

Organica

Cotton fabrics treated with airbrush and pen; machine quilted; 34 x 47 inches (86.4 x 119.4 cm).

I consider Organica *as representing the interconnectedness of all life—the Universal Oneness. I didn't set out to make this particular statement. It just evolved and took its own direction as if the quilt were already out there in the ether and it was my task to help it materialize. Airbrushes constantly clog and splatter, requiring constant problem solving. You have to develop a sort of "happy masochism" in order to stay with this technique, I think.*

LESLIE GABRIËLSE

ROTTERDAM, NETHERLANDS

Enlarged Apple

Fabric and acrylic paint; hand appliquéd, quilted, and painted; 85 x 53 inches (215.9 x 134.6 cm).

Enlarged Apple *was influenced by a work by French Impressionist painter Pierre Bonnard. That work was almost entirely orange except for some small additions of other colors. The yellow fabric used in this piece was recycled from one of the environmental sculptures by Christo, a well-known contemporary artist.*

JANE BURCH COCHRAN

RABBIT HASH, KENTUCKY

Life Line

Various fabrics and old clothing that have been treated with paint and colored pencils, beads, and buttons; hand appliquéd, hand beaded and embellished; 82 x 68 inches (208.3 x 172.7 cm).

In rural Kentucky, you still see a few clotheslines. I love to see the clothes waving in the breeze. They tell a story about a family. Life Line is a self-portrait: part gypsy butterfly, part pearly queen, part moon chaser. The pearly kings and queens are a group of Cockney English who cover their clothes with buttons and collect alms for the poor. The turkey buzzard is a bird I see every day. It looks so beautiful when it is flying and soaring, but up close it is ugly by our standards. Perhaps made of beads and silks, it seems more beautiful

66

NANCY N. ERICKSON

MISSOULA, MONTANA

The Models Have Been Waiting for Some Time, But No Artist Is in Sight

Cotton, satin, and velvet fabrics embellished with fabric paint; machine stitched and appliquéd; 60 x 60 inches (152.4 x 152.4 cm).

This work, the ninth in a series about studio life, illustrates the true situation in my own work room, where my companions (and I) are sometimes late, or not ready, when the model is. I move back and forth from painting with paintsticks to working on a larger scale with quilting and fabrics. Each approach enhances the other.

JANET STEADMAN

CLINTON, WASHINGTON

Local Color

Cotton fabrics, most of which
were hand dyed by Liz Axford and
Connie Scheele; machine pieced
and hand quilted; 58 x 58 inches
(147.3 x 147.3 cm).

*Early in 1994, I returned to my island home from Houston with a
suitcase filled with hand-dyed fabrics and an idea for a new quilt. As
I worked on the quilt, the name* Local Color *came to me. Living on an
island buffered from the mainland by Puget Sound, I find the importance
of local people is magnified. The variety of colors in the quilt reflects
the diverse, vibrant personalities of the island population.*

C661

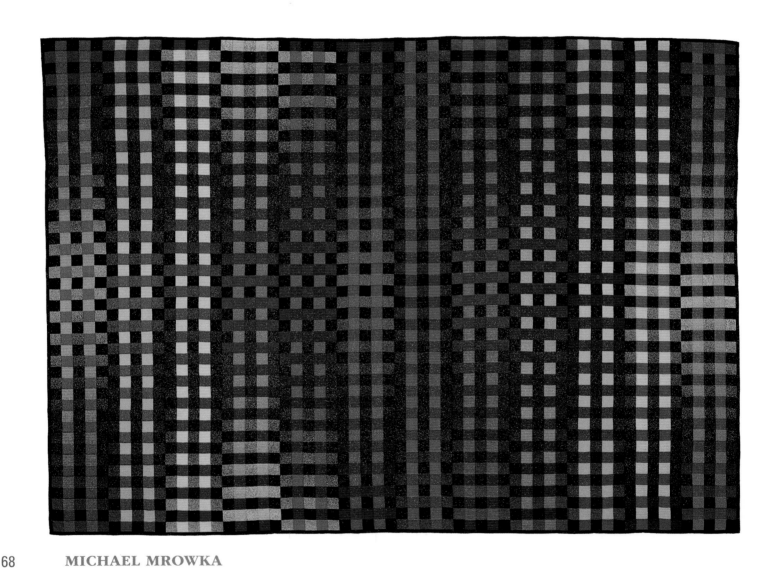

MICHAEL MROWKA

LANCASTER, OHIO

Michael's Excellent Color Adventure

Pointillist Palette (a signature line of fabric designed by Michael Mrowka and Debra Lunn for Robert Kaufman Co. Inc); machine pieced and quilted with assistance by Elaine Cottingham; 87 x 64 inches (221 x 162.6 cm).

Using principles of color theory, with gradual gradations of color moving from selvage to selvage, Pointillist Palette puts "paint in a tube" for quilt makers. The 264 different colors used in this quilt were cut from only 24 colorways. Taking advantage of the gradations and using strip piecing techniques, this quilt— my third—was truly a color adventure.

NEW IMAGE*

VIRGINIA AND MARYLAND

Never Done

Various fabrics and materials embellished with rubber stamps, fabric crayons, embroidery, Inkoprinting, and cyanotype; hand and machine pieced, appliquéd, and quilted; 54 x 72 inches (137.2 x 182.9 cm).

Never Done is the fifth in a series of collaborative works by New Image members. We worked from a photograph taken by Dominie Nash who initiated this piece. Keeping the shape, size, and placement the same, each artist approached the ironing board image with her own style, technique, and emotions. Ironing boards symbolically stand astride the line between our personal and artistic lives for those of us working with fabric.

*New Image members include: **Pat Autenreith, Barbara Bockman, Carol Gersen, Lesly-Claire Greenberg, Dorothy Holden, Dominie Nash, Sue Pierce, Mary Ann Rush, Judy Spahn, Linda Tilton, Michele Vernon,** and **Caroline Wooden.**

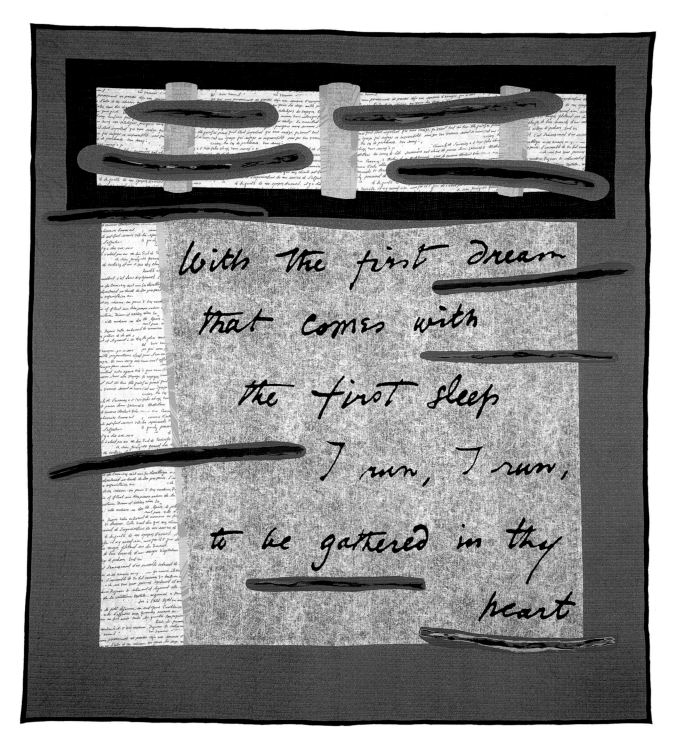

ROBIN SCHWALB

BROOKLYN, NEW YORK

First Dream

Commercial and stenciled cottons and cotton/linen blends; machine pieced, hand appliquéd, and hand quilted; 77 x 89 inches (195.6 x 226.1 cm).

I liked the idea of making a quilt about sleeping and dreaming. I also wanted the chosen text, after a poem by Alice Meynell, to be a major design element. Begun in May 1992 while visiting Susi Shie and Jimmy Acord (a.k.a. "Zombie Quilt Camp"), First Dream was an exercise in working with only the limited palette of fabrics I had brought from home.

CLARE M. MURRAY

CANTON, OHIO

Interior #5

Various fabrics including nylon net, cheesecloth, and sheers, painted with fiber reactive dyes; machine appliquéd and machine quilted; 90 x 68 inches (228.6 x 172.7 cm).

Interior #5 is from a series of quilts and paintings based on doors and chairs. I was interested in discovering a connection between oil painting on canvas and painting with dyes on fabric. Initially I bought a pair of French doors and an old chair that I drew, photographed, photocopied, and collaged. The resulting quilts are based on the fractured black and white collage. Metaphorically, they refer to not only a physical interior, but also to the interiors of the mind.

PATRICIA MINK

ANN ARBOR, MICHIGAN

Relic Vessels

Hand-dyed cotton, discharged
acetate, netting, gold leaf, fabric
paint, and beads; appliquéd;
38 x 20 inches (96.5 x 50.8 cm).

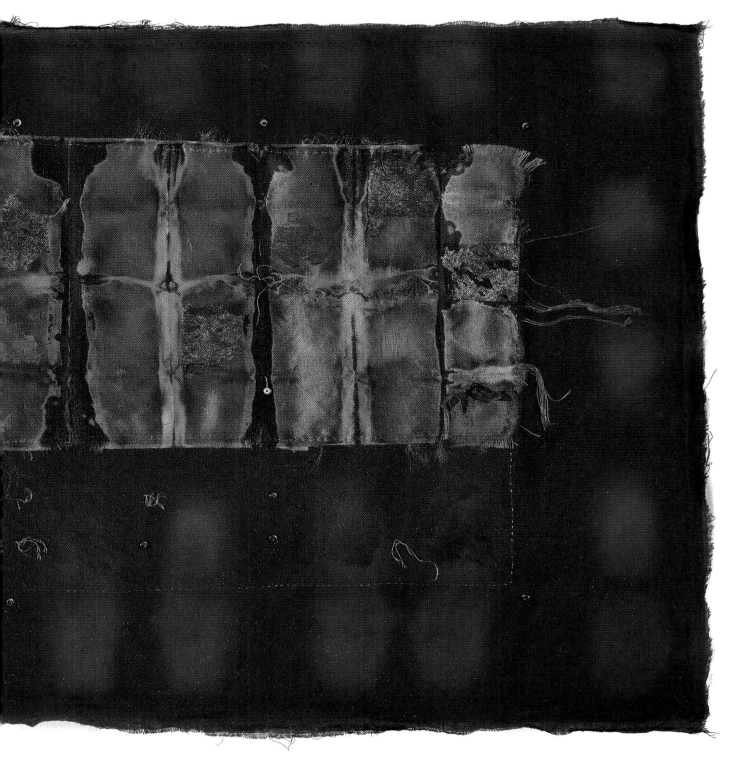

*In my work I have been exploring the use of visual
grid structures.* Relic Vessels *refers to the forms
suggested in the discharged fabric; fragments
of ritual, relics obscured by layers of time.*

NANCY CONDON

STILLWATER, MINNESOTA

Idols of Reality

Cotton and linen fabrics embellished with chalk, fabric paint, and embroidery threads; mostly hand sewn with some machine construction and hand tied; 90 x 70 inches (228.6 x 177.8 cm).

This quilt was made by drawing directly on the material with chalk and tearing away part of the double fabric to expose a figure beneath. The construction was minimal with simple tying leaving exposed edges and frayed fabric. This approach was intended to be direct, to explore the qualities of the materials, and mostly to enhance the strength of the images. Even reality is raw and direct sometimes.

KAREN FELICITY BERKENFELD

NEW YORK, NEW YORK

Where There's Smoke

Cotton printed with collagraph printing plates on an etching press using Grumbacher MAX water-soluble, oil-based paint; machine pieced and hand quilted; 36 x 46 inches (91.4 x 116.8 cm).

In 1993 I received a grant from the Empire State Crafts Alliance to explore nontoxic intaglio printing on cloth. I bought an etching press and began making collagraphs using environmentally safe printing methods. I was more concerned with materials and process than content and subject matter. But as the prints emerged, I realized that I had unconsciously incorporated images that reflected my concern for the environment and my own health as an artist, the motivating idea behind the project.

SUSAN WEBB LEE

WEDDINGTON, NORTH CAROLINA

Red Threads

Hand-dyed cotton fabrics; machine pieced and machine quilted; 39 x 51 inches (99.1x 129.5 cm).

Dyed fabrics are placed in small compartments of varying sizes and shapes. The red edging emphasizes certain areas or lines, and the erratic quilting pattern flows from one "block" to another, connecting and integrating the shapes. The circular motifs represent continuity and security while the squares refer to diversity, exploration, and the search for an adventurous spirit.

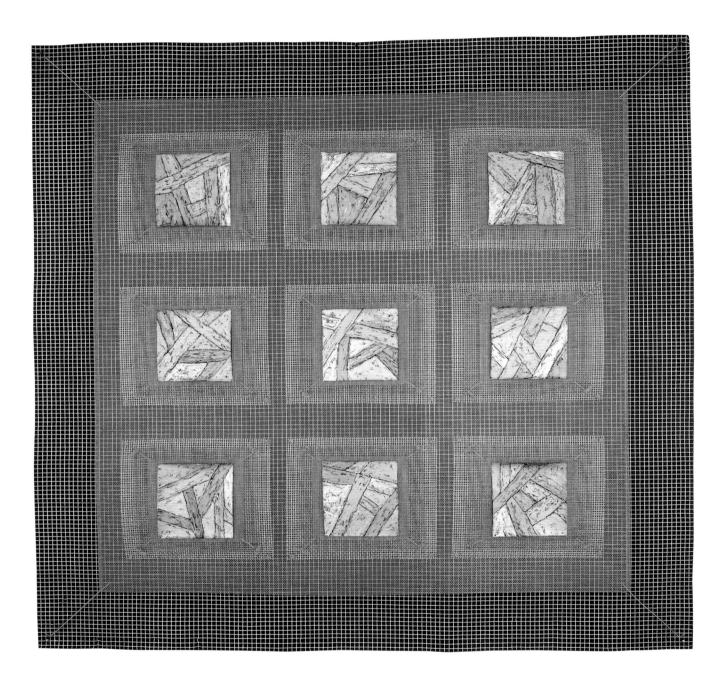

ANNE MARIE KENNY

HOOKSETT, NEW HAMPSHIRE

Woven II
Industrial Quilt

Acrylic paint on cotton canvas, steel and bronze wire cloth, fiberglass mesh, spray paint, wire, and thread; paintings stitched by hand with wire and thread; 37 x 36 inches (94 x 91.4 cm).

Art parallels progress, modern industry, and invention. These influences create new forms of expression and aesthetics. My Industrial Quilts embody the aesthetic quality and confusion of machine-made versus hand-made. I use unconventional materials that complement each other yet provoke the controversy surrounding the way things of value are made. Contrasts such as delicate versus durable, structure versus freedom, decorative versus conceptual, intimate versus impersonal aim at a new aesthetic influenced by tradition and progress.

MARGE HURST

PUKERUA BAY, WELLINGTON, NEW ZEALAND

Tribute to John Wesley Powell

Commercial and hand-dyed cotton and blended
fabrics; machine pieced and machine quilted;
78 x 49 inches (198.1 x 124.5 cm).

Conscious and unconscious absorption of color and pattern drive my quilt making. When the April 1994 issue of National Geographic *arrived on my doorstep just after I finished a quilt of the New Zealand bush colors, the completely different desert colors shown with the article on John Wesley Powell said to me, "Another quilt." Representation of the juxtaposition of colors in nature through a "double colorwash" of lattice and picture has evolved from a variety of experiments.*

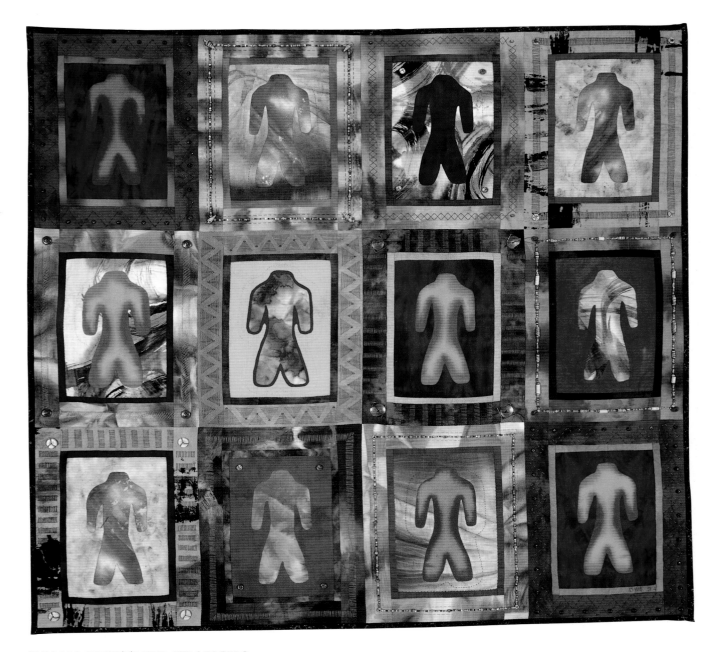

DIANA WHITMER-FRANCKO

OXFORD, OHIO

Trade Routes (Ancient Culture Series)

Commercial and hand-dyed cotton fabrics embellished with beads, shells and hand-made copper buttons; reverse appliquéd, machine pieced, and hand quilted; 38 x 36 inches (96.5 x 91.4 cm).

I have been fascinated and intrigued by the images associated with ancient cultures, especially the Hopewell and Adena cultures in Ohio. This particular quilt is the third in the series on Ancient Cultures. *It is my visual concept of the trade routes through which ancient tribes were able to procure materials not native to their own environments.*

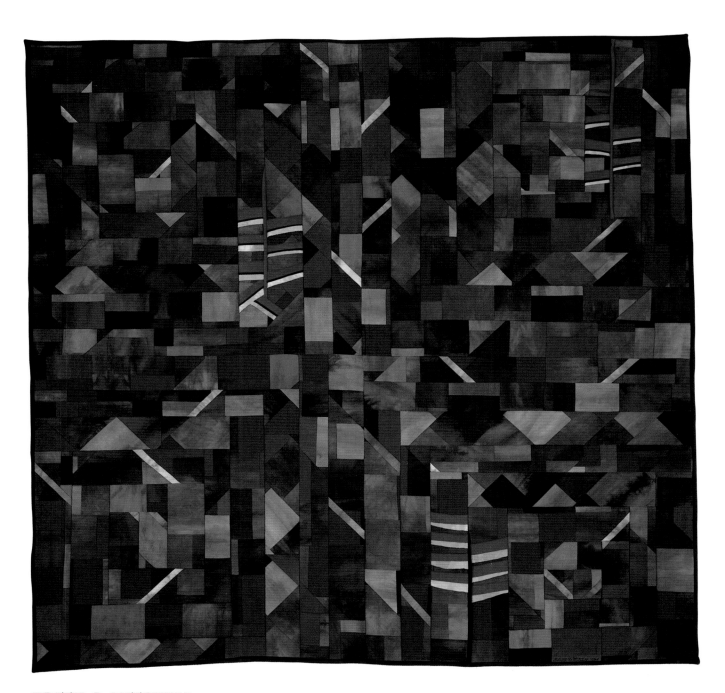

EDITH C. MITCHELL

TUPPER LAKE, NEW YORK

Intuit Square IV:
Heliconia

Hand-dyed cottons by Lunn Fabrics and
Fabrics to Dye For, cotton batting; machine strip-pieced and repieced, machine
stitched and quilted in one operation;
44 x 44 inches (11.8 x 111.8 cm).

Making a quilt frees me up intuitively to develop an idea.
The inspiration for this piece arose from a recent trip
to the rain forests of Costa Rica. Thank you, Walter.

PATRICIA KENNEDY-ZAFRED

PITTSBURGH, PENNSYLVANIA

Innocenza Persa

Commercial fabrics and fabrics
hand dyed by Jan Myers-Newbury,
Kodalith negatives and positives
transferred to acetate; machine
pieced and machine quilted;
16 x 20 inches (40.6 x 50.8 cm).

*This piece reflects on issues of betrayal, entanglement, and lost
innocence. My recent work involves personal experiences that are
universal human emotions. Each piece is interpreted within the
context of the viewer's own experiences, thus allowing a multitude
of impressions and conclusions. There is no right or wrong answer.
I seek to provoke thought and create impact, even if momentary.*

LAURA WASILOWSKI

ELGIN, ILLINOIS

Crazy Rose

Cotton fabrics that have been hand dyed, painted, stamped, and silk screened; machine pieced and machine quilted; 41 x 35 inches (104.1 x 88.9 cm).

Crazy Rose *resulted from two classic housekeeping problems: an inability to throw anything away and a lack of storage space. For years, my garment business, Kaleidoscope Clothing, has generated boxes of my hand-dyed and printed fabric scraps.* Rose *grew from those boxes. She didn't deplete the boxes by a long shot but she did grow to be my inspiration for more quilts. Her sisters may emerge during spring cleaning.*

1995

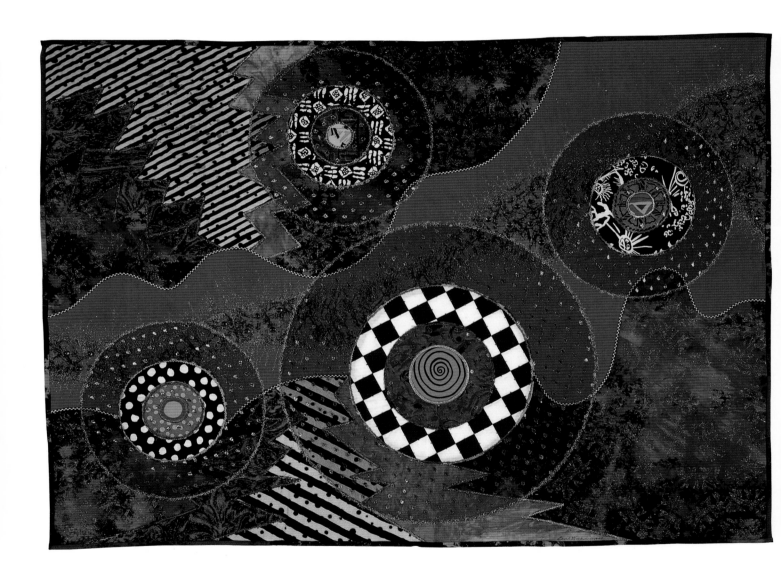

DAVID WALKER

CINCINNATI, OHIO

Passing Through

Netting and cotton fabrics, some of which have been bleached and overdyed; machine appliquéd, machine quilted, and machine embroidered, hand stamped and embellished with beads; 48 x 41 inches (121.9 x 104.1 cm).

This quilt is dedicated to my friend Charlie Bolan who died on May 30, 1993 from complications of the AIDS virus. Exactly one year later, Passing Through, *the first in a series of three quilts, began as a simple statement of how I had tired of grieving. I decided to throw all my unexpressed grief out into the universe, a fitting container, large enough for the stars and the planets and surely large enough to care for my grief as well. I believe that a new constellation now brightens the night sky. I know that Charlie would have it no other way.*

1993

BARBARA OTTO

LAKE ELMO, MINNESOTA

Space:
Grains of Sand

Cotton muslin stamped with thickened Procion H dyes, resist; machine quilted whole-cloth piece; 63 x 72 inches (160 x 182.9 cm).

The title was chosen upon finishing the piece and is used to suggest the connection between the number of grains of sand on a beach, the number of people that have walked upon this earth, and the number of stars that we can see in the sky. I want my quilts to be beautiful, but also to suggest various ideas, meanings, and metaphors to different people. Using a whole-cloth, dye-painting technique blurs the distinction between painting and quilting, and encourages people to wonder about how we define art.

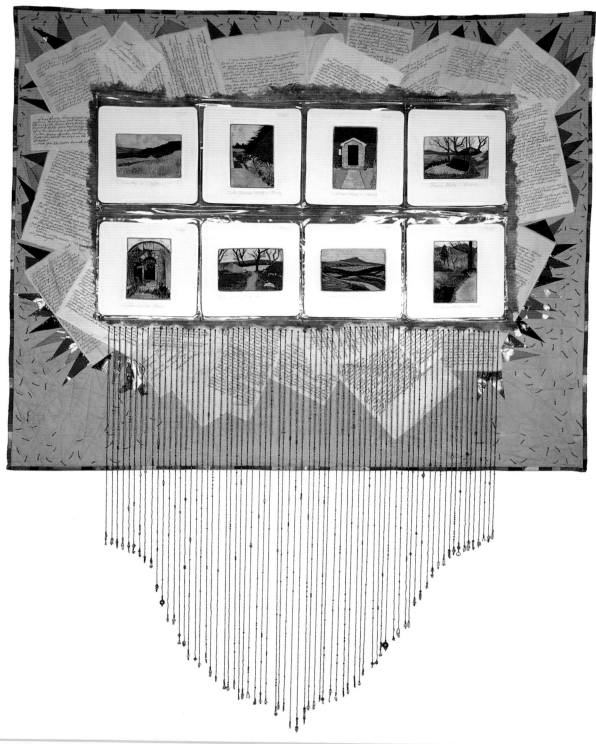

DURANGO, COLORADO

Reredos,
Prayer for Return...

Cotton fabrics dyed with commercial and vegetable dyes, metallic threads, theater gels, plastic beads and buttons; hand appliquéd, hand quilted, and a variety of other techniques necessary to achieve the desired look; 54 x 74 inches (137.2 x 188 cm).

To bring a dream to life, one must first make an act, sort of open a door into this world through which the dream can "become." Reredos, a chronicle of a pilgrimage to ancestral lands, is that first step. That step is the first in the journey to Ireland, the fulfillment of a lifelong dream. A prayer, "reredos," opens the door for my return.

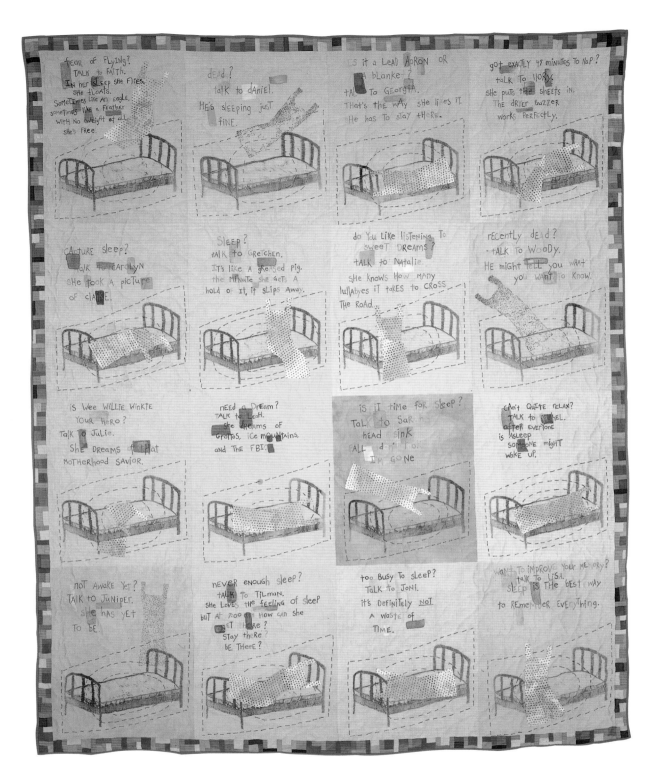

RACHEL BRUMER

SEATTLE, WASHINGTON

Conked Out

Commercial and hand-dyed cottons by Lunn Fabrics and Fabrics to Dye For, paint, fabric sensitizer; contact painted, hand appliquéd, machine pieced, and hand quilted; 61 x 75 inches (154.9 x 190.5 cm).

I collected these sleep epigrams from a group of friends over the course of several months. They are reflections on that most wonderful activity— sleep. In some cultures, sleep is seen as a rehearsal for death. I composed two of these epigrams in memory of two friends who recently died.

LINDA R. MACDONALD

WILLITS, CALIFORNIA

My Friends 2

Cotton fabric that has been
hand dyed, airbrushed, and
hand painted; hand quilted;
40 x 36 inches (101.6 x 91.4 cm).

*These shapes were familiar to me once they became visible.
They allude to the micro yet seem at home in their actual
size. This piece is part of a series of Friends of mine.*

GERRY CHASE

SEATTLE, WASHINGTON

Sampler I: Dream House

Cotton fabric, photo transfers, India ink, acrylic paint, and various embellishments; hand appliquéd, machine pieced, and machine quilted; 53 x 42 inches (134.6 x 106.7 cm).

In Sampler I: Dream House, *I am referring to the idea of home as an embodiment of idealizations which can range from nostalgia to idealized utopia. This piece is based on the "sampler" quilt format.*

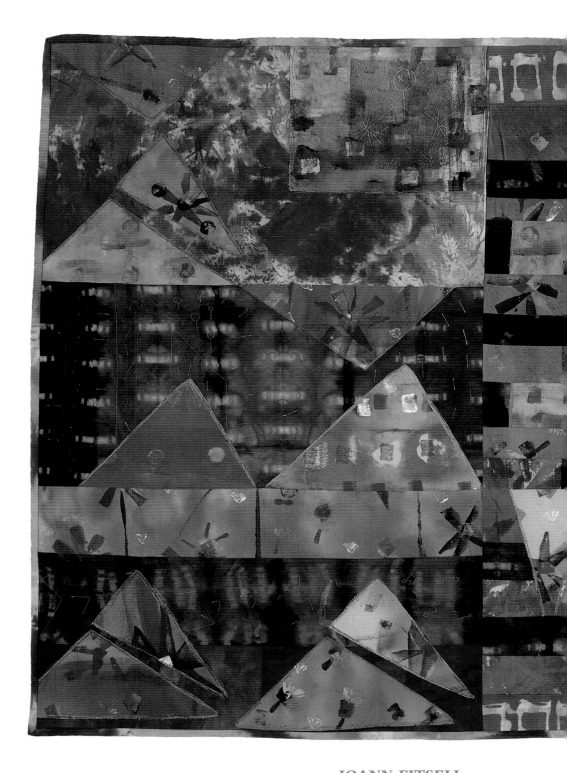

JOANN FITSELL

DENVER, COLORADO

The Meadow Above Me

Canvas and cottons treated by batik and stamping with acrylic paint and Procion dyes; machine pieced, appliquéd, and quilted; 76 x 43 inches (193 x 109.2 cm).

*Every year I climb to a high mountain meadow as an emotional pilgrimage
to reflect on my search for romantic love. Everything seems possible up
there. I have experienced perfect beauty along with doubt, disbelief, and
danger. I have gotten lost and scared and have been run off the mountain
by a dangerous storm. In this piece I am reminding myself as I climb/search
to appreciate the beauty of both the mountain flowers and the rocks below.*

LIBBY LEHMAN

HOUSTON, TEXAS

Free Fall

Cotton, purchased hand-dyed fabrics embellished with machine embroidery using rayon metallic and Sulky Silver threads; machine pieced and machine quilted; 41 x 41 inches (104.1 x 104.1 cm).

INVITATIONAL WORK: QUILT NATIONAL '95 JUROR

I am currently exploring the design possibilities of machine embroidery. Some embroidery was done prior to piecing and some was added later. I like to work intuitively, letting the quilt emerge rather than planning ahead.

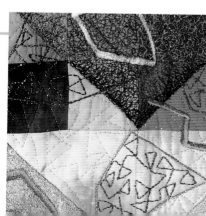

KATHERINE L. MCKEARN AND DIANE MUSE

TOWNSON, MARYLAND AND MADRID, IOWA

DON'T BUG US.

Psycho-Moms at Rest

Commercial cottons and various found items including a pot holder, old tablecloth, and '50s drapery fabric; hand appliquéd, machine pieced, and hand quilted; 59 x 80 inches (149.9 x 203.2 cm).

NINA MORTI

CARBONDALE, ILLINOIS

Sityatki Whales

Cotton fabric hand dyed by Eric Morti, silk, Sulky threads, batting; fabric collage with hand and machine stitching; 32 x 42 inches (81.3 x 106.7 cm).

When my son was three years old, he gave me a picture of "whales" that he had drawn with markers. He had simply sprawled on the floor and gone to work. I watched as he worked with the pure abandon I envied. I had been reading about petroglyphs and his "whales" reminded me of ancient art, so I decided to use his drawing as a basis for a representation of painting on rocks.

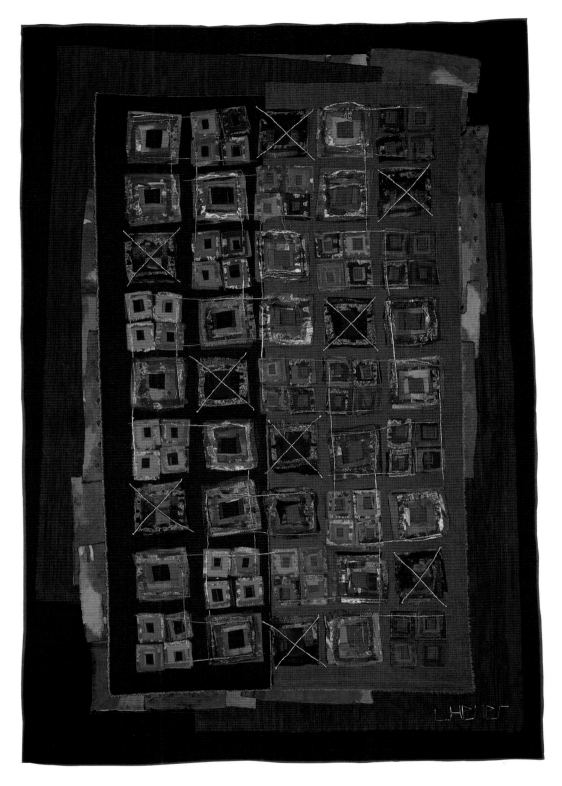

LYNNE HELLER

TORONTO, ONTARIO, CANADA

Blue/Orange Mola/Quilt

Cotton, silk, silk organza, polyester organza, rayon, and wool; hand and machine stitched; 36 x 54 inches (91.4 x 137.2 cm).

The tactile pleasure of manipulating fabric has encouraged me to explore age-old techniques of layering and stitching to create a hybrid of quilt making and molas (reverse appliqué) technique. I used the grid motifs and repeat patterns of quilts to establish a visual structure. Then, by cutting through the fabric, I expose the layers underneath the surface, creating depth and interest with an improvisational quality.

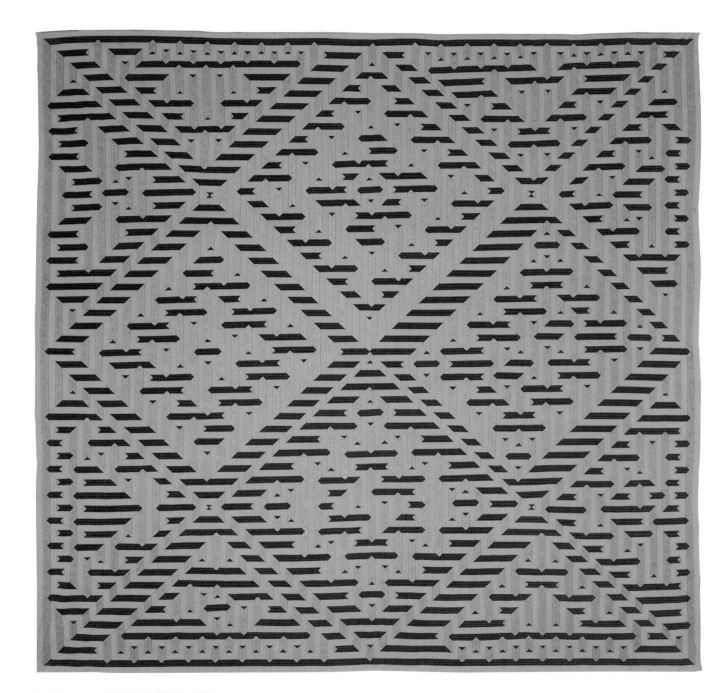

ELLEN OPPENHEIMER

OAKLAND, CALIFORNIA

Head Gasket Maze

Silk-screened and hand-dyed
fabric; machine sewn and
hand quilted; 60 x 60 inches
(152.4x 152.4 cm).

In 1990 I began a series of quilts that were concerned with lines and stripes. These frequently take on the quality of a labyrinth or maze. The series has been immensely satisfying because I am able to address color, form, and content in a compelling format. I feel these pieces also refer to various historical or ethnic textiles. In Head Gasket Maze *I am particularly interested in exploring a new palette of dyes and inks.*

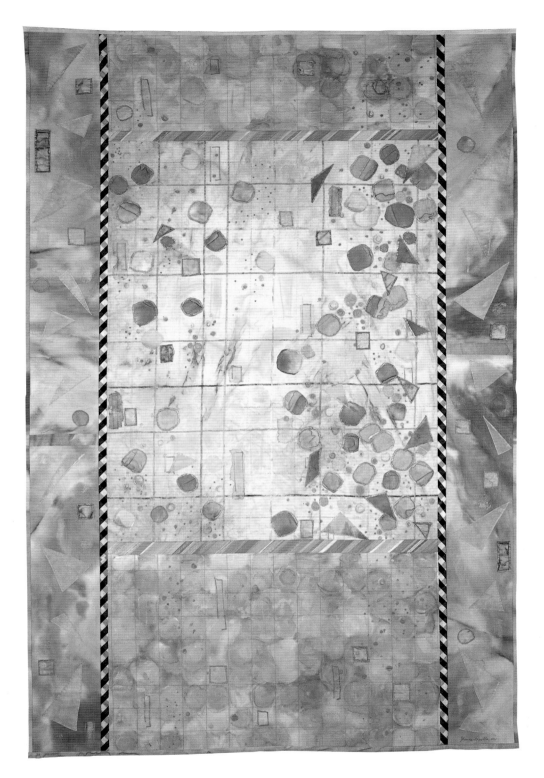

C661

YVONNE PORCELLA

MODESTO, CALIFORNIA

Yo Yolanda

Silks, cottons, cotton blends,
silk ribbon, metallic inks;
hand painted, hand and
machine quilted; 42 x 64
inches (106.7 x 162.6 cm).

*A basic grid configuration anchors the design, circular brush
strokes and appliquéd shapes are confined within the geometric
form of the grid. Rectangles, squares, and triangles also appear
as appliquéd and painted shapes. A variety of techniques were
used to paint the different fabrics. The narrow black and white
vertical bands echo the subtle pastel diagonal painted horizontal
bands adding an element of surprise to the composition.*

SUZAN FRIEDLAND

SAN FRANCISCO, CALIFORNIA

Savannah Cloth

Linen and silk; machine pieced and quilted, hand painted, laced with linen twine; 59 x 79 inches (149.9 x 200.7 cm).

Savannah Cloth was inspired by African mud cloth from Bamako in Southern Mali and strip weaving from the savannah lands of Western Africa. A combination of physical constraints (e.g. loom size) and aesthetic criteria (e.g. means of combining strips) leads to the unique relationship between individual pieces and the whole. In more than any other art form I have encountered, the pieces push the limits of maintaining an individual integrity while still working together as a whole.

JAN MYERS-NEWBURY

PITTSBURGH, PENNSYLVANIA

Ophelia's Dream

100 percent cotton muslin tie-dyed with Procion fiber reactive dyes; machine pieced and machine quilted; 76 x 68 inches (193 x 172.7 cm).

Ophelia's Dream *is the current omega of a year-long evolution in my work from the geometric to the organic. I have never been as excited about the potential of applying transparent color to fabric as I am now. I have always been interested in manipulating color to create luminosity and the illusion of depth, and more and more of this seems to be happening in the dyepot, less in the piecing. And the layering of color upon color in a single yard of cloth seems a perhaps not accidental metaphor for the portion of my life that has fed these 18 years of quilt making.*

JULIA E. PFAFF

RICHMOND, VIRGINIA

#109, Why Have We Come Here?/Dashur

Hand-dyed and painted cotton, zinc plate intaglio printing; machine pieced, hand embroidered, hand and machine quilted; 84 x 61 inches (213.4 x 154.9 cm).

*This quilt is based on my experience working at the archeological site of Dashur located
south of Cairo, Egypt. The form of the mud brick pyramid was distorted by erosion,
but underground, where I worked drawing the sarcophagi, the burial chambers were
left intact. These mysterious chambers seemed haunted by the royal princesses who
had intended to inhabit them for eternity. My interest lies in the nexus of the physical
and spiritual, the known and the unknown, the found and the sought.*

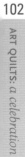

JANICE FASSINGER

CAMBRIDGE, OHIO

Our Lives—Our Work

Wool felt and photos; knotted;
34 x 40 inches (86.4 x 101.6 cm).

I came to understand the great strength and comfort of quilts by learning to make them from women who knew: knew the determination required by a project so complex; knew and accepted the pain of fingers that quilt (no cry-babies); knew how each quilt marks, not time, but our lives—secrets shared or sewn into each piece, events which, for Everywoman, become a record of her life. This work pays homage to my sisters.

EMILY RICHARDSON

PHILADELPHIA, PENNSYLVANIA

Night Clock

Textile paint on silk and cotton,
nylon net, silk suture thread, and
cotton embroidery floss; direct
and reverse hand appliquéd
and embroidered; hand quilted;
60 x 82 inches (152.4 x 208.3 cm).

*Night Clock is a bed-size quilt made from painted strips of
sheer and lightweight fabrics, woven together in a way that
suggests dreams and thoughts weaving through a mind as it
sleeps: transparent, merging and dividing, creating and altering
time.* Night Clock *measures the unbalanced hours of our
sleep—forward, backward, lingering on one thing, leaping
to another, indifferent to any time but its own.*

The path to the Giant Pines is a hiking/skiing trail in Tahquamenon State Park in Michigan's Upper Peninsula. Here, I continue my work with layering by exploring the detritus of the forest floor. Ignoring organic shapes and relying on the grid for structure allowed me to fully explore the play of color, light, and texture, as well as what is revealed and what is concealed.

BARBARA BUSHEY

ANN ARBOR, MICHIGAN

Path to the Giant Pines IV

Cotton, acetate, cheesecloth, and polyester; dyed, painted, discharged, layered, and machine stitched; 13 x 26 inches (33 x 66 cm).

ALISON SCHWABE

SHELLEY, AUSTRALIA

Obiri

Hand-dyed commercial fabrics; reverse appliquéd, machine pieced, and machine quilted, hand embroidered; 20 x 28 inches (50.8 x 71.1 cm).

A recurring theme in some of my quilts is the fascination with man-made marks and patterns on natural surfaces. In the Northern Territory, Australia, stands Obiri Rock, surrounded by green. Rock overhangs protect ancient markings from annual torrential rains and fierce sunlight. The visitor looks far out across the plains, and behind, sees far back into history through painted images there. The gold embroidery represents the value to us of all such legacies.

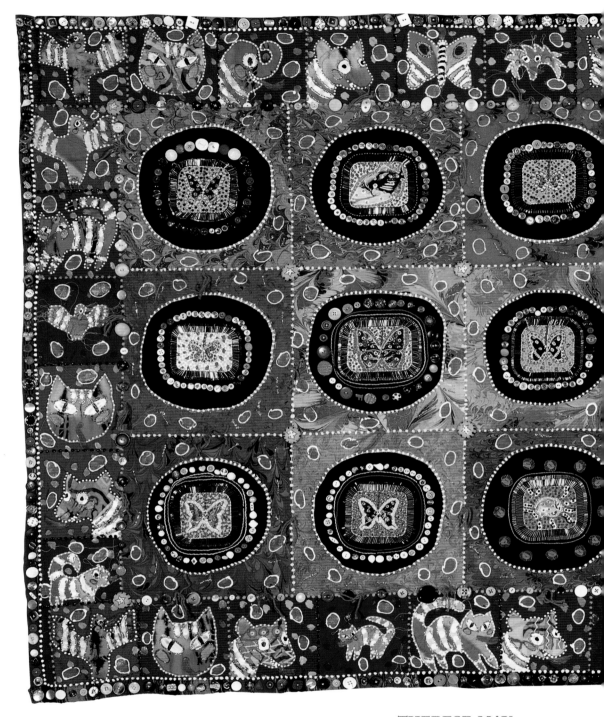

THERESE MAY

SAN JOSE, CALIFORNIA

Contemplating the Nine Patch

Painted panels on mat board; hand quilted and tied, embellished with paint, beads and buttons; 90 x 50 inches (228.6 x 127 cm). Courtesy of Mobilia Gallery.

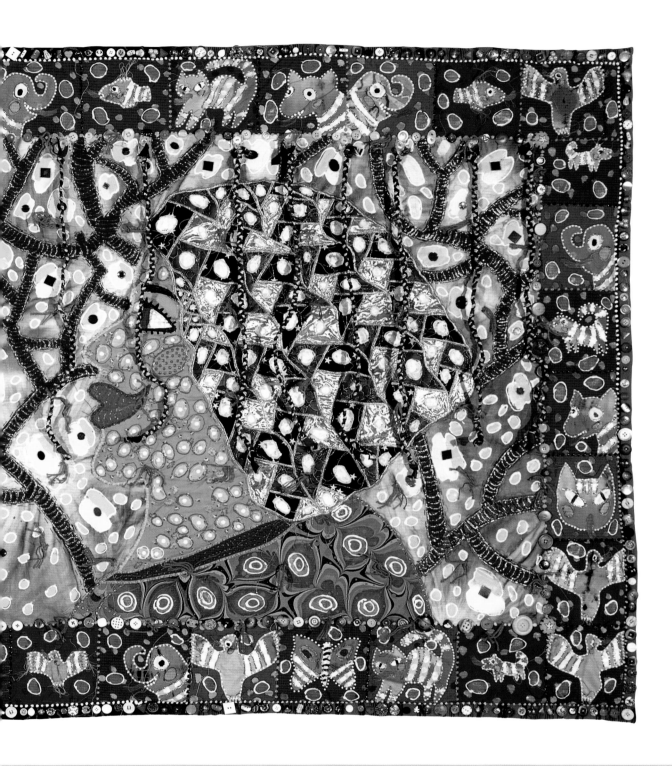

This quilt emerged as I thought about the traditional quilt versus the art quilt. Even though this quilt is based more on a painting concept, I wanted to express something about the beauty of the traditional quilt and the idea of sewing squares together.

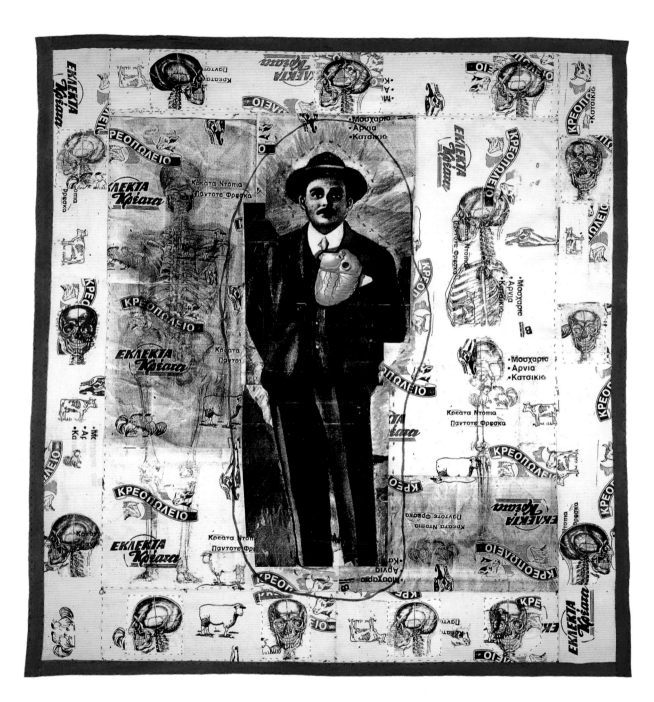

LISA CLARK

BURNSVILLE, NORTH CAROLINA

Blood and Bone

Paint, paper, fabric, thread, and
ink; phototransfer, monoprint,
hand stitched and painted,
35 x 38 inches (88.9 x 96.5 cm).

*This piece is part of a series in which I am exploring the question,
"What is it to be human?" Are we merely blood and bone? I am
looking for spirit in the body through the physical. Feeling my
blood as the source of life, finding its source at the heart, feeling
bones as physical structures that remain as imprints after life.*

Overlay 1 *is one of several quilts in which I have tried to present a grid composed of pieces varied in shape, pattern, color, and size, floating above an irregularly pieced background. I work with a method of curved strip piecing that introduces some unpredictability into my quilting. Never knowing exactly what to expect as I bring the quilt together, I remain intrigued throughout the construction process.*

RUTH GARRISON

TEMPE, ARIZONA

Overlay 1

Cotton fabrics, some hand dyed; machine pieced and machine quilted; 40 x 79 inches (101.6 x 200.7 cm).

HOLLIS CHATELAIN

HILLSBORO, NORTH CAROLINA

Changes

Commercial fabrics printed in
Mali, Western Africa; machine
pieced, hand quilted, and then
hand painted; 90 x 67 inches
(228.6 x 170.2 cm).

*The beauty and contrast of Africa influence me in everyday life. This
quilt is the starting point of my evolution from African prints to colored
fabrics (that I also paint). Extensive use of the prints taught me how to
use bold colors.* Changes *has also helped me to discover my own style.*

PAULA NADELSTERN

BRONX, NEW YORK

Kaleidoscopic XIII: Random Acts of Color

Cottons and blends; machine pieced and hand quilted; 59 x 56 inches (149.9 x 142.2 cm).

Kaleidoscope: the very word promises surprise and magic, change and chance. In choosing fabrics, I seek a random quality to imitate the chance interlinkings and endless possibilities synonymous with kaleidoscopes. The notion that there isn't an absolute or best selection is liberating. After all, a breathtaking collision of color in a scope's interior will maneuver into something different, something slightly new, during even the instant it takes to hand it to you.

MIDGE HOFFMANN

COBURG, OREGON

Cosmic Garden

Silk dupioni that has been painted, stamped, and stenciled; fused and machine quilted; 25 x 35 inches (63.5 x 88.9 cm).

Design, pure color, and pattern are my passions. This piece is the first I have produced with a method new to me—painting silk, cutting, fusing, and random machine stitching. This method suits me. It is quick and spontaneous, painterly with a sense of quiltness. This work reflects the interconnectedness of life and matter throughout the universe. Stars, planets, and comets are growing in this garden.

MARY ALLEN CHAISSON

SOUTH HARPSWELL, MAINE

Pecos

Indonesian batik and assorted commercial cottons and blends that have been hand painted, dyed, and stamped; machine pieced and hand tied; 46 x 58 inches (116.8 x 147.3 cm).

The Pecos National Monument sits on a low mesa amidst a magnificent landscape in the Southwest. Having visited this splendid Pueblo ruin with its two mission churches, kivas, and multiple domed adobes, one can only imagine life between A.D. 1450 and 1838 for the Native Americans and the Spanish conquerors.

JANE A. SASSAMAN

CHICAGO, ILLINOIS

Overgrown Garden

Commercial and hand-stencilled
cotton fabrics; machine appliquéd
and machine quilted; 27 x 41
 inches (68.6 x 104.1 cm).

Overgrown Garden *attempts to capture the inex-
haustible vitality of nature. This garden is organized
but has become a gloriously undisciplined field
of energy, each flower contributing its glory to the
overall radiant effect. We are all flowers in the garden.*

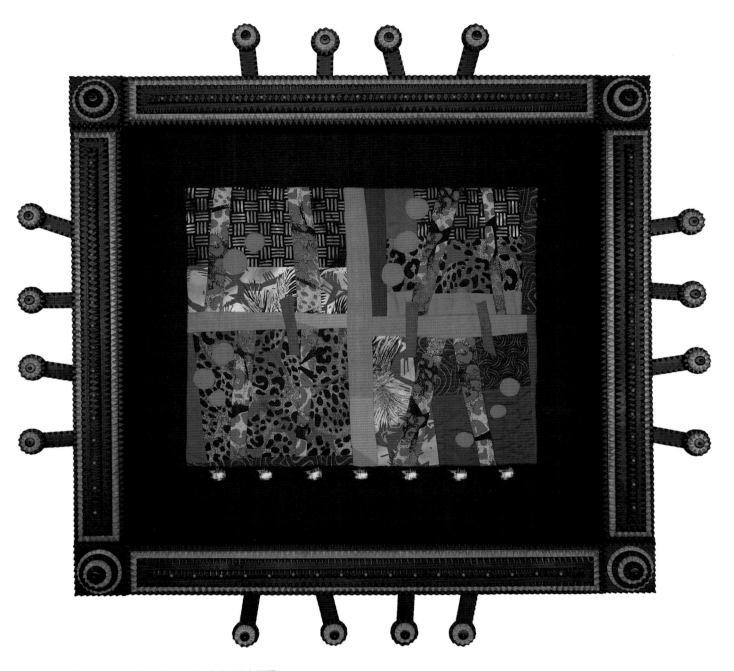

MARILYN AND HERB DILLARD

LONGMONT, COLORADO

Naive Art

Cotton fabrics; machine pieced, hand quilted, and embroidered; aspen wood frame, chip carved and painted, embellished with map tacks; 40 x 37 inches (101.6 x 94 cm).

Sometimes a new work knows what it wants to become and dictates its own transformation. Naive Art, our first collaboration, is such a quilt. After spontaneously cutting and piecing fabrics, Marilyn developed this small stitchery that has a primitive folk art quality. In order to give the small piece integrity, Herb constructed and beautifully carved the frame. The completed work seems warm and friendly—happy that it came into being.

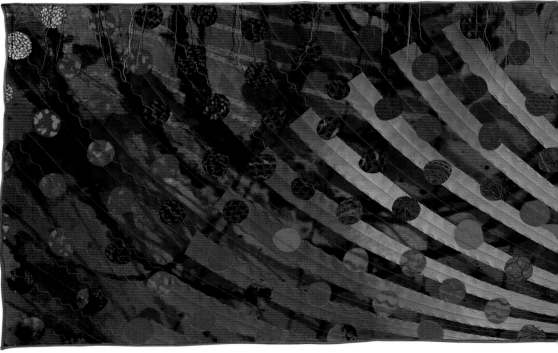

SUE BENNER

DALLAS, TEXAS

Sink or Swim #21 & #22

Commercial silks treated with dyes; fused and
machine quilted; 61 x 35 inches (154.9 x 88.9 cm).

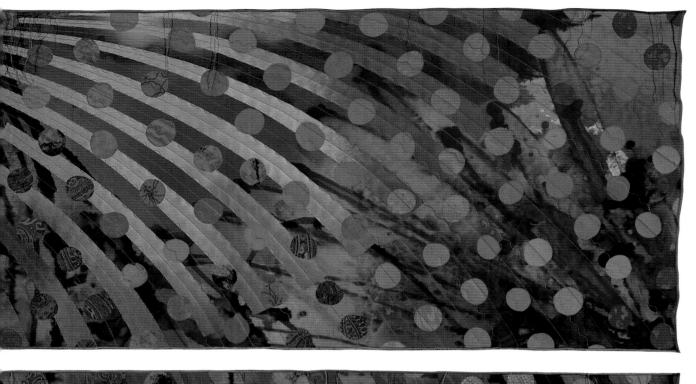

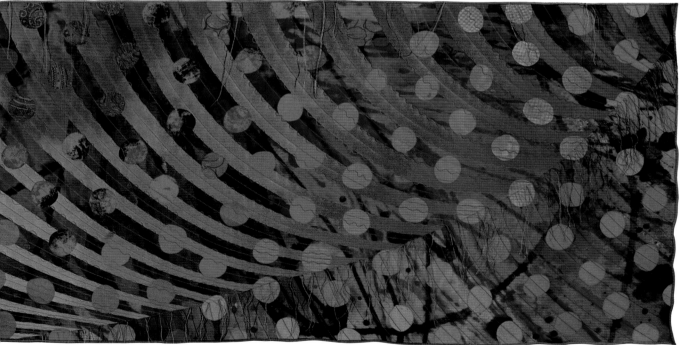

Two ideas came together at the inception of the Sink or Swim *series. I had recently given birth to my first son and found myself alternately floating and sinking in a sea of motherhood. Also, my dye-painted silks began to remind me of underwater environments. Later in the series, as I gained confidence, I added elements of tropical fish. After the birth of my second son, I am still swimming.*

FRAN SKILES

PLANTATION, FLORIDA

Red Landscape

Cotton duck fabric and woven printed hemp treated with oil stick, acrylic, and fabric paint; machine stitched; 63 x 52 inches (160 x 132.1 cm).

My assemblages are about old, decaying materials—old wooden piers, buildings and the stuff found therein. Traditionally, I turn to landscapes for design. My thoughts and elements are abstract. The imagery I use in my quilts is from my own photography. I want the image to lose its identity and become a part of the whole.

ELIZABETH BRIMELOW

MACCLESFIELD, CHESHIRE, ENGLAND

Elsworth

Dyed, discharged, and screen-printed fabric; appliquéd (direct and reverse) and embroidered, hand quilted and tied; 70 x 70 inches (177.8 x 177.8 cm).

The inspiration for my work is the landscape and man's mark on it. I am very aware of earlier cultures and times and how man has left behind evidence of his presence. Disclose, lay open, reveal, discover and uncover are key words and have influenced my textile techniques. I stitch and manipulate cloth, which I use for its tactile quality, it substance, and its intimacy.

REVERSE VIEW

JILL PACE

GLENDALE, ARIZONA

Heaven's Gate

Cotton fabric; machine pieced,
hand appliquéd, hand embroidered,
hand beaded, and hand quilted;
82 x 82 inches (208.3 x 208.3 cm).

I was inspired to make Heaven's Gate *after viewing a television program about people's near-death experiences. I was amazed by how similar the stories were. All described themselves floating down a corridor with colorful squares of light and the glowing outline of a figure reaching out to them. All of the people reported that the experience was very peaceful and that they no longer feared death. After the show, I also felt more peaceful about death and what happens after…it truly is only "another horizon."*

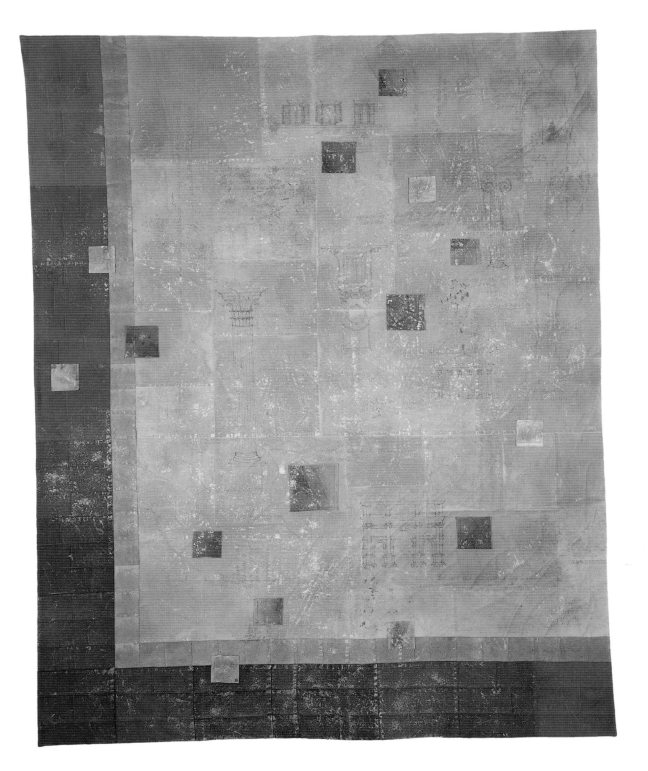

JANE REEVES

CANTON, OHIO

Borghese

Hand-dyed cotton embellished with paint and ink; machine pieced and appliquéd, hand quilted; 43 x 55 inches (109.2 x 139.7 cm).

Borghese *is meant to look like an old stucco wall: peeling, crumbling and spotted with mud. Drawings of architectural fragments and written quotations are partially obscured by layers of paint. The quilting outlines a street map of Rome. I want the quilt to show the layers of meaning which accumulate around buildings, places, and ideas with the passage of time.*

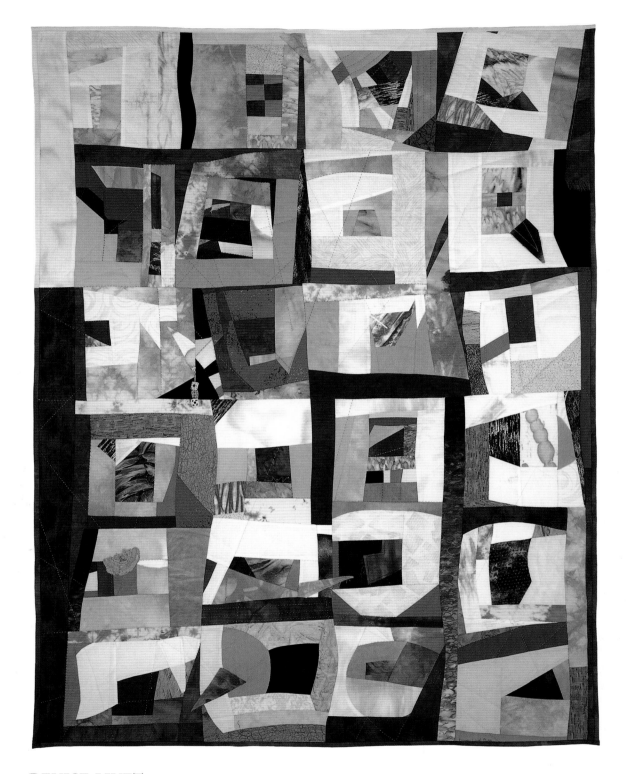

DENISE LINET

CENTER HARBOR, NEW HAMPSHIRE

Zen Circles

Commercial and hand-dyed cotton
and linen fabrics; machine pieced
and hand quilted, embellished with
beads and found objects; 41 x 55
inches (104.1 x 139.7 cm).

This quilt was inspired by Sue Bender's book Everyday Sacred.
*Each morning I would go into my studio to compose a "circle,"
and I'd wait to see how my muse would fill the void. I eagerly
looked forward to the new inspiration that quickly filled the
empty space on my design wall. The challenge was to take
each individual "circle" and create a coherent whole.*

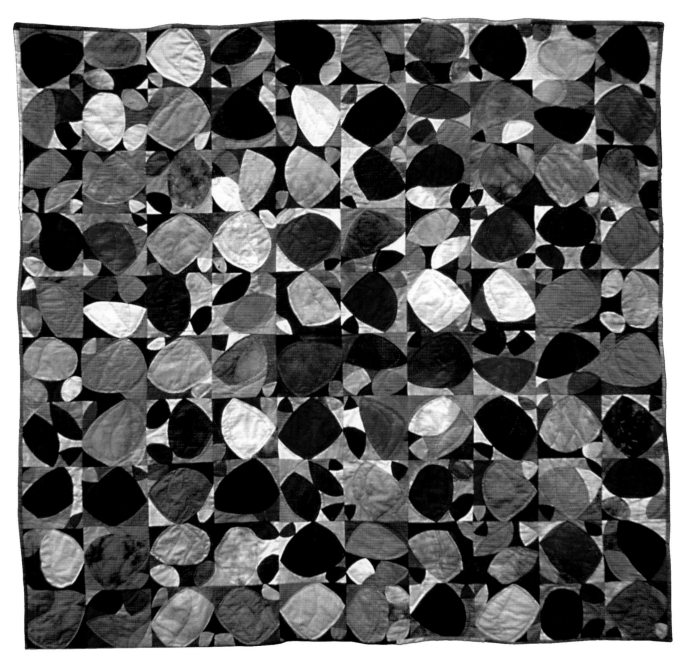

CONNIE SCHEELE

HOUSTON, TEXAS

611 River Rocks

Hand-dyed cotton fabrics,
cotton batting, silk and cotton
quilting threads; machine pieced
and hand quilted; 60 x 60 inches
(152.4 x 152.4 cm).

*This is the third quilt in a series inspired by river rocks. I have
canoed the Brule River in Northern Wisconsin since I was
a young girl, and love the look of the river rocks through
clear water. After dyeing a wide range of neutral fabrics, I felt
compelled to create quilts that incorporate the wonderful
colors of nature and the fascinating shapes of the river rocks.*

NIKI BONNETT

GREENWICH, CONNECTICUT

American in Asia:
A Fabric Diary of Hong Kong, Thailand, The Easter & Oriental Express, Singapore, Tokyo, & Kyoto

Various fabrics and found objects; pieced, appliquéd, collaged, and quilted; 83 x 53 inches (210.8 x 134.6 cm).

*In 1995, I spent four weeks in Asia. Before going, I made a diary—an American
flag—from a painter's drop cloth and divided it into one "page" for each day.
I expected that each day my parochial American outlook would be overlaid with
uniquely Asian impressions, and I wanted to record them. The fabric diary does
show some of my experiences, but, primarily, it reminds me of how this trip has
changed the way I see everything. I think of it as a sampler. If I could think of
a technique, I tried it; if I could get a medium to stick, I used it.*

SYLVIA H. EINSTEIN

BELMONT, MASSACHUSETTS

Spring

Cottons and blends; machine
pieced and machine quilted;
36 x 36 inches (91.4 x 91.4 cm).

*My quilts are autobiographical and a tribute to the resilience of the human
spirit. I like arranging scraps—found materials of someone else's design—
into a new form. With printed, eccentric fabric I peruse chance encounters
of lines and colors, and out of this dialogue with the material comes the
finished product. Quilts have a history and a language of their own.
I am joining the many women who have written their diaries in cloth.*

12

JANE A. SASSAMAN

CHICAGO, ILLINOIS

Weeds

Cottons and various threads; machine appliquéd and machine quilted; 42 x 42 inches (106.7 x 106.7 cm). Private collection.

Restless weeds, persistent in their divine right to flourish. Are they calamitous pests or triumphant flowers? I'm sure they are unaware of their sinister reputation as they weave their way to the sun. Are they not as majestic as a delicately cultivated blossom? Shouldn't they be admired for their tenacious energy, determination, and shameless pride? Love them or hate them, you must be fascinated by their stunning life force and uninhibited creativity.

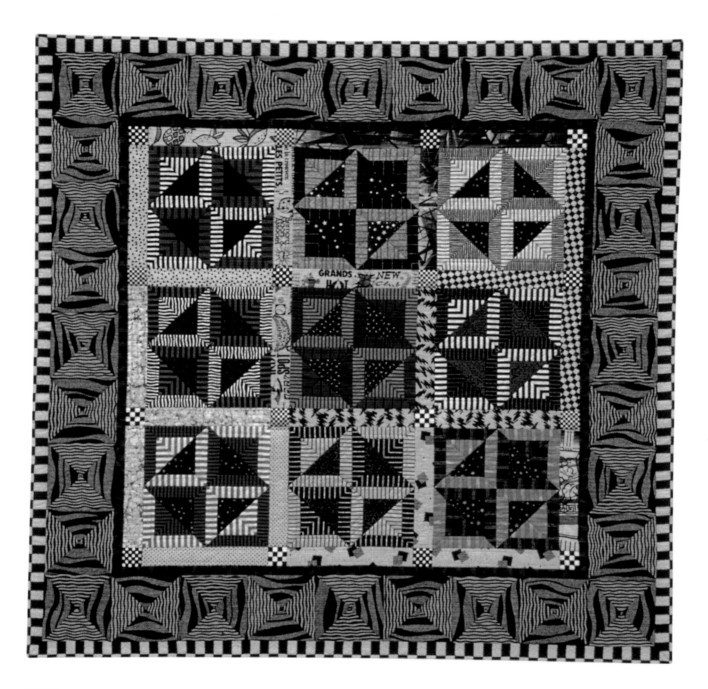

MARY MASHUTA

BERKELEY, CALIFORNIA

Checker Cab:
New York City, 2 A.M.

Commercial and hand silk-screened
(by Katie Pasquini Masopust) fabrics;
machine pieced and machine quilted;
64 x 64 inches (162.6 x 162.6 cm).

*New York City fascinates me, and I wanted to make a story quilt
that would capture an impression of the place. On one trip I awoke
at 2:00 A.M. and was amazed to hear the cacophony of sounds outside my window...taxis and cars still going strong with their horns.
I decided to work with this sound memory.*

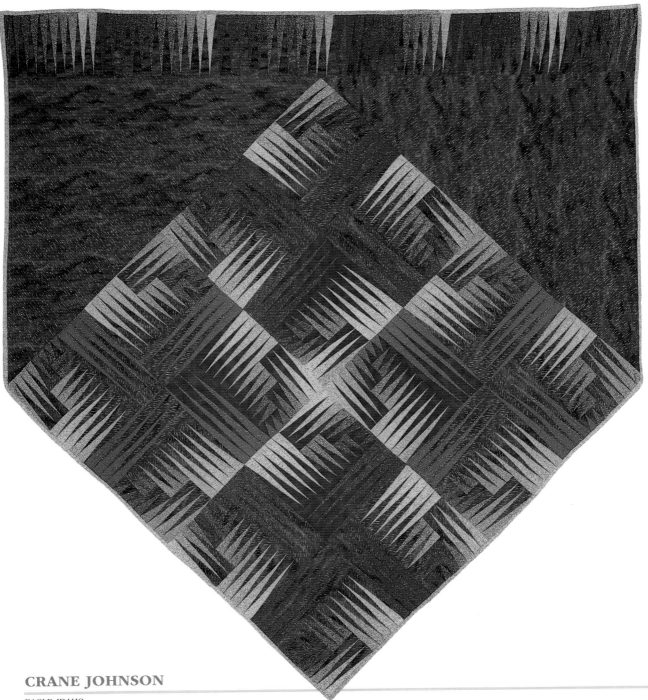

CRANE JOHNSON

EAGLE, IDAHO

Calyx 2

Commercial cotton; machine
pieced and hand quilted with
metallic thread; 55 x 61 inches
(139.7 x 154.9 cm).

*Love of botany and quilting join forces in my Calyx series, a
study of the outer floral envelope reduced to its simplest elements.
Cultivation of flowers in my garden and my quilt making process
requires time and care; I've learned patience from both.*

13

ERIKA CARTER

BELLEVUE, WASHINGTON

Traces V

Hand-painted cotton and silk
organza; machine appliquéd and
machine quilted; 46 x 67 inches
(116.8 x 170.2 cm).

*As a metaphor for time, the cave can be seen as both a
timeless and a time-filled environment. On the walls in*
Traces V *are machine-stitched counting marks, reminiscent
of marks scratched by a survivor. The counting, however,
becomes less accurate near the top of the quilt, challenging
the meaning of counting as it relates to time.*

GERRY CHASE

SEATTLE, WASHINGTON

Repeat Block IV: Vessels

Cotton fabric embellished with ink, acrylic paint, and computer process; machine pieced, hand and machine quilted; 29 x 25 inches (73.7 x 63.5 cm).

The world of postage stamps, with its array of multiple images and its abundance of borders and text, is a rich source of inspiration for me. Also, I find the sampler and repeat block formats together irresistible for their invitation to express "sameness within difference" and "difference within sameness." Repeat Block IV: Vessels reflects my penchant for making the border an active part of my compositions and for using the visual qualities of text.

JUDY TURNER

CHAPMAN, AUSTRALIA

Desert Sky

Wool fabric embellished with
couched woolen yarns; machine
pieced and machine quilted;
41 x 36 inches (104.1 x 91.4 cm).

*Desert Sky was inspired by my memory of a camping trip
in Central Australia many years ago. Despite the rich, vast
landscape, the land is still overwhelmed by the clear blue sky.*

TERESA BARKLEY

MAPLEWOOD, NEW JERSEY

Tea Will Make It Better

Commercial cotton and rayon, found
textile objects; machine pieced, hand
appliquéd, and machine quilted; 61 x 71
inches (154.9 x 180.3 cm).

*I did not drink tea at all when I first met my husband, but
I finally yielded to his frequent offerings to have a cup. Over
the years, tea has been a great source of enjoyment. Through
both its delicious flavors and its ritualistic preparation, the
experience of tea is a comfort. Whether faced with exhaustion,
tension, confusion, anxiety, or cold, tea will make it better.*

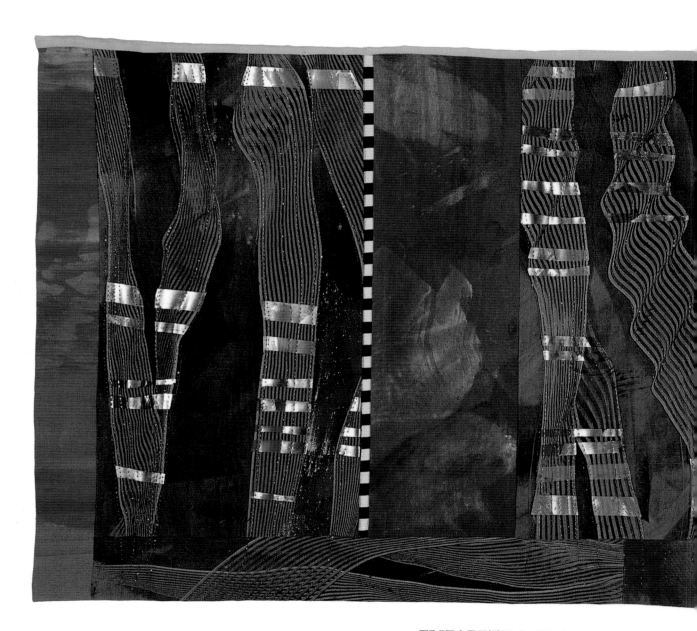

ELIZABETH A. BUSCH

GLENBURN, MAINE

Great Barrier Reef: Submerge

Textile inks on canvas, embellished with acetate, metal leaf, and mica powders; machine pieced and machine quilted; 49 x 20 inches (124.5 x 50.8 cm).

This spring I had the good fortune to teach for several weeks in Australia.
At the end of this time I spent a day on the Great Barrier Reef. I was
awestruck by the unreal color of both water and fish, and I attempted to
remember and put such color to canvas as soon as I returned to Maine.

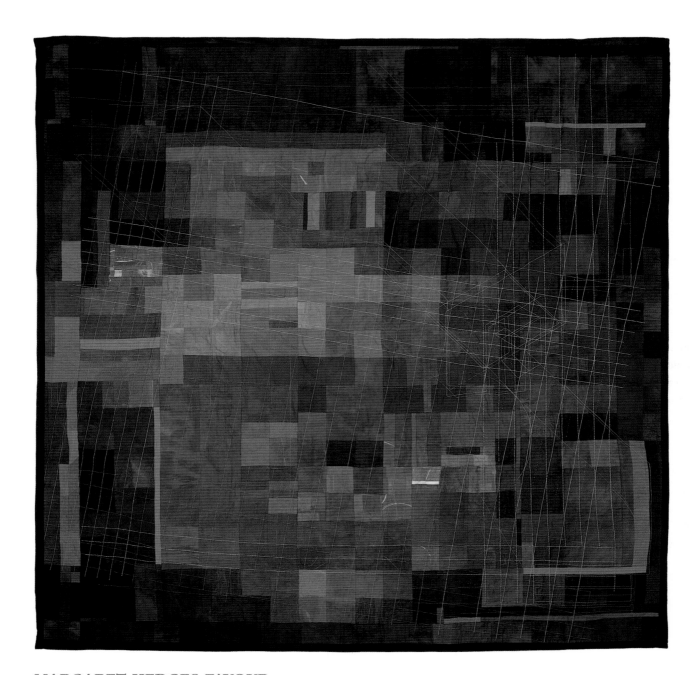

MARGARET HEDGES FAVOUR

ALBUQUERQUE, NEW MEXICO

House at Abiquiu Lake

Hand-dyed cotton fabrics; machine
pieced and embellished with hand and
machine topstitching, machine quilted;
52 x 52 inches (132.1 x 132.1 cm).

*Years ago I regularly traveled back and forth between Albuquerque
and Northern New Mexico to take my children to their father's house
at Abiquiu Lake. The experience translated into a blue field where
linear objects give reference to enclosure, while the composition alludes
to dissolution of boundaries. Superimposed and dissociated systems
of stitched lines, pieced patterns, and bleached marks interface and
associate the urban grid of one world with the rural landscape of another.*

An artist friend's courageous battle with breast cancer inspired a series of works entitled Shields for Women Warriors. *The idea of soft armor that provided psychological protection with its positive energy soon grew into a visual way to deal with my own realities: menopause, hot flashes, and a mother with Alzheimer's.* For the Tribe of the One-Breasted Women *is for Lee and all heroic souls surviving with humor and grace.*

BERNIE ROWELL

KNOXVILLE, TENNESSEE

For the Tribe of the One-Breasted Women

Painted cotton canvas; machine appliquéd and collaged, hand and machine quilted, embellished with buttons, beads, and metallic fabrics; 37 x 60 inches (94 x 152.4 cm).

BEATRIZ GRAYSON

WINCHESTER, MASSACHUSETTS

Village Street

Commercial cottons; machine pieced, hand appliquéd, and machine quilted; 43 x 53 inches (109.2 x 134.6 cm).

Currently I am using architectural themes developed mostly from memories of places visited and some never seen. Sometimes I record the exact delight I felt in a particular place; other times reality and fantasy mingle. By and large, all of my quilts reflect loves and interests, past and present.

NANCY HERMAN

MERION, PENNSYLVANIA

Spring

Woven fabric strips; woven in six parts, adhered to interfacing, then woven together and sewn to a backing; 52 x 77 inches (132.1 x 195.6 cm).

For many years I have been exploring color progressions. I am fascinated by the way colors change each other as they move together in a sequence. Recently my work has involved smaller units combined to make larger forms. I model my work from music and growth patterns in nature.

**LESLIE A. GOLOMB
LOUISE SILK**

PITTSBURGH, PENNSYLVANIA

Tallit for
Maurycy Gottlieb

Photo silk-screened silk noil;
machine pieced and hand
quilted; 48 x 76 inches (121.9
x 193 cm). Private collection.

*This Jewish prayer shawl honors the 19th-century
artist Gottlieb and his painting* Jews Praying in the
Synagogue on Yom Kippur. *We made it as part of a
protest against the Museum of the Diaspora in Tel Aviv,
where an altered reproduction of the painting (the women looking
on in the background were removed) was mounted. It was an
outrage both to artists and women that required our reflection.*

SUSAN SHIE & JAMES ACORD

WOOSTER, OHIO

Rainbow Garden—
A Green Quilt

Painted canvas, found objects and materials, including bottle caps, wooden spoons, and clothespins; hand embroidered, hand appliquéd, and hand quilted; 94 x 78 inches (238.8 x 198.1 cm). Courtesy Mobilia Gallery, Cambridge, Massachusetts.

This is our diary of the gardening season in our rainbow-shaped garden. We offer it as a healing blessing for all gardens of the Earth, embodied in the central garden goddess, our Irish friend and artist, Bridget O'Connell. Her pincushion harvest befits a quilter. The leather raccoons were caught together (and freed) as we struggled to get rid of a groundhog. Sewn-in paintings on wood honor our cat, Vikki, and the trapping of the groundhog.

SUE BENNER

DALLAS, TEXAS

Hostess with the Mostest II

Commercial cottons and blends treated with
immersion dyeing, direct application of dyes
and paints, and stamping; machine pieced and
machine quilted; 70 x 45 inches (177.8 x 114.3cm).

The series began with a black and white cotton piqué print from the skirt of a 1970s floor-length hostess dress I rescued from a garage sale at my mother's house. My mother led me to fabric. She taught me to sew. She made me rip seams out and do them again. This quilt is a tribute to my mom, Joanne Benner, the hostess with the mostest.

JOCELYNE PATENAUDE

MONTREAL, QUEBEC, CANADA

Taboo

Recycled 100 percent silk fabric;
English paper-pieced, hand quilted;
55 x 51 inches (139.7 x 129.5 cm).

"Taboo," a Polynesian word for menstruation, also means sacred, valuable, magic, and frightening. It connotes immutable law and the forbidden, expressing recognition of the female origin of the power of blood. Using scraps of recycled clothing, I attempted to express an awareness of inner body/mind or "feeling tones" that otherwise are difficult to communicate.

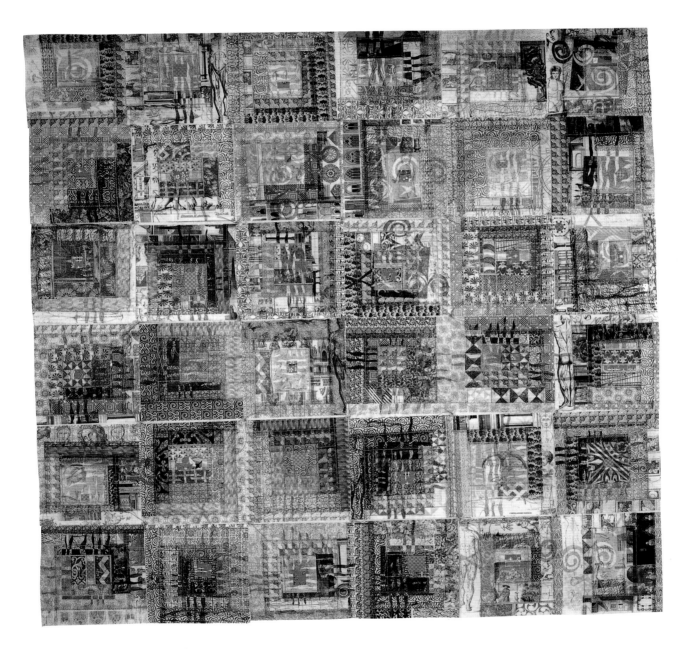

JANE DUNNEWOLD

SAN ANTONIO, TEXAS

Log Cabin for
Hildegard von Bingen

Photocopied and hand-painted interfacing and clear transparencies; fused,
machine and hand stitched, and beaded; 50 x 50 inches (127 x 127 cm).

*I like to listen to the music of Hildegard von Bingen, a 12th-century
Christian mystic. It is ethereal, pure, and beautiful. I also like to interpret
traditional designs in new materials. Industrial interfacing and imagery
on transparencies are natural media to use as we speed toward the end
of this century. Hildegard's Log Cabin cannot physically warm anyone,
but it can be a visual "comforter" because it speaks of the wealth of
human experience and diversity that precedes us, much as an old
quilt comforts us with reminders of a familial past.*

ANNE MARIE OLLIVIER

AUBAGNE, FRANCE

Regard

Commercial and hand-dyed
cottons, lamé; machine pieced
and hand quilted; 64 x 61 inches
(162.6 x 154.9 cm).

*I started with my own photographs of a flower arrangement…precise images that
became increasingly blurred. My aim, as I sewed the small blocks together, was to
begin with a "destructured" image and end with a structured one. Why Regard?
Because I wanted to lead the "spectator" to think about the meaning of my work.
At first and from a distance, one would only see smooth outlines. With a closer
viewing, one would see the jagged lines that simulate the look of live flowers.*

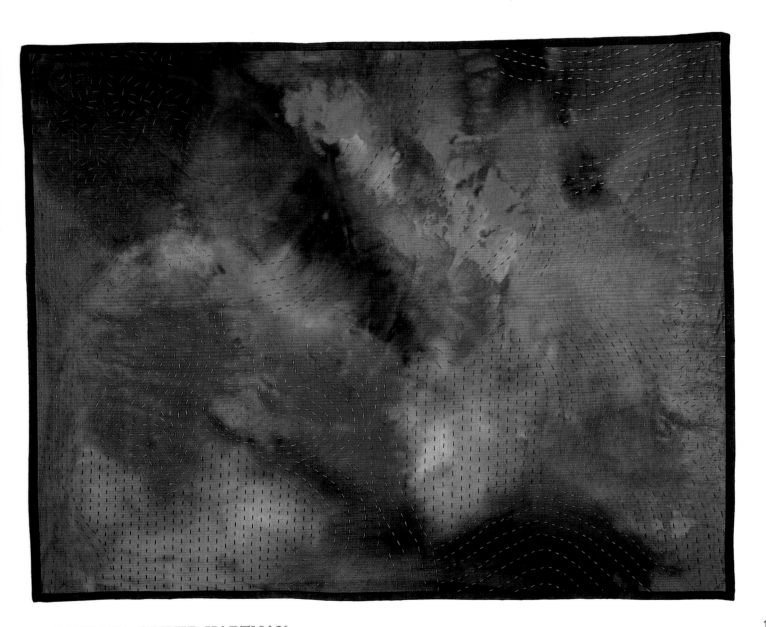

BARBARA OLIVER HARTMAN

FLOWER MOUND, TEXAS

Atmospheric Event

Dye-painted cotton fabric; hand
stitched and hand quilted;
44 x 36 inches (111.8 x 91.4 cm).

*This quilt is part of an ongoing series about global warming. When an
accident or emergency occurs at a nuclear power plant, the public is
informed of an event. When atmospheric conditions reach critical stages,
will they be described as events? We already have "Ozone Action Days."*

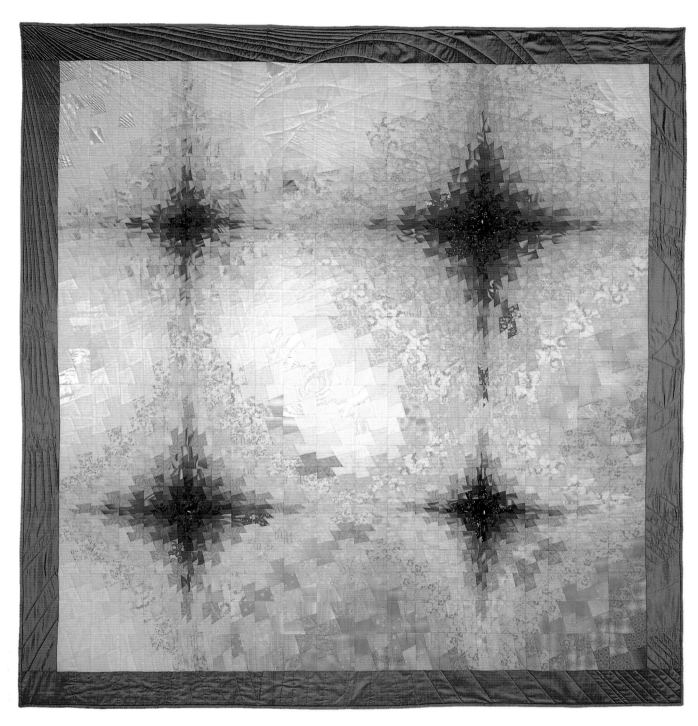

MIWAKO MIYAMOTO

KANAGAWA, JAPAN

A Gust of Wind

Cotton, blends, and silk fabrics;
hand and machine pieced,
hand quilted; 84 x 88 inches
(213.4 x 223.5 cm).

*I like to create a sense of movement by using a variety
of fabric piece sizes in my quilts. I always hope that
people will think that the quilt tells a story.*

I'm still playing with language and layering. After Boris Yeltsin won the July 1996 presidential election, the Russian newspaper Izvestia ran the headline "Democracy Wins/What Next?" Having been in Russia a few months earlier, that phrase had a certain resonance for me. I hope this quilt—despite its surreal, floating shapes—captures some of the color and feel of Moscow.

ROBIN SCHWALB

BROOKLYN, NEW YORK

What Next?

Photo silk-screened, stenciled, overdyed, and commercial cottons; machine pieced, hand appliquéd, and hand quilted; 38 x 74 inches (96.5 x 188 cm).

15

MICHELE VERNON

FALLS CHURCH, VIRGINIA

Intersections #5

Cottons, hand-dyed fabrics
(by Michele Duell), some embellished with acrylic paint; machine
pieced and machine quilted;
57 x 58 inches (144.8 x 147.3 cm).

*Intersections are where the action is, where two lines cross,
where streets cross, where things overlap. Intersections are
symbolic of connection. In some cases, though, such as
where two wide, busy streets cross, intersections can be
alienating. For me, the symbolic meaning enriches work
that can be enjoyed on purely visual terms.*

LORRAINE ROY

LONDON, ONTARIO, CANADA

Shadow

Needlepoint panels with thread
and fabric collage; machine
appliquéd and machine quilted;
37 x 37 inches (94 x 94 cm).

*My quilts mark the path of a spiritual journey. The images
come from dreams and are influenced by research into their
symbolic messages. The fish, which is often in my dreams,
is thought to act as a guide to the unconscious because it
never closes its eyes. As such, it inspired a series of pieces
that acknowledge and honor a part of my nature that is
wild, mysterious, and filled with potential.*

CYNTHIA CORBIN

WOODINVILLE, WASHINGTON

Bare Root

Commercial and hand-dyed cotton
fabrics; machine pieced and machine
quilted; 61 x 37 inches (154.9 x 94 cm).

*I am interested in abstract images and the expression of something
intangible through this medium of fabric. This is my language.
My quilts are my poems. They allow me to say something.*

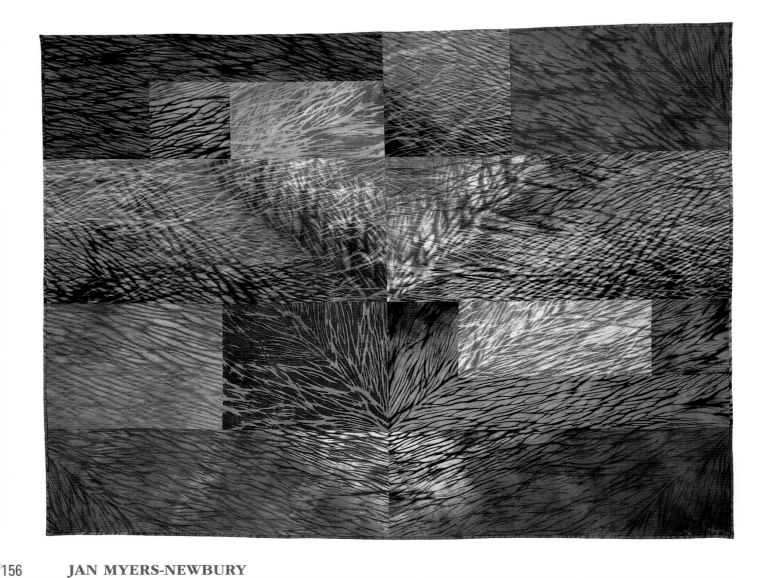

JAN MYERS-NEWBURY

PITTSBURGH, PENNSYLVANIA

The Trysting Tree

Cotton muslin that has been
tied, dyed and (sometimes)
bleached; machine pieced
and machine quilted; 76 x 58
inches (193 x 147.3 cm).

*I love creating these fabrics—layering color on color, then removing
some. I love the way depth and light saturate each individual piece.
I cut them as little as necessary…the fabrics themselves are so
evocative that the challenge for me is to hear their message and
combine them in ways that increase their strength and beauty.
The title refers to an image from the novel* Snow Falling on Cedars.

DOROTHY FUSSELMAN

CHAGRIN FALLS, OHIO

Drains and
Falling Waters

Samples of cotton decorator fabrics and photo transfers; pieced and hand quilted; 20 x 20 inches (50.8 x 50.8 cm).

The use of the photo transfer technique is just another way to enhance fabric with surface design. The photographs of the drains and pond were taken on the grounds of the Pontifical College Josephinum while attending the Quilt Surface Design Symposium in Columbus, Ohio. The Fallingwater photograph was taken years earlier on the grounds of Frank Lloyd Wright's famous house in Pennsylvania. It seemed appropriate to combine the two into this simple nine-patch quilt.

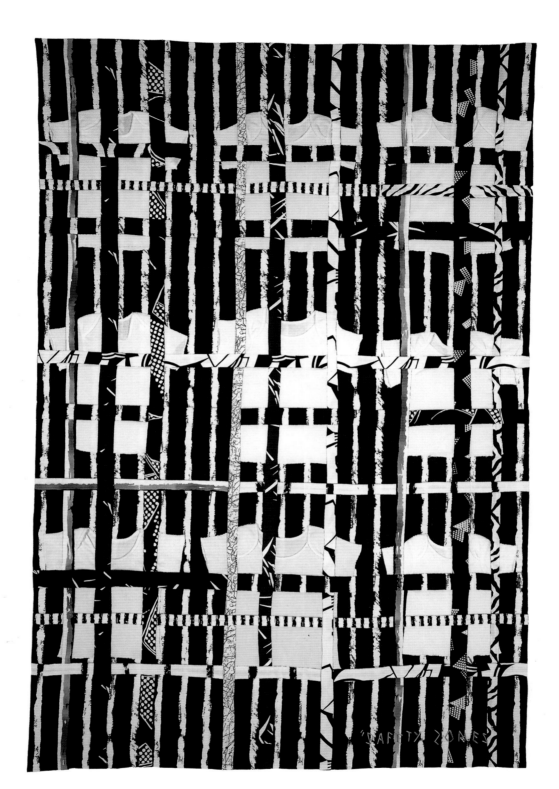

GERRY FOGARTY

YELLOW SPRINGS, OHIO

Safety Zones

Commercial fabrics and used
infant T-shirts; hand appliquéd
to a whole cloth background;
42 x 63 inches (106.7 x 160 cm).

*I have strong concerns about the issue of child abuse. Safety Zones
is part of a series which uses the generic imagery of the infant shirt to
explore issues of vulnerability and protection. My desire to symbolically
hold and secure our children by "weaving" them into the protective
surface of the quilt is expressed in Safety Zones. Paradoxically,
however, such restrictive protection often stunts children's emotional
development. Perhaps Safety Zones? would be a better title.*

SHARON HEIDINGSFELDER

LITTLE ROCK, ARKANSAS

Friends on the Other Side

Cotton fabrics, some silk-screened by the
artist; machine pieced and machine quilted;
46 x 49 inches (116.8 x 124.5 cm).

*So you think everything that happens
to you is of your own making?*

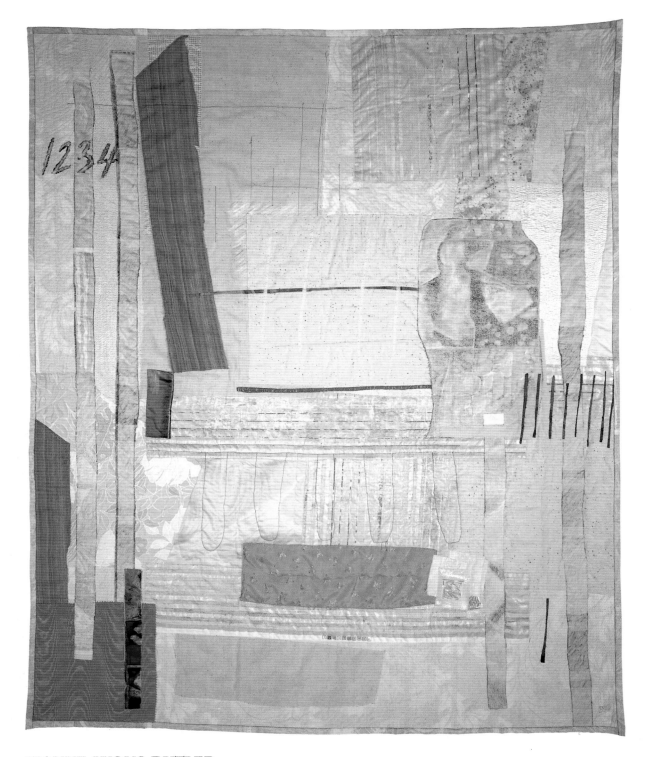

JEANNE LYONS BUTLER

HUNTINGTON, NEW YORK

1–2–3–4

Cottons and silks; machine
appliquéd and machine quilted;
54 x 66 inches (137.2 x 167.6 cm).

Beat. 1–2–3–4. Shadows, crooked lines, a reflection. Beat.
Something added, a change. The balancing act doesn't stop.
Life, it throws you a curve. Take the next step. Beat.

SHARON HEIDINGSFELDER

LITTLE ROCK, ARKANSAS

Friends on the Other Side

Cotton fabrics, some silk-screened by the artist; machine pieced and machine quilted; 46 x 49 inches (116.8 x 124.5 cm).

So you think everything that happens to you is of your own making?

1997

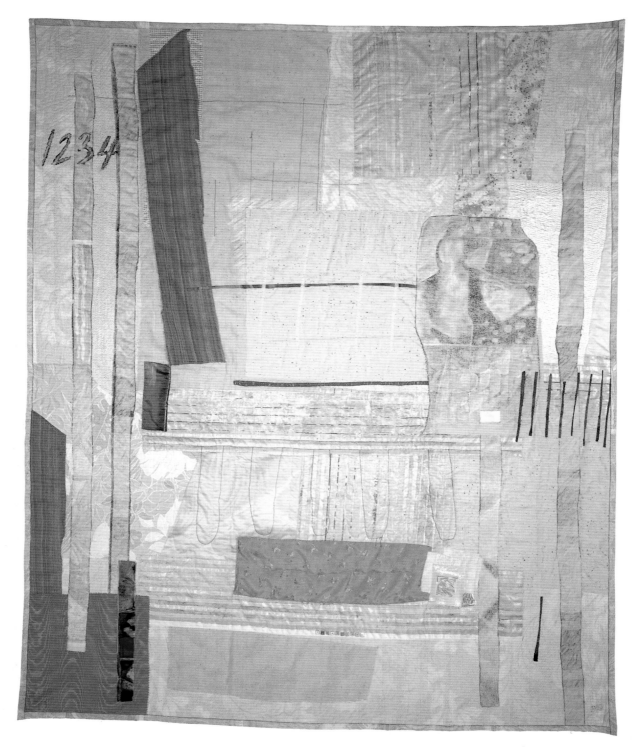

JEANNE LYONS BUTLER

HUNTINGTON, NEW YORK

1–2–3–4

Cottons and silks; machine
appliquéd and machine quilted;
54 x 66 inches (137.2 x 167.6 cm).

*Beat. 1–2–3–4. Shadows, crooked lines, a reflection. Beat.
Something added, a change. The balancing act doesn't stop.
Life, it throws you a curve. Take the next step. Beat.*

KYOUNG AE CHO

MILWAUKEE, WISCONSIN

Aged: Covered by Wisdom

Fabric, construction board, pieces of pine;
hand stitched and tied; 108 x 108 inches
(274.3 x 274.3 cm).

*Time and nurturing are carried through rings of wisdom.
These rings are displayed in their natural form through
geometric cuts. The patterns allow the viewer to visualize
the existence and environmental history of this tree
and how it has sheltered and nurtured the earth.*

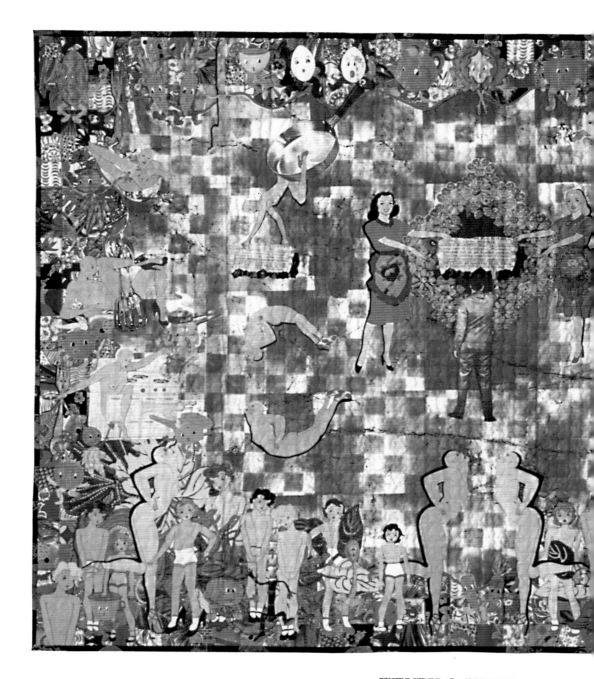

WENDY C. HUHN

DEXTER, OREGON

Wife Wanted

Various fabrics embellished with stencils, T-shirt transfers, screenprinting, and airbrushed paint; machine quilted; 67 x 47 inches (170.2 x 119.4 cm).

I found this ad in a magazine from the 1940s: "Wife wanted:
Must be graduate engineer in electronics. Preferably checked
out on jet bomber controls. Sardine packing experience
valuable. Should be accomplished contortionist." To me
this clearly states the talents women possess.

ANN STAMM MERRELL

CUPERTINO, CALIFORNIA

Untitled

Cotton, wool, silk, and blended
fabrics; fused, appliquéd,
embroidered, and quilted;
50 x 48 inches (127 x 121.9 cm).

*Of all the really bad things that can happen to you, making a mistake
with a piece of fabric is not one. This perspective—newly acquired as
a result of a 1993 breast cancer diagnosis—allowed me to do such
things as cut into expensive fabric without having a plan, leave edges
unfinished and raw, and defiantly stitch "outside the lines," reflecting
both the truly awful times and the wonderful new freedoms.*

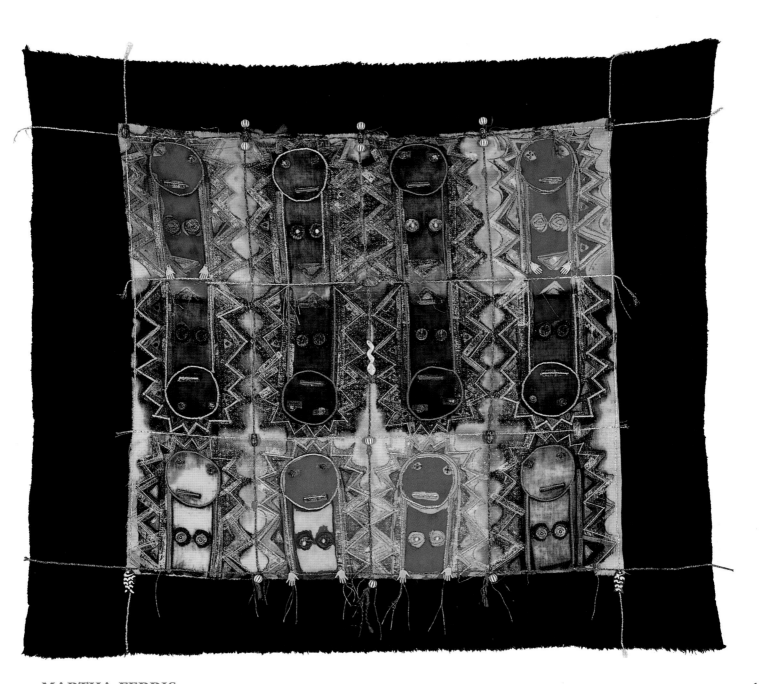

MARTHA FERRIS

VICKSBURG, MISSISSIPPI

Reliquary

Tritik-discharged cotton treated with wax resist, dyes and pearlescent paints applied with stamps; hand and machine stitched, and embellished with beads, cords, and charms; 52 x 48 inches (132.1 x 121.9 cm). Private collection.

Making Reliquary *involved many basic techniques of manipulating fabric, some dating back thousands of years and most traditionally performed by women. For me, the piece brings to mind relics sometimes seen in Italian cathedrals: a bit of some saint's shroud, a lock of another saint's hair. I wanted to create the feeling of a small chapel in a large cathedral: ancient and rich, mysterious, and quiet.*

RACHEL K. TURNER

MARYVILLE, TENNESSEE

We're Never Really Alone...

Commercial fabrics as well as others created
through color xerography and lithography;
machine pieced and quilted; laced with
cotton yarn through brass eyelets;
48 x 50 inches (121.9 x 127 cm).

*Are we ever really alone? Life takes many forms. What about your
religious beliefs? Do you believe in ghosts? And in this obsessed, techno-
saturated society of World Wide Webs, cellular phones, televisions, and
video cameras, how can we be alone? Whether we like it or not, we're
all connected. So then…is "alone" more a mental than a physical state
of being? Well, I'll leave you alone with your thoughts now…or maybe not…*

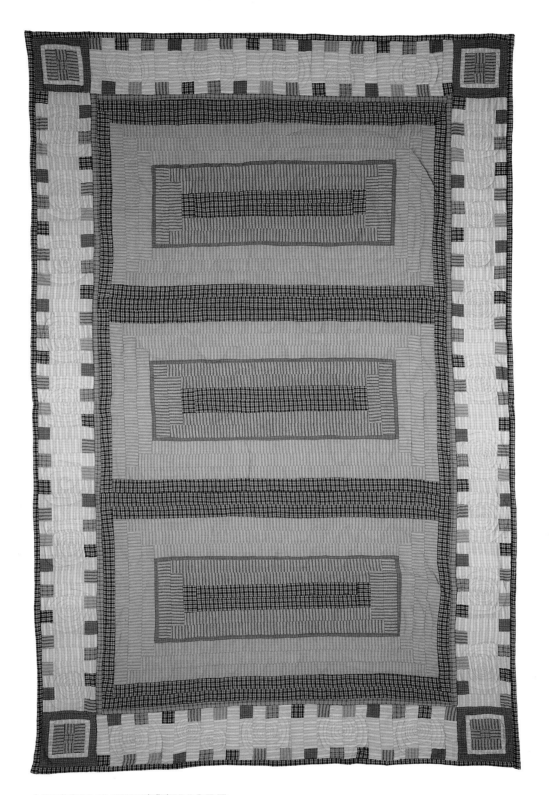

ALISON F. WHITTEMORE

SAN ANTONIO, TEXAS

Metaphor for a Bed

Commercial fabrics; machine
pieced and machine quilted;
44 x 70 inches (111.8 x 177.8 cm).

*I started making quilts because I love combining two disparate
things—old and new, traditional and contemporary, staid
and quirky. In this quilt I took the traditional log cabin block,
skewed it into huge rectangles (using old fashioned fabrics),
and added an old-timey pieced border. Then I started freestyle
quilting in fanciful, fun spirals and squiggles.*

1997

When I was young, I would go to the end of the hall and open the mirrored door to the linen closet. As I approached with the week's clean towels and sheets, my reflection would usher me in. Here's a place where the fabrics, usually intimate and functional in our lives, are neither. The linen closet is layers of folds and shadows, softness and textures, surprises of color, all contrasted against hard, narrow strips of shelves.

EMILY RICHARDSON

PHILADELPHIA, PENNSYLVANIA

Linen Closet

Silk, cotton, nylon net, and linen embellished with acrylic and textile paints; hand appliquéd, embroidered, and hand quilted; 29 x 65 inches (73.7 x 165.1cm).

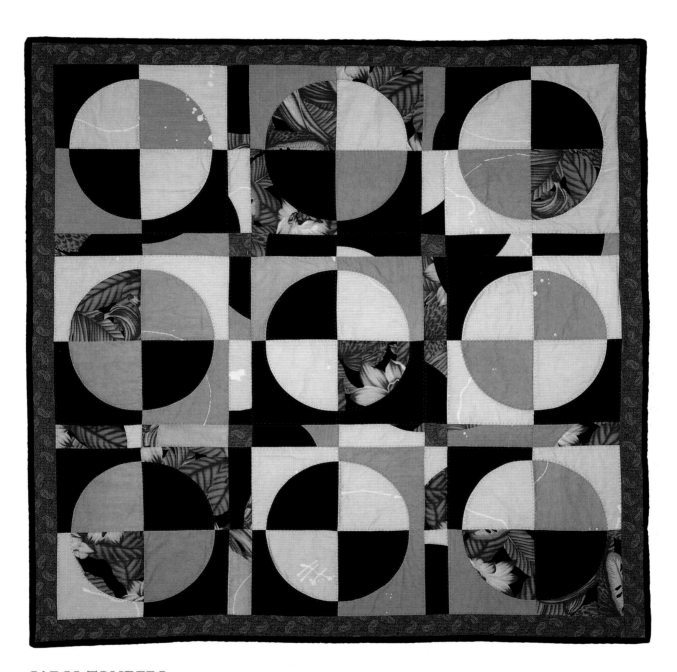

CAROL TOMBERS

ST. PAUL, MINNESOTA

The Southern Moon

Hand-dyed and hand-batiked
cotton fabric; machine pieced
and hand quilted; 51 x 51 inches
(129.5 x 129.5 cm).

*To fully experience and understand the world is to find patterns
and relationships that are unique, while still being identifiable and
repeatable. To make art is to do this with an object as evidence of
the search. Below the surface of conscious seeing, art may speak
specifically about what is universal, just as the inexactitude of a
quilt may be masked to suggest an energy that cannot be calculated.*

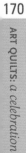

NELDA WARKENTIN

ANCHORAGE, ALASKA

Chinese Tiles

Semi-transparent ribbon folded and encased in plastic; machine stitched and hand tied; 44 x 54 inches (111.8 x 137.2 cm).

Unlike most quilts, this quilt emphasizes the inner layer. Both sides of the quilt are transparent, allowing the colorful inner layer to show. Changing the background color, which also shows through the quilt, alters the viewer's reaction to the quilt.

ADRIENNE YORINKS

NORTH SALEM, NEW YORK

Resistance to Tyranny is Obedience to God

Cotton, silk, vintage American fabrics from the mid-1800s through the 1920s, photo transfers; machine pieced and quilted; 71 x 79 inches (180.3 x 200.7 cm).

This quilt celebrates the 75th anniversary of women's suffrage. It illuminates and pays homage to the suffrage movement in America from its beginnings in 1848 to its passage in Congress in 1920. With historical photos and images, vintage fabrics, and the full text of the Declaration of Sentiments, I wanted this quilt to be a testament to the people who fulfilled Susan B. Anthony's statement, "Resistance to Tyranny is obedience to God."

YVONNE FORMAN

HASTINGS-ON-HUDSON, NEW YORK

Einstein & Tomatoes

Cotton fabric and laser printer photo transfers; machine pieced and hand quilted (by Grace Miller); 41 x 41 inches (104.1 x 104.1 cm).

Einstein & Tomatoes *reflects my continued fascination with geometry, found objects, nontraditional art materials, and the transformation that occurs when an ordinary object is placed in an unexpected context. In this piece I juxtapose the high-tech, laser-printed photo transfer with the traditional nine-patch block, dissolving boundaries and reordering fragments in pursuit of what can happen when two unlikely elements meet.*

MICHAEL JAMES

LINCOLN, NEBRASKA

Ikon

Cotton fabrics; machine pieced
and machine quilted; 74 x 79
inches (188 x 200.7 cm).

*This quilt was motivated in part by a desire to simplify,
to return to elemental forms and relationships, and
was inspired by a 15th-century Russian icon.*

BONNIE PETERSON-TUCKER

ELMHURST, ILLINOIS

Burnt Pine Forest #3

Cotton photocopy transfers cut and fused or stitched to cotton fabric; machine quilted; 56 x 42 inches (142.2 x 106.7 cm).

In June, 1995, eight years after the Yellowstone fire, I expected to be saddened by the sight of the vast burned forest. I thought it would look like a commercial clear-cut forest, ravaged and raw, exposed. But far from being ugly or boring scenery, the burned area appeared to be part of the forest's natural life cycle. Perfectly formed little pine trees grew abundantly amidst the still-standing timber "snags" and fallen branches. The contrast between the blue sky, blackened trees, and lush green forest floor was striking and unexpected.

KATHERINE KNAUER

NEW YORK, NEW YORK

At the Pond

Single-use stencil on sponge-printed fabric;
trapunto, hand embroidery, hand quilting;
20 x 56 inches (50.8 x 142.2 cm).

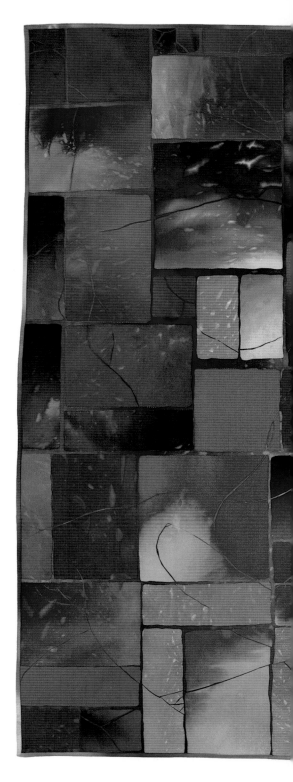

MELODY JOHNSON

CARY, ILLINOIS

Streetdance

Hand-dyed cotton; fused and
machine quilted; 69 x 51 inches
(175.3 x 129.5 cm).

Strolling on an upstate New York campus last summer, I thought I saw a figure formed by the cracks in the sidewalk under my feet. I photographed the pavement and later began a series of quilts based on those intriguing cracks. I love the way the cracked line is sustained from block to block as it deteriorates. My contribution was to change the color from utilitarian concrete gray to the vibrant colors of the fiesta.

SUSAN WEBB LEE

WEDDINGTON, NORTH CAROLINA

A Prayer for Sylvain

Hand-dyed and/or painted cotton fabrics; machine pieced and machine quilted; 35 x 42 inches (88.9 x 106.7 cm).

This quilt is part of a series about my relationship with a dear friend who died of AIDS in May of 1995. When I first heard of Sylvain's illness, I was so frightened about what would happen to him and to his partner, John. I had horrible nightmares, waking up terrified every morning, as though I were on the brink of death myself. I said many prayers for Sylvain, hoping somehow to make life easier, and hoping he knew I cared.

BETH P. GILBERT

BUFFALO GROVE, ILLINOIS

Lest We Forget

Cotton fabric that has been stamped, painted, stenciled, and embellished with heat transfers; machine pieced, machine appliquéd, machine embroidered, and machine quilted; 67 x 77 inches (170.2 x 195.6 cm).

This work expresses my feelings about the Holocaust as we pass the 50th anniversary of the liberation of the camps. After visiting Yad Vashem, the Holocaust museum in Israel, I had to express these feelings. It is a tribute to those who died and to those who continue to die because of prejudice. Notice that the swastika is not quilted into the quilt.

NOËL M. RUESSMANN

STROUDSBURG, PENNSYLVANIA

Snow

Cotton, silk, and wool fabrics
embellished with acrylic paint;
machine pieced and hand quilted;
89 x 46 inches (226.1 x 116.8 cm).

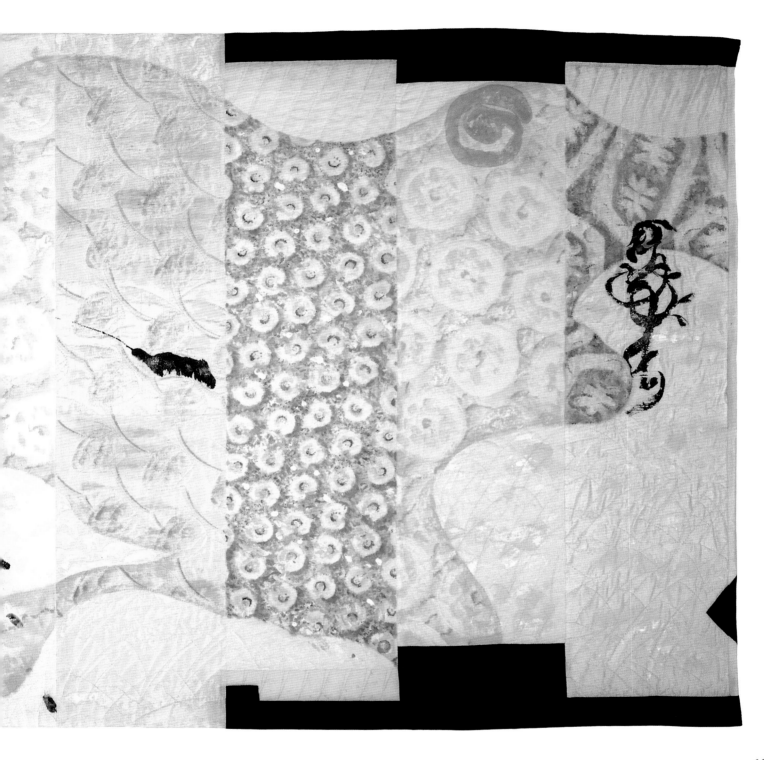

*In snow, shapes and patterns become abstractly detached and isolated
by the delicately wind-chiseled drifting snow. Billowing snowfall in
rapidly changing descents has designs and rhythms of rich luxuriance;
the airy weightlessness of massing clumps, the smooth gliding of
sharp, perfect flakes, the rapid descent of heavy snowdrops.*

KATHERINE MCKEARN & DIANE MUSE

TOWSON, MARYLAND AND MADRID, IOWA

This is it.

Psycho Moms Bake a Cake

Commercial cotton, vintage fabrics, and old clothing; hand and
machine pieced, embroidered, stamped, appliquéd, and hand
quilted (by Katherine McKearn); 81 x 77 inches (205.7 x 195.6 cm).

JANE BURCH COCHRAN

RABBIT HASH, KENTUCKY

Looking for God

Painted canvas embellished with beads, button, sequins, and found objects; hand stitched and tied; 64 x 74 inches (162.6 x 188 cm).

I wanted to do a quilt about my black lab, Barker, who was my studio companion for 13 years. I've sketched and pondered and dreamed on this for several years. While finishing a name quilt of historical Kentucky women, I thought of a name quilt using dog names. What finally came together was a background for another quilt I'd started called Looking for God *(for which I could not find the central image), the dog names I had collected, and a desire to bead this dog head. The dog is my current lab, Belle. I couldn't imagine beading the body, too; thus the dress. My husband asks, "Why the potholder?" It represents the unknown. I had fun, fun, fun making this quilt. I even said aloud, "I don't care if anyone likes this quilt; I like it." I kept the title because of what "God" spells backward.*

CLARE FRANCES SMITH

WELLINGTON, NEW ZEALAND

Mozzies:
Don't You Just Hate 'Em!

Textile inks applied to cotton fabric;
machine pieced and machine quilted;
41 x 41 inches (104.1 x 104.1 cm).

*It's late at night and your body craves sleep. You lie
still in the darkness. Suddenly, you hear a whining
noise, and before you know it, you are up on the bed,
trying to smash that sound through the ceiling.*

JACQUELYN NOUVEAU

CHAPEL HILL, NORTH CAROLINA

Veiled Sunrise

Foreground piece: silk and polyester organza, hand-dyed silk chiffon, netting; hand quilted with "silver" and other threads; background piece: cotton fabric; hand quilted with pear cotton thread; 42 x 58 inches (106.7 x 147.3 cm).

Each morning I watch the sun emerge through a veil of trees, sometimes shrouded by fog or rain. The squares and circles represent the splitting atom releasing its energy and dissipating into forces not so readily seen as in this special time of day. The circles on the backdrop heighten the sense of energy, and depending on the light source, shadows are cast from the foreground to the background, subtly demonstrating the presence of a power source.

I gathered these sticks while walking the shore of Lake Superior, thinking about pollution and our water system. We have come dangerously close to destroying our home, the planet Earth. This bed (with the wolves peering out behind the sticks) represents the environmental bed we have made, and now must sleep in.

TERRIE HANCOCK MANGAT

CINCINNATI, OHIO

Lake Superior Stick Bed

Assorted fabrics; hand appliquéd, hand embroidered, hand quilted (by Sue Rule), beaded, and embellished with paint. The bed was decoupaged with fabric, paint, and sticks; quilt, 64 x 78 inches (162.6 x 198.1 cm); bed, 80 x 45 x 42 inches (203.2 x 114.3 x 106.7 cm).

JOY SAVILLE

PRINCETON, NEW JERSEY

Summer's End

Cotton, linen, and silk; machine
pieced and stitched to muslin backing, mounted on hidden frame;
67 x 48 inches (170.2 x 121.9 cm).

*Summer's End is a response to the brilliance of color seen in gar-
dens and landscapes around the country at the end of summer. The
light at that time of year is just beginning to take on the intensity and
clarity that comes in autumn, and all color seems especially vivid.
Since the focus of my work is color and the continued development
of a piecing process that allows color and fabric to be used in a free,
painterly manner, I enjoy the drama of seasonal change.*

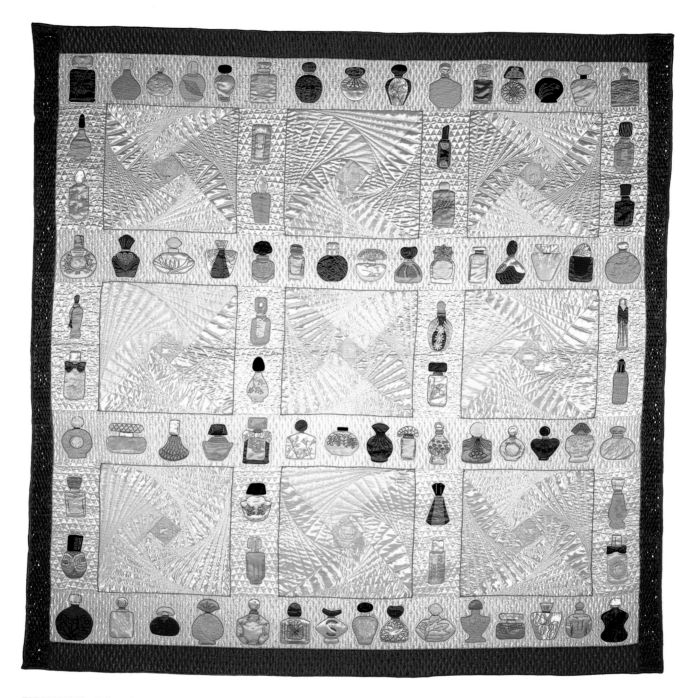

KUNIKO SAKA

TOKYO, JAPAN

Perfume

Various fabrics embellished with buttons and lace; pieced, appliquéd, smocked, and hand quilted; 81 x 82 inches (205.7 x 208.3 cm).

I used luminous fabrics to express the mysterious scent and beautiful transparent colors of charming perfume bottles. Cording enhances the sense of perspective in the center of the work, and the pearl buttons in the smocked border give the work a wonderful visual appeal.

ANN RHODE

BERKELEY, CALIFORNIA

Exploring Bali

Bali batiks and airbrushed
cottons; machine pieced
and machine quilted; 58 x 70
inches (147.3 x 177.8 cm).

*I put a selection of Bali batiks on my design wall to admire, and
without my conscious involvement, a nearby pile of airbrushed
samples migrated to the wall. They formed small abstract pictures
within batik frames. Tradition became a frame for the future.
The quilting enhances the contrast between the fabrics without
competing for attention. The fabrics are the quilt.*

DIANA LEONE

SANTA CLARA, CALIFORNIA

Earth Series—Ice

Commercial cotton and lamé
fabrics; machine pieced and
machine quilted with rayon,
metallic, and cotton threads;
63 x 51 inches (160 x 129.5 cm).

The Earth *series exemplified my deep appreciation of the gifts the Earth continues
to give me. These quilts are impressionist reminders, made as memorials of my
favorite places and the Earth's bounty.* Ice *illustrates my love of the snow. I love
the knowledge that I will be warm in the cold. I love to see the variety of colors
reflected in the crystal flakes. I seek the contrast in the seemingly low-contrast
landscapes. I love to ski in the quiet solitude of the big mountain landscape.*

DARCY L. FALK

FLAGSTAFF, ARIZONA

Windmill

Hand-dyed and/or dye-painted commercial cotton fabrics; hand and machine pieced, hand and machine quilted; 76 x 81 inches (193 x 205.7 cm).

Windmill tells stories about both the Midwest, where I have strong roots, and the Southwest, where I now live. It tells of Don Quixote's obsession. It's the wheel of fortune, the roulette wheel, the wheel of life. Windmill is from my series of quilts about machinery. Machines both enable and handicap by giving us the ability to work alone. The elegant shapes in obsolete machinery often remind me of the human figure.

1997

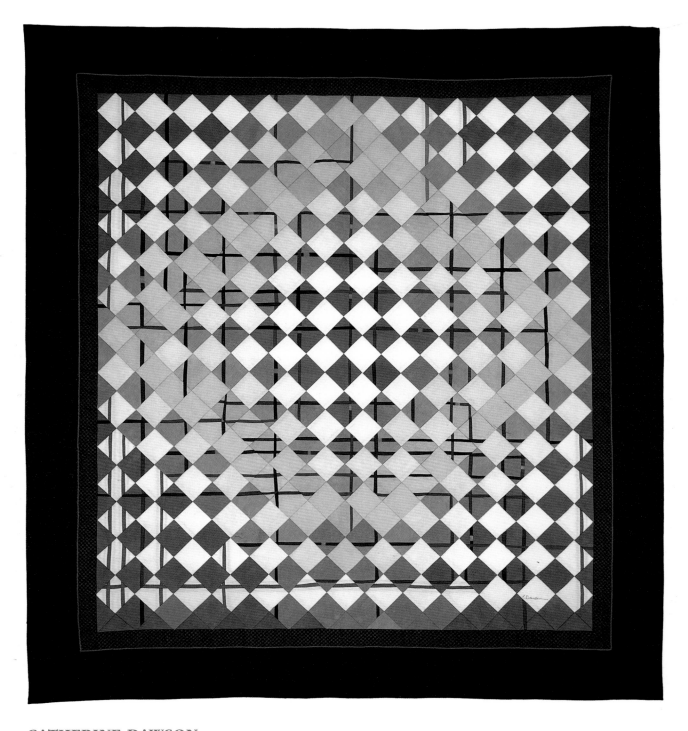

CATHERINE DAWSON

CALAIS, MAINE

Plane Dreams

Commercial and hand-dyed cotton; machine pieced and quilted, embellished with embroidery floss; 46 x 50 inches (116.8 x 127 cm).

This piece is part of a series exploring space and dimension. It draws the viewer into a space beyond the surface with lights to beckon and mark the way. This quilt is dedicated to my grandfather, an inventor, who never faltered in his disciplined and enthusiastic search for knowledge and his quest for his dreams.

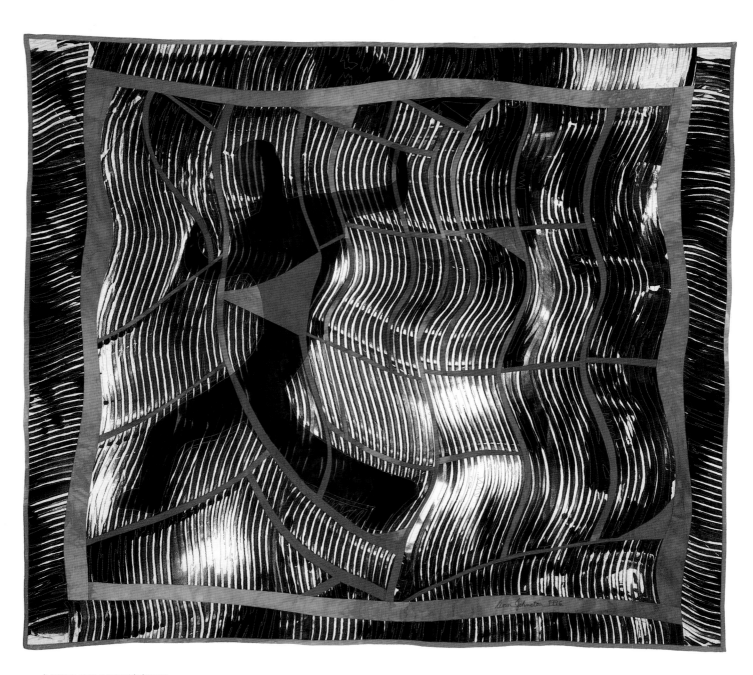

ANN JOHNSTON

LAKE OSWEGO, OREGON

Shock Waves

Hand-dyed cottons; machine pieced and machine quilted; 47 x 41 inches (119.4 x 104.1 cm).

Shock Waves *came from the images embedded (accidentally) in the fabric I dyed. When I cut, pieced, quilted, and dyed the fabric again, I did have a specific idea in mind, but I do not want to limit the meanings of them by defining them. I enjoy knowing that my work may mean something very different to viewers, and I regret that I do not hear their interpretations more often.*

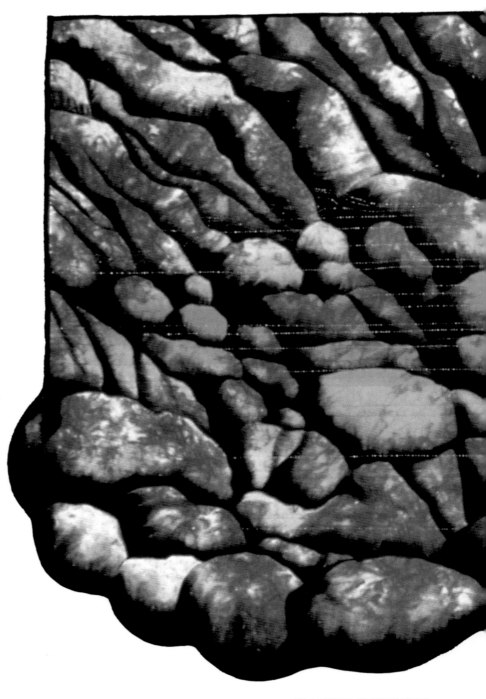

KAREN PERRINE

TACOMA, WASHINGTON

Pool

Cotton fabric treated with Procion dye and metallic pigment; hand and machine quilted; 56 x 31 inches (142.2 x 78.7 cm).

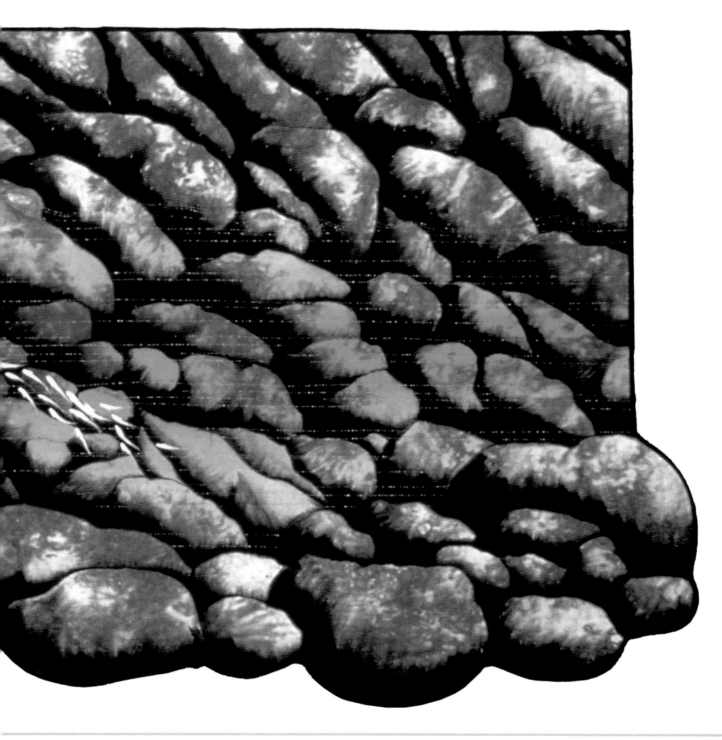

This imaginary view of a quiet pool seems a bit strange and mysterious.
The interface between air and water is obscure—where does one end and
the other begin? The ideal pool of cool, clear, clean water filled with life is
shown in an almost surreal setting. It is a contrast to reality. It is a dream.

CAROL ANNE GROTRIAN

CAMBRIDGE, MASSACHUSETTS

Inside/Out: Chairs

Cotton fabrics hand-dyed using
variations of shibori techniques;
machine pieced and quilted;
38 x 29 inches (96.5 x 73.7 cm).

*Peake's Island, Maine. A memory of time at the shore where everything
is change—tides, light, life, even rocks…marking time by the minute
and the millennium. Now frozen in shape and line, pattern and color,
a breathing space is recreated with layers of meaning both universal
and personal. The organic pattern of shibori led my art to the coast!*

ART QUILTS: *a celebration*

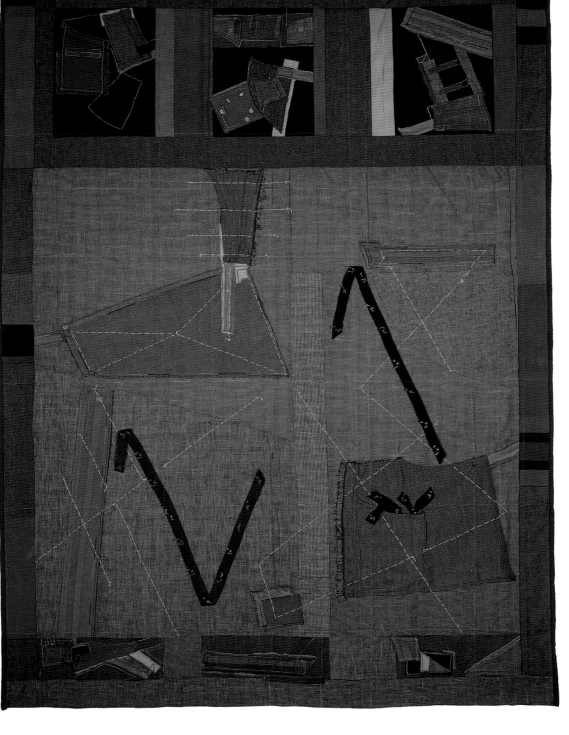

MARYVONNE DEVILLE GUILLOT

RENNES, FRANCE

Constellation II
or
The Dressmaker's Workshop

Commercial fabrics and clothing remnants; hand and machine stitched and quilted; 43 x 59 inches (109.2 x 149.9 cm).

The French Larousse Encyclopedia *defines a constellation as a group of scattered objects on a limited space. This quilt is a poetic reminder of the sky and the earth, of the astral influence the stars have on human life. The background and foreground elements serve as a link between the two worlds. I included the old apron as a way to honor the humble work of the hands that created the gardens and crafts of the old days.*

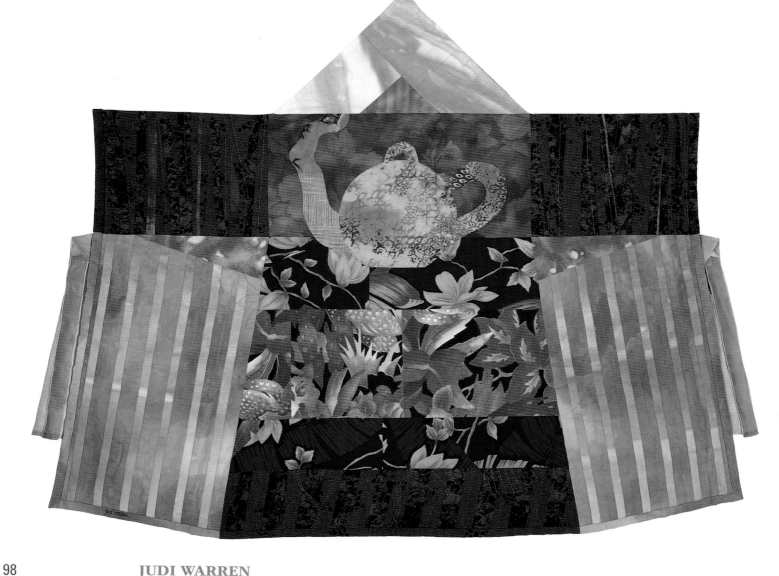

JUDI WARREN

MAUMEE, OHIO

Triptych:
Some Like It Hot

Commercial and hand-painted
cottons and ribbon; machine
pieced, machine appliquéd,
and hand-quilted; 40 x 33 inches
(101.6 x 83.8 cm).

*Some Like It Hot is a kitchen triptych: a household altar
recalling the comfort and coziness of flowered tablecloths,
pots of tea, and curls of steam that warm a room.*

RACHEL BRUMER

SEATTLE, WASHINGTON

Bread; Staple, Fourth Removed

Hand-dyed fabrics printed and embellished with textile paint; hand appliquéd, hand pieced, and hand quilted; 62 x 50 inches (157.5 x 127 cm).

In some cultures, it is considered a breach of natural law to harm a person with whom one has broken bread.

CHRISTI TEASLEY

MONTEAGLE, TENNESSEE

Forest Cloth One

Silk fragments; machine-stitched to
rayon/silk velvet and hand-dyed rayon
viscose twill, painted with waterbased
polyurethane and polyacrylic; 56 x 36
inches (142.2 x 91.4 cm).

Forest Cloth One *maps connections between art and place. Silk fragments were hidden in tree hollows, creeks, and crevices of the forest for eight months to collect the marks of their place. Stained by maple innards, soil fungus, and creek algae, the fragments bear the effects of their site. The stitches suggest topography, perhaps the contours of the plateau from which it was created. Strata constructed of contrasting surfaces honors the significance of place to the process of creating.*

SHULAMIT LISS

YOKNEAM MOSHAVA, ISRAEL

Beyond the Bars II

Hand-dyed cotton; direct
appliquéd; machine stitched
and machine quilted; 44 x 56
inches (111.8 x 142.2 cm).

*Bars: a metaphor for personal and social barriers. Curiosity: a
fundamental aspect of the human mind. Curiosity encourages us
to cross barriers, to find what is hidden by the barrier. Occasionally
we are satisfied with our findings, but sometimes we are left frustrated.
The urge to cross barriers, to explore the other side, is mixed with
fear of failure. Is it safer to stay on the known side?*

WENDY LUGG

BULICREEK, AUSTRALIA

Smoke Veil

Commercial and hand-dyed cotton
fabrics; machine pieced, discharged,
slashed, and hand quilted; 42 x 53
inches (106.7 x 134.6 cm).

Like the black wedding veil worn on the Palestinian bride's symbolic
journey to her husband's home and her new life, bush fires signify
not only the end of life, but also regrowth and new beginnings.

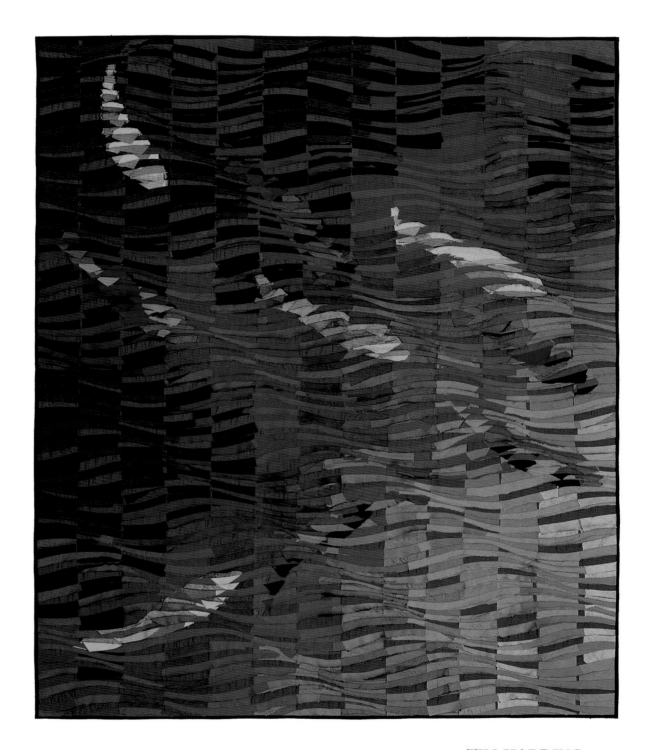

TIM HARDING

STILLWATER, MINNESOTA

Koi Diptych

Three layers of silk on two cotton
backing layers; reverse appliquéd
(stitching, cutting, and pressing by
Shawn Behrends); 88 x 52 inches
(223.5 x 132.1 cm).

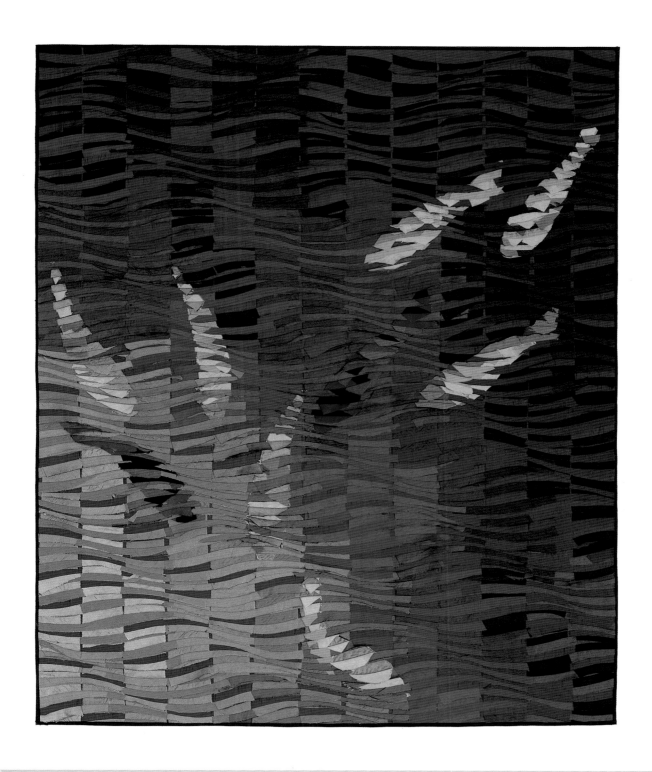

I wanted to create the illusion of depth and movement, to capture the way goldfish appear to flicker through the moving, reflective surface of water. Silk has the reflective quality of water. Reverse appliqué helps to create depth through contrast between layers. The offset wavy-line quilting and cutting create an illusion of wave motion. Composition and placement of fish between layers gives depth and motion. The specific cutting and pressing within the fish helps create the flickering quality.

RHODA R. COHEN

WESTON, MASSACHUSETTS

Attachments

Cotton, blends, and rayon fabrics, ric-rac, sequins, metallic thread, buttons, and brass fittings; stitched by hand and machine; 70 x 88 inches (177.8 x 223.5 cm).

This is an enterprise of elements collected over a long period. Pockets salvaged from used clothing are doing new service as weights for colored strips, evoking an African healer's cloak. The pockets symbolize the wearer/donors; the whole celebrates salvage, diversity, inclusiveness, culture, and health-giving vibrations.

KAREN DUNPHY

CINCINNATI, OHIO

Unexpected Baby Quilt

Hogscreening, vinyl, wool, cane, clothespins, roofing nails, fishing line, and batting; quilted with roofing nails and fishing line; 40 x 40 inches (101.6 x 101.6 cm).

For years I have collected various materials common to everyday life, but not typically destined for quilt making. These materials provide unique and interesting metaphors for aspects outside their ordinary context. My work seems to translate the traditional to the contemporary while pushing the boundaries of the conventional quilted form.

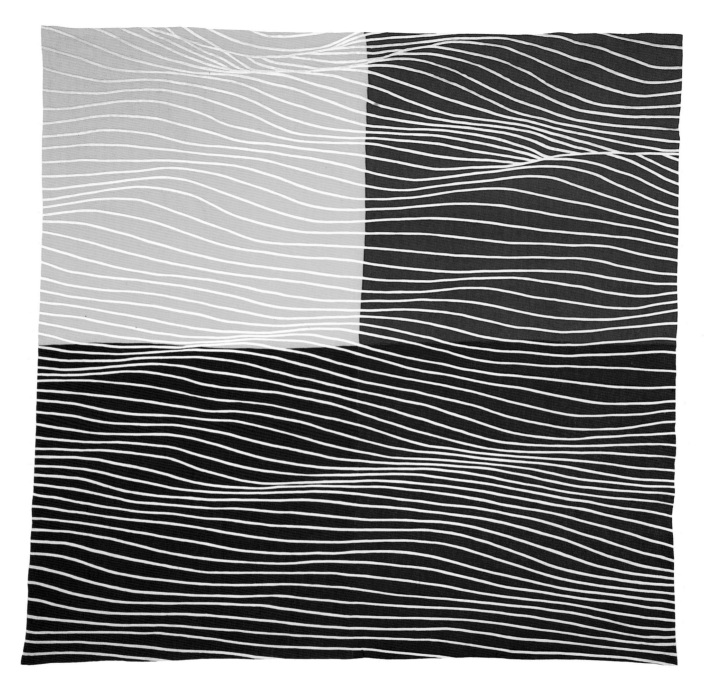

ANNELIESE JAROS

VIENNA, AUSTRIA

Waves

Cotton fabric and bias tape; machine pieced and machine quilted; 72 x 72 inches (182.9 x 182.9 cm).

I wanted to experiment with wave-like designs and create a three-dimensional impression. The design was inspired by Robert Dixon's Mathographics.

EMILY PARSON

ST. CHARLES, ILLINOIS

I'm Buggin'

Hand-dyed (by artist and Cynthia Bonner) cotton fabric; machine appliquéd and machine quilted; 51 x 50 inches (129.5 x 127 cm).

For the past year, I have been working on whimsical quilts that depict images of important objects in my life. The Volkswagen bug was an especially fun quilt to make, bringing back memories of the cream-colored bug I had in college that my friends affectionately nicknamed "The Egg."

1999

RUTH GARRISON

TEMPE, ARIZONA

Overlay 4

Hand-dyed and commercial
cottons; screen printing, machine
piecing, machine quilting; 54 x 54
inches (137.2 x 137.2 cm).

Overlay 4 *contrasts the rigidity of the grid and the
controlled value gradation of the background with
the playful unpredictability of irregular strip piecing.*

LINDA LEVIN

WAYLAND, MASSACHUSETTS

Maine /
Frenchman's Bay II

Synthetic fabrics treated with transfer dyeing, fabric overlays, and machine stitching;
machine pieced, appliquéd, and quilted;
56 x 44 inches (142.2 x 111.8 cm).

Maine/Frenchman's Bay II *is part of a series inspired by a*
special place in northern Maine. I'm interested in the changeable
quality of light and its effect on water, land, and sky.

BARBARA SCHULMAN

KUTZTOWN, PENNSYLVANIA

49 Vignettes on Turning 50

Dyed and pieced industrial wool felt; handstitched; 67 x 68 inches (170.2 x 172.7 cm).

Memories of travel, encounters, and visions, including fragments of baskets, woven cloth, quilts, landscapes, seasons, and textures as I approach age 50.

HARUE KONISHI

TOKYO, JAPAN

Miyabi

Japanese kimono silk; embroidered,
hand and machine pieced, hand
and machine quilted; 76 x 76
inches (193.0 x 193.0 cm).

*This is the reproduction of my parents' kimonos from about 70 years ago,
which could have otherwise been thrown away. This work allowed my
thoughts to fly back to the times when artisans carefully created those
kimonos, thus reminding me of a sense of duty to pass a piece of history
on to the next generation. In today's high-paced world dominated by
technology, it is nice to know that at least something never changes.*

1999

This quilt is one from a group I have made using a childhood puzzle as a design format for quilt blocks. The puzzle has ten pieces that can be arranged to create a square from a seemingly infinite number of solutions. In this composition the square of ten shapes has shifted into a flow where figure and ground mingle. I am investigating environmentally friendly dye resists. Vegetable resists, especially potato dextrin, wash out with water and make patterns unlike any other.

ANN M. ADAMS

SAN ANTONIO, TEXAS

Chroma Zones V

Silk noil, fiber reactive dye, potato dextrin resist (front) and hand-printed wax resist (back); appliqué and reverse appliqué by machine and machine quilted; 33 x 71 inches (83.8 x 180.3 cm).

ELIZABETH BARTON

ATHENS, GEORGIA

Walmgate, November

Hand-dyed, silk-screened, painted, and commercial cottons; fused (occasionally), machine pieced, and quilted; 51 x 64 inches (129.5 x 162.6 cm).

While walking through the old city (York, England) on a dreary November afternoon, I was struck by the warm yellow, amber, and pink glow of the windows. The contrast of the gold and gray, warmth and dank cold, and light and shadow reflected my own feelings of loss and sorrow, and—finally—peace.

MAYA SCHÖNENBERGER

MIAMI, FLORIDA

Heartwood

Commercial cottons and blends, hand-dyed and painted cottons, knitting material, rayon, silk, and cotton threads; machine pieced, appliquéd, and quilted; 60 x 37 inches (152.4 x 94.0 cm).

Humans will always be part of nature. Similar to the growth of trees in the rain forest, where in regular cycles sapwood turns into heartwood and old, fallen trees turn into nurse trees, generation after generation of humans develop and change our world.

PAT SIMS

ANCHORAGE, ALASKA

Back Yard: The Flats— Lowest Low Water

Cotton fabric hand dyed by artist;
hand pieced and hand quilted;
61 x 60 inches (154.9 x 152.4 cm).

*Living atop a 300-foot cliff overlooking Turnagain Arm of Cook Inlet,
I am presented with views of Arm's stunning seasons, tides, mountains,
and skies. Part of an on-going series,* Back Yard: The Flats—Lowest
Low Water *depicts a rare occurrence of the very lowest tide when
tidal-pool depths expose primogenital sources.*

DIRKJE VANDER HORST-BEETSMA

TEGELEN, NETHERLANDS

Cobblestones

Commercial and hand-dyed cotton, silk, and polyester fabrics; freehand cutting, directly stitched on a foundation, and machine quilted; 52 x 61 inches (132.1 x 154.9 cm).

MOST INNOVATIVE USE OF THE MEDIUM
SPONSORED BY FRIENDS OF FIBER ART INTERNATIONAL

221

My goal in playing around with fabric is to tell a story. This quilt is a walk in the garden on a sunny day. You see the colors of the flowers, shadows, trees, and the colors of the stones. The stones are old and can also tell us stories.

1999

SYLVIA H. EINSTEIN

BELMONT, MASSACHUSETTS

Requiem for an Ashtree

Cottons (many Marimekko fabric
scraps); machine pieced and machine
quilted; 40 x 40 inches (101.6 x 101.6 cm).

*The battle of wills between the bold Marimekko fabrics from the ´60s
and my idea of a quilt was fought on my design wall while a beloved
old ash tree was taken down after a slow death over a number of years.*

CAROL TAYLOR

PITTSFORD, NEW YORK

Shattered

Cotton fabrics dyed commercially and by the artist; machine pieced, quilted, and embroidered; 80 x 81 inches (203.2 x 205.7 cm).

Nancy Crow's improvisational techniques have inspired my creativity and encouraged further experimentation with my own designs. A result of this experimentation is a quilt with a powerful electric center that emits charged black lines seeking to ignite combustible colors. Contact creates the illusion of a multicolored fabric explosion, as if tiny pieces of fabric are being ripped from the quilt, propelled toward the dark edges, and blown onto the floor.

I used all three essential layers of quilt making to build this piece. The batting is reused fabric and handwork between two layers of cheesecloth— loaded with textile making tradition. The hand stitching is its skeleton, but also a visual part of the work. This is an unusual quilt, because normally invisible elements (batting and stitching) play a major role; in this quilt, though, the surface and backing are invisible. I did not use any expensive new material. This work is my visual/sensual statement about the beauty of waste.

ANNA TORMA

HAMILTON, ONTARIO, CANADA

Lullaby II

Found objects, discarded cloth, horsehair, and cheesecloth; hand embroidered and quilted; 50 x 78 inches (127.0 x 198.1 cm).

PAT OWOC

ST. LOUIS, MISSOURI

Earth and Soul "To Go"

Commercial cotton fabric, plastic, paper, and photographs shaped into plastic-stuffed biscuits, embellished with plastic covered pictures on earring wires; machine quilted; 42 x 56 inches (106.7 x 142.2 cm).

Plastic, it's everywhere! When we're done with it, we throw it away and it becomes permanent landfill. Plastic also denotes meaninglessness, stiff, false. How much of our world, both physical and spiritual, is plastic? Are we sealing off earth, humanity, and belief in plastic-covered "to go" bundles?

JANIS V. JAGODZINSKI

BALTIMORE, MARYLAND

Sea Goddess

Tapestry and drapery fabrics;
fused, pieced, machine appliquéd,
machine stitched; 43 x 27 inches
(109.2 x 68.6 cm).

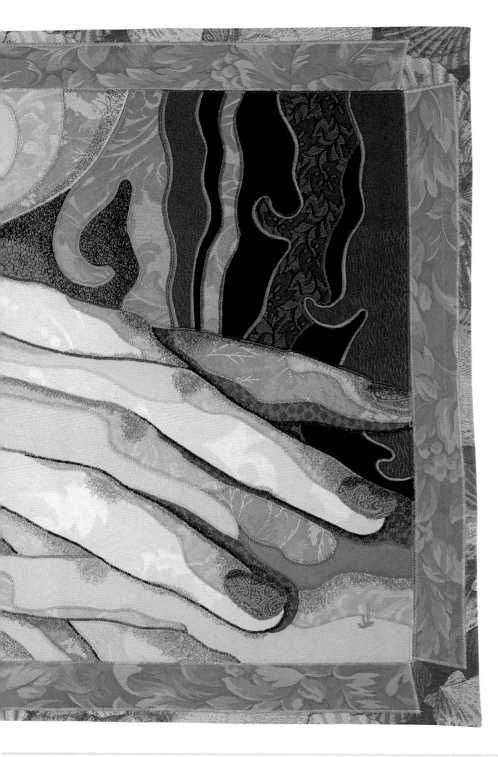

Sea Goddess *is a mystical mermaid waiting near the shore, her body nestled between rocks and boulders as waves lick against jagged cliffs. Gazing out at the ocean, she anxiously awaits her lover's return from a distant voyage. Seaweed tangled in her hair, cool blue lips smiling in anticipation of his arrival. Chin propped on clasped hands, dreaming of the future they may someday share, and silently praying for his safe journey home.*

ERIKA CARTER

BELLEVUE, WASHINGTON

Flow VI

Cotton and silk organza fabrics
painted with pigment; machine
appliquéd, hand embroidered,
hand and machine quilted;
39 x 46 inches (99.1 x 116.8 cm).

This work developed out of a personal history of creating artwork that addresses structure, growth, and connections through surfaces composed of small, torn squares and rectangles. The emphasis in my current work is on the painted surface (versus directing the work through construction methods). I want to "see what's happening," rather than to direct "something to happen." Simple structure is balanced with painted and stitched surfaces, allowing the elements of simplicity and complexity to coexist. Flow VI *continues my series referencing "being with the moment."*

ROSANNA LYNNE WELTER

SALT LAKE CITY, UTAH

African Violets

100 percent cotton and frayed chiffon
fabrics, metallic thread; discharge
dyed, painted, and machine quilted
with free-motion style; 50 x 55 inches
(127.0 x 139.7 cm).

*I am currently consumed with contrast and texture. Discharge dyeing,
which I use extensively, is perfectly suited to create high-contrast fabrics.
I added further contrast to African Violets by simply positioning lines
against curves. The quilting of primitive/geometric images over the
entire surface, along with raw edges and hanging threads, created
extensive texture and ultimately defined this piece. My goal was
to create dimension and movement away from a flat wall.*

MIRIAM NATHAN-ROBERTS

BEST OF SHOW

BERKELEY, CALIFORNIA

Spin Cycle

Commercial and hand-dyed, hand-painted, and airbrushed fabrics; machine appliquéd and machine quilted; 66 x 71 inches (167.6 x 180.3 cm).

This quilt is the latest in the Interweave Series *started in January 1983. Every time I finish one I think it is the last of that series, but then yet another beckons me. I have been interested in structure and illusions of depth all my life. My father was interested in bridges, and Pittsburgh (where I grew up) is a city of bridges. He often pointed out the differences in their structures to me. I have no real depth perception because my eyes don't achieve fusion (one is near-sighted and the other is far-sighted.) Most of the fabrics were hand dyed by me. All of the pieces were individually airbrushed by me. The quilt was named by my friend Nancy Halpern.*

ALICE NORMAN

BOISE, IDAHO

The Chevy: '57 Bel Air Coupe

Commercial and hand-dyed cotton
fabrics; machine-stitched raw-edge
appliqué with machine quilting;
76 x 90 inches (193.0 x 228.6 cm).

*Intrigued by the design possibilities of the raw-edge appliqué technique,
I chose a subject with complex planes, transparent elements, and highly
reflective surfaces. For the first glance, I wanted the image to convey the
spirit and romance of this popular model, compelling viewers to step
closer to examine details. In 1950s America, this car epitomized the
"baseball, apple pie, and Chevrolet" slogan for social optimism.*

HOLLIS CHATELAIN

HILLSBORO, NORTH CAROLINA

Rolling Toys

Whole cloth quilt, hand dye-painted with Procion dyes and acrylic paints; machine quilted; 54 x 48 inches (137.2 x 121.9 cm).

Happy, playful images come into my mind when I think of the children in West Africa. Tires provide hours of endless pleasure and are perhaps the most common toy.

MARLA HATTABAUGH

SCOTTSDALE, ARIZONA

Yon and Beyond

Hand-dyed and commercial fabrics;
machine pieced and hand quilted;
51 x 48 inches (129.5 x 121.9 cm).

On a spring 1998 trip to South Africa I traveled about 4,000 miles by car,
and the beautiful directional arrows on the pavement were the inspiration
for this motif. The colors of Northern Arizona inspired the colors.

233

1999

JUDITH ANTON

WARDSBORO, VERMONT

Discourse

Hand-dyed pima cotton, muslin, and cotton sateen fabrics; machine pieced, appliquéd, and quilted; 63 x 25 inches (160 x 63.5 cm).

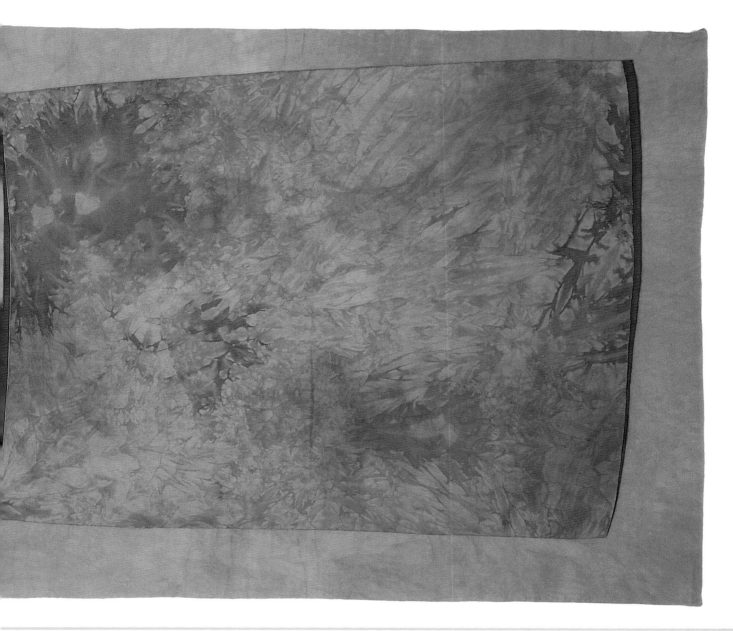

This work begins and ends with the fabric. My technique is called "sliding."
I place fabrics over and under each other and slide them until I begin to feel
the direction to take. No sketch was used in forming the basic concept. This
way of working gives me complete freedom in creating the piece. It gives the
fabric placement "maximum flow," by allowing the colors, textures, and
shapes to bounce off each other, thereby creating the piece's own energy.

236   **NANCY GIPPLE**

AFTON, MINNESOTA

Night Fliers

A wide variety of new and recycled fabric, ribbon, and found materials that were machine collaged and embellished with paint; machine pieced, appliquéd, and quilted; 72 x 57 inches (182.9 x 144.8 cm).

Night Fliers is one of a series of pieces inspired by watching my young niece and nephew draw. I was so impressed with the open and spontaneous nature of their approach. The preciousness was in the freedom of an open and spontaneous mind-set, not in the preciousness of the material goods or in a rigid perfection of technique. To me, the most meaningful work is when I find this same attitude in the quilt tradition. Watching them freed me, if just for a moment.

SANDRA ALTENBERG

SEATTLE, WASHINGTON

Collage II

Silk tissue and fabric that was
hand dyed, painted, glued, and
stitched; hand and machine
pieced and stitched; 15 x 18
inches (38.1 x 45.7 cm).

*I was challenged creatively by working within the two-layer
requirement for this show. I developed a way of bringing together
this tissue, fabric, and stitching as one texture and surface. This
was accomplished through a process of dyeing, painting, and
layering the materials. I then utilized piecing techniques in
reconstructing the materials into this unique composition.*

FAYE ANDERSON

TRAILBLAZER AWARD
SPONSORED BY AN ANONYMOUS DONOR IN MEMORY OF AMY GREGERSON

BOULDER, COLORADO

Dreams

Artist canvas, fused cotton fabric, and candlewick thread; free-motion machine stitchery, hand and machine quilting; 48 x 60 inches (121.9 x 152.4 cm).

It's not that encouraging to be voted Most Talented in a high school that didn't offer a single art class, but at age 17 the gap between fantasy and reality doesn't seem that wide. There's a lot of room to dream, and sometimes the dreams do come true. This quilt was created in a reflective mood. I haven't been in touch with anyone from the PineCrest class of '63 for many years, but I enjoyed rereading their yearbook quips and notes while stitching the portraits, and hope that they have shared my good fortune. P.S. Those who wrote that they didn't think that I was all that talented somehow vanished between the worktable and the sewing machine.

MALKA DUBRAWSKY

Chaim's Tree

Hand-dyed and discharged
cottons; machine pieced
and machine quilted; 26 x 34
inches (66.0 x 86.4 cm).

Chaim's Tree *grew out of a love for nature. The circular forms
that are the "trunk" of my tree honor nature lessons learned
from watching my garden grow, bloom, freeze, and reemerge to
bloom anew. The title, however, blossomed only after the piece
was quilted. The Hebrew word for life is* chaim *and it was also
my grandfather's name. This tree of life is dedicated to him.*

DOMINIE NASH

BETHESDA, MARYLAND

Red Landscape 2

Cotton and silk fabric treated
with textile paint, fiber reactive
dye, and Theox (discharge)
paste; monoprinted, screenprint-
ed, machine appliquéd, and
machine quilted; 61 x 40 inches
(154.9 x 101.6 cm).

*Color and texture are the dominant elements in my work. This piece
is an exploration of the interaction of large areas of subtly textured
saturated color with graphically patterned black and white sections.
The color becomes more emphatic by contrast, while the black-
and-white patterning compensates for the absence of color.*

JUDITH LARZELERE

BELMONT, MASSACHUSETTS

Tumbling Reds

100 percent cotton hand dyed by
Heidi Stoll-Weber; machine strip
pieced, machine strip quilted in
quilt-as-you-go technique; 60 x
60 inches (152.4 x 152.4 cm).

*I see myself as one of many artists working in a medium that was once
considered only a craft, and a woman's craft at that. I struggle to use all the
basic tools of art and design theory, but I express myself with fabric rather
than pigment on canvas. I make images that would be next to impossible to
create with paint, but can quite easily be accomplished using the techniques
natural to cloth, such as cutting apart and reconnecting with thread.*

ANNE SMITH

WARRINGTON, CHESHIRE, ENGLAND

Passing Harbin's

Cotton blends and recycled fabrics;
machine pieced, painted, appliquéd,
embroidered, and hand quilted;
60 x 37 inches (152.4 x 94.0 cm).

*Harbin's was an old textile mill in my home town. I used to
pass it every Sunday and peep through a gap in the big wooden
door to see and smell the machinery. As I grew up, the old
door decayed and then disappeared, along with the mill.*

244

SALLY A. SELLERS

VANCOUVER, WASHINGTON

Irregular
Thought Patterns

Hand-dyed and commercial
cottons and silks; machine
appliquéd onto canvas and
machine quilted; 39 x 39
inches (99.1 x 99.1 cm).

*I do not like lines that are exactly parallel. I do not understand junctions
that are entirely smooth. I have not experienced many journeys of note
in which it was revealed early on what the final destination would be.*

MELODY JOHNSON

CARY, ILLINOIS

Aquifer

Cotton fabrics that have been hand dyed and painted by the artist; fused and machine quilted; 25 x 27 inches (63.5 x 68.6 cm).

Aquifer is part of a series based on cracked pavement, which became pathways and rock walls. The fabric I dye sometimes develops air bubbles which can look three dimensional when cut away from the whole. These "rocks" were piled into pastel geological formations and layered between sunrise skies.

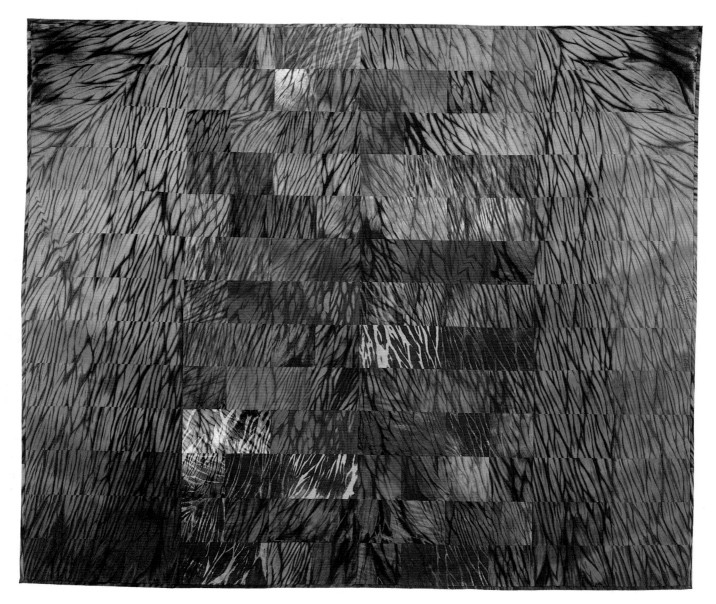

JAN MYERS-NEWBURY

PITTSBURGH, PENNSYLVANIA

Agape

Cotton fabric shibori dyed with
Procion dyes, some discharged;
machine pieced and machine
quilted; 60 x 52 inches (152.4 x
132.1 cm). Private collection.

*My dyeing techniques continue to be relatively primitive with
gradual changes and an occasional lurch forward, always in
the context of what I have done before. Discoveries made
while creating one piece generate a starting point for the next.
The depth and beauty of the fabrics excite and inspire the
design. Agape is a Greek word for love, referring to the love
that extends outward and is freely given, the grace of God.*

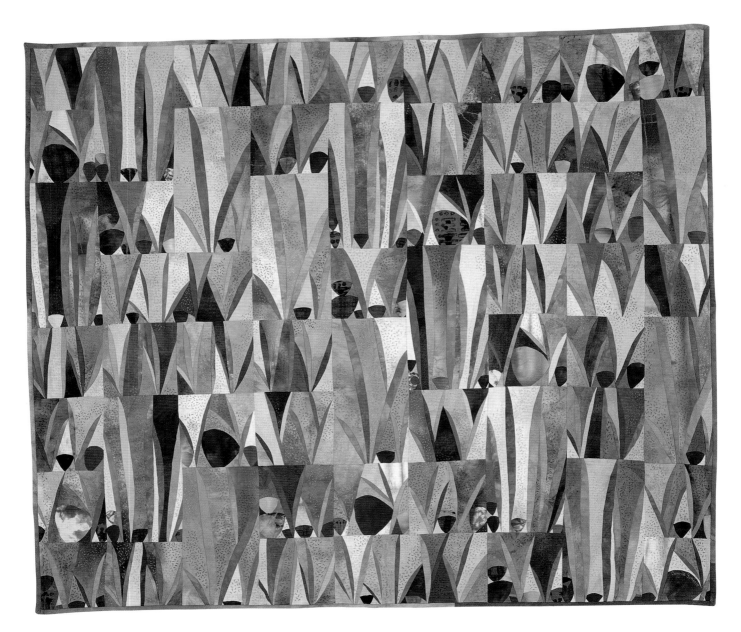

CONNIE SCHEELE

HOUSTON, TEXAS

In the Shallows

Hand-dyed cottons; machine pieced and hand quilted; 53 x 46 inches (134.6 x 116.8 cm).

After doing a number of River Rocks *quilts, I did a few quilts of foliage and grasses. This quilt is an integration of the two, and is reminiscent of the northern Wisconsin lake country that is very important to me.*

JANET STEADMAN

CLINTON, WASHINGTON

Breaking Ground

Hand-dyed cottons and commercial fabrics; machine pieced and machine quilted; 56 x 56 inches (142.2 x 142.2 cm).

After a devastating fire destroyed my next-door neighbors' house, I looked out of my studio window at an ash-covered lot for 18 months. Finally, work began to rebuild the house. I started the quilt Breaking Ground *the day the construction equipment moved onto the lot and started moving ground for the house foundation.*

VITA MARIE LOVETT

MARIETTA, GEORGIA

Primitive Door Series— VIII Keep Out

Canvas, cotton, acrylic paint, various threads; machine thread painted and machine quilted; 27 x 29 inches (322.6 x 73.7 cm).

In the foothills of the Tennessee Smoky Mountains, in an area known as Piney Branch, I came upon a weathered barn with a "Keep Out" warning. Barns are a landmark of rural America that are fast on their way to disappearing. These old structures have inspired me to create vignettes of the past through fabric and thread.

ANN STAMM MERRELL

CUPERTINO, CALIFORNIA

Celtic Crosses
3.1, 3.2, 3.3

Cotton, silk, linen, and blend fabrics, screen door netting, old embroidered tablecloth, patchwork from my Great Aunt Lena Tomlinson; fused and machine stitched; 22 by 21 inches (55.9 x 53.3 cm), 21 by 23 inches (53.3 x 58.4 cm), 24 by 22 inches (61.0 x 55.9 cm).

The construction method for these abstract Celtic crosses involves starting with squares of fabric and going through several iterations of cutting, swapping, and sewing, without any predetermined outcome. In this case I started out with 24 pieces of fabric, each associated in some way with the Trinity: the color red for Sustainer/Holy Spirit, schools of fish for Creator/God, a cross for Redeemer/Jesus, or by some unarticulated feeling of mine.

**SUSAN SHIE
AND JAMES ACORD**

WOOSTER, OHIO

The Teapot/High Priestess
(Card #2 of The Kitchen Tarot)

Fabric, beads, gemstones, Mardi Gras beads, shells,
buttons, antique jewelry, and assorted collectibles
and found objects; painted, airbrushed, embroidered, appliquéd, quilted, and embellished by
hand; 87 x 55 inches (221.0 x 139.7 cm).

This piece is the third quilt of The Kitchen Tarot. *In this quilt,
Susan's invented saint, St. Quilta the Comforter, makes her first
appearance in the deck. She wears an entire teapot (instead of her
usual tiara of a Fiestaware teacup), which is in the top of the quilt
now. She has her ever-present Lucky Tomato Pincushion. (When-
ever one is around a room, St. Q can spontaneously manifest!)*

JANE BURCH COCHRAN

RABBIT HASH, KENTUCKY

Je t'aime

Fabric, beads, buttons, paint, clothing, gloves, gold leaf, color pencil, china markers, pastels, playing cards; machine pieced, hand appliquéd with beads, embellished, and monoprinted; 63 x 60 inches (160.0 x 152.4 cm).

The working title for this quilt was Nearly New, *a term referring to used clothing in good condition. I started intuitively putting images together from materials I had collected and received as gifts (in this quilt special thanks to Betsy Cannon, Anita Corum, and Beth Kennedy). I made a monoprint from the blouse and rickrack glove, using the originals as plates and acrylic paint to print. Suddenly I realized the quilt was just a big old nine patch about romantic love. I had found a handkerchief that said both* I love you *and the beautiful French companion* Je t'aime. *It is in the painted denim pocket in the upper right corner.*

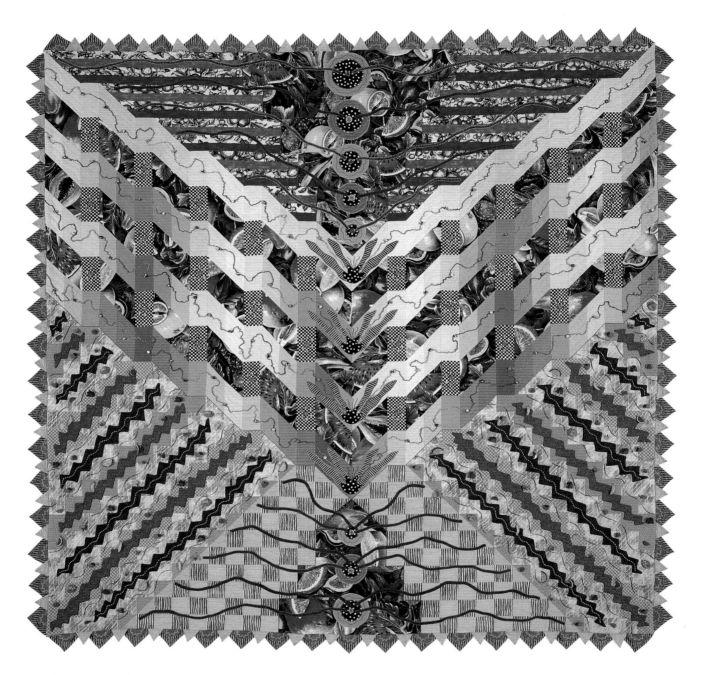

JILL PACE

GLENDALE, ARIZONA

Tutti Frutti

Various materials including cotton
fabric, embroidery floss, buttons,
beads, chenille fiber, and perle cotton;
machine pieced, hand quilted, hand
appliquéd, hand embroidered;
72 x 72 inches (182.9 x 182.9 cm).

*This piece represents the rich cornucopia of life choices the world offers
us. Though there may be many twists and turns in this "mixed salad,"
if you really want to, you can find a way to accomplish anything.
All your opportunities are there in front of you for the tasting.
Open your eyes, reach out, pick one, take a bite, seize the day!*

BARBARA BARRICK MCKIE

LYME, CONNECTICUT

Floral Symphony #2: Foxgloves

Hand-dyed cottons and discharge-dyed polyester computer transfers; machine pieced, appliquéd, and quilted; 24 x 29 inches (61.0 x 73.7 cm).

As a photographer and former computer consultant, I have been experimenting with computer fabrics since 1994. Realistic images from my photographs become computer-disperse dye transfers. Abstract backgrounds and semirealistic parts of the design are my hand-dyed fabrics. Themes involving nature and still lives are my usual, though not exclusive, subject matter. Foxgloves in my cousin's garden inspired Floral Symphony #2: Foxgloves, *the second in a series of floral studies.*

1999

KUNIKO SAKA

TOKYO, JAPAN

Wisteria

Cottons and blends; machine
pieced, hand appliquéd, and
hand quilted; 88 x 88 inches
(223.5 x 223.5 cm).

*In Japan, the wisteria are in full bloom every spring. The purple
flowers and fresh, verdurous leaves are beautiful swaying in
the wind. This quilt is one picture of scenery in Japan.*

SARA NISSIM

RAMAT-GAN, ISRAEL

Hamsa

Silks, velvets, embroideries, and
embellishments; hand appliquéd,
embroidered and quilted; 36 x 46
inches (91.4 x 116.8 cm).

*I trained as a painter and art teacher, arriving from abstract
oil paintings to mixed media collage. When I felt the need to look
back into my past, I realized that I could express my childhood
memories of Iraq only in a textile medium. To me, composition
takes the lead, while the colors and textures follow on.*

1999

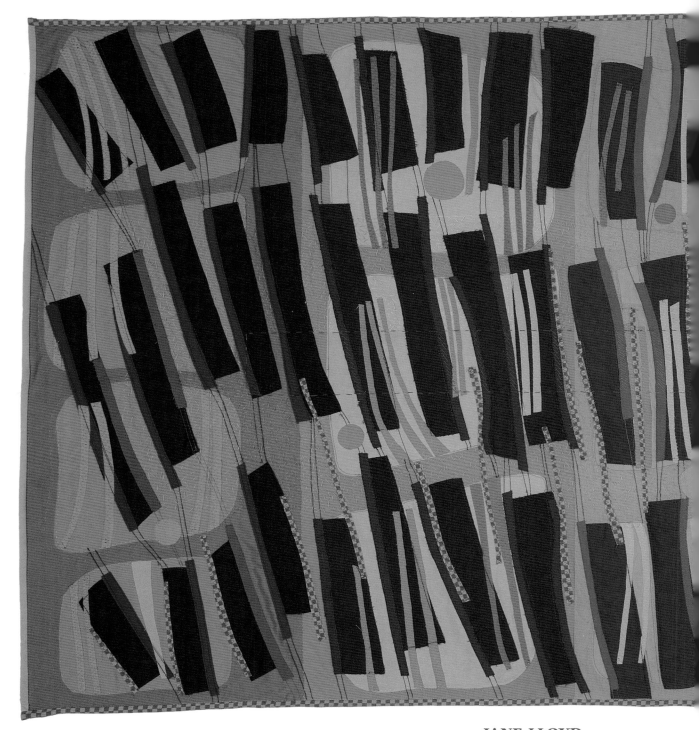

JANE LLOYD

BALLYMENA, COUNTY ANTRIM,
NORTHERN IRELAND

Trick Track

Commercial hand-dyed cotton/poly
fabrics; direct appliquéd, fused, embroidered, hand and machine stitched;
58 x 35 inches (147.3 x 88.9 cm).

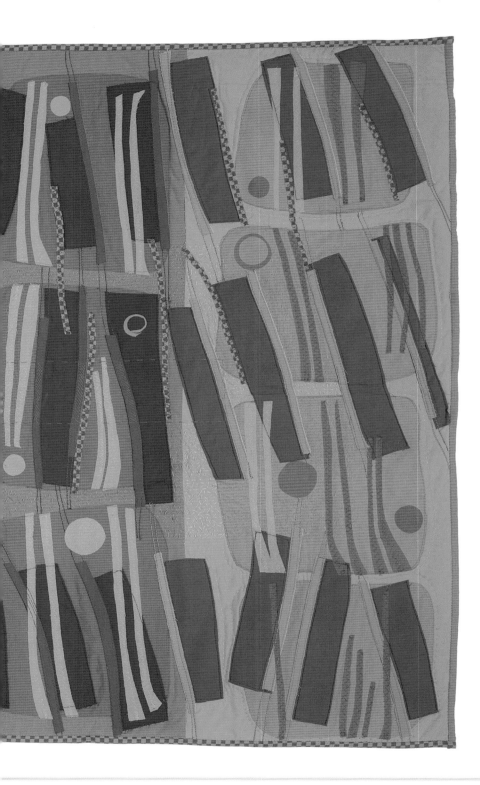

Treating the fabric like paper collage gave me great design freedom, thus making it more exciting to create. I liked the idea of using large seeding stitches to form a different texture and embroidery emphasizing some parts.

JUDITH H. PERRY

WILMETTE, ILLINOIS

Garden Fantasy

Cotton fabrics hand dyed by the artist
and Kathy Sorenson and/or painted by
the artist with metallic pens; machine
pieced and machine quilted; 54 x 56
inches (137.2 x 142.2 cm).

Dirt doesn't hold my dreams-
Fabric does-
Flowers seen in splendor and brilliance-
Leaves and dragonflies-
Butterflies and birds-
Sunshine and moon glow-
All this and more-
My garden fantasy.

ANNE MCKENZIE NICKOLSON

INDIANAPOLIS, INDIANA

In Perspective

Cotton fabrics; machine pieced,
hand appliquéd, and hand quilted;
57 x 57 inches (144.8 x 144.8 cm).

*My inspiration for this particular piece was my favorite Johannes Vermeer
painting,* A Lady at the Virginal with a Gentleman (The Music Lesson).
*I tried to capture and use in my own way the palette of colors and the way
the light streams in the open window, letting the golden light settle on the
objects inside the room. And I thank Her Majesty, Queen Elizabeth II, for
letting me see this painting at the National Gallery in Washington, D.C.*

ART QUILTS: *a celebration*

JANE A. SASSAMAN

CHICAGO, ILLINOIS

Seeds and Blossoms

Hand-printed fabric; machine
appliquéd and machine quilted;
43 x 43 inches (109.2x 109.2 cm).

QUILTS JAPAN PRIZE SPONSORED BY QUILTS JAPAN MAGAZINE

*We have a dense garden in our small city yard. Every year we grow
several varieties of angels' trumpets, also called jimsonweed or thorn
apple. This plant is poisonous, yet incredibly dramatic. It has huge,
white, sweet-smelling trumpet blossoms, dusty gray-green leaves, and
wonderfully evil-looking prickly seed balls the size of Christmas orna-
ments. I absolutely love them so it was an obvious subject for a quilt.*

BARBARA W. WATLER

HOLLYWOOD, FLORIDA

Print Series:
"Her Very Own #5"

100 percent pima cotton fabric; direct appliqué machine stitched to hold all layers together; 36 x 36 inches (91.4 x 91.4 cm).

A decision to try a series of quilts using only black and white focused my attention on fingerprints. Each fingerprint is a unique and identifying design appealing to my need to never repeat a design. Examining my own prints proved how quickly everyday tasks would subtly overlay the print design. Because I do hand stitching without a thimble, several of my own prints have distorted, torn skin patterns, depending on which finger's print and which hand I used for a particular quilt. When hung all together, this series of 20 machine-stitched quilts has an ebb and flow of line and rhythm that reminds me of music.

JUDY HOOWORTH

TERREY HILLS, NEW SOUTH WALES, AUSTRALIA

Mothers/Daughters #6...
Lines of Communication

Cotton blends, torn fabrics; layered and
machine stitched to cotton batting, machine
quilted; 78 x 78 inches (198.1 x 198.1 cm).

*Family relationships are fragile at times of stress and emotional
upheaval. The bond between mother and daughter is stretched to
the fracture point. To help preserve a special and loving relationship,
the lines of communication, though tenuous, need to be kept open.*

YASUKO SAITO

TOKYO, JAPAN

Movement #4

Commercial and hand-dyed fabrics, some treated with paint; 81 by 74 inches (205.7 x 188.0 cm).

The vision of the third millennium: In one moment all the stages of life are connected to 3,000 worlds. All existence in the universe is connected to and affected by each other fundamentally, deep down at the roots. And thus, an eternal harmony ultimately results from the cycle of life and death. White lines are the symbol of one such universe. I believe we could be the source of the harmony rather than chaos.

B. J. ADAMS

WASHINGTON, D.C.

Hand Tools

Hand-dyed and commercial fabrics (cotton, silk, and wool), cotton, polyester, and metallic threads, acrylic paint; machine embroidery using a boil-away stabilizer, photo transfer, appliqué, and machine stitching; 75 x 46 inches (190.5 x 116.8 cm).

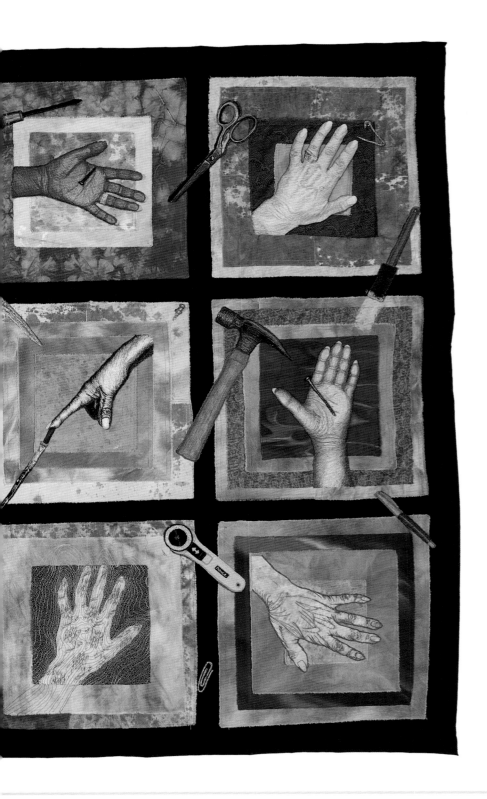

Machine embroidered hands are part of a theme in an ongoing series of my work. Hand Tools *is an homage to creativity. The hands are created in a variety of colors and techniques to illustrate the varieties of people in our world. The tools are a small representation of the diversity of vocations and avocations available.*

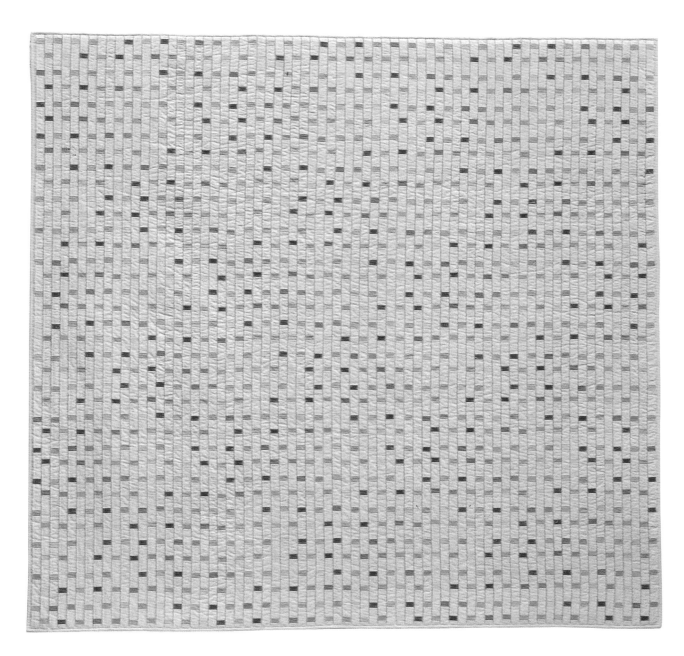

INGE HUEBER

COLOGNE, GERMANY

Ikat Quilt/Rhythm II

Hand-dyed cotton; machine pieced and machine quilted; 79 x 78 inches (200.7 x 198.1 cm).

This is an attempt to transform one old textile technique (ikat weaving) into another (piecing and quilting). I enjoy the contrast between a rigid concept and the floating pattern of the 11 rainbow colors.

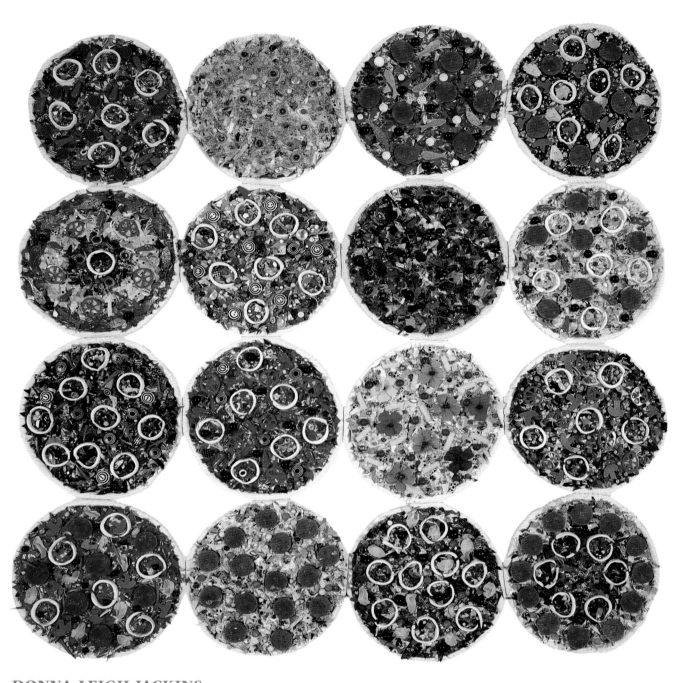

DONNA LEIGH JACKINS

BIRMINGHAM, ALABAMA

Laissez-les Manger du Gâteau Pizza

Assorted materials including fabric, thread, buttons, rubber, wire mesh, leather, silk flowers, plaster, beads, and wood; machine stitched and hand quilted; 52 x 52 inches (132.1 x 132.1 cm).

Pizzas! They came to me in the middle of the night. Lately I've been traveling extensively with my husband, and the pizzas with ingredients are quite portable compared to the larger quilts I had been transporting. While sewing feta cheese in the Tokyo airport, I had a conversation with a Japanese quilter. She spoke no English. I spoke no Japanese. I've no idea what she said except for the word "pizza."

1999

ELIZABETH BRIMELOW

MACCLESFIELD, CHESHIRE, ENGLAND

Appletreefield

Silk and cotton fabrics, some hand dyed; direct and reverse appliqué, slashing, hand and machine stitching; 54 x 54 inches (137.2 x 137.2 cm).

Landscape is my inspiration. I study its history, archaeology, geology, and botany. I am interested in man's mark on it and the results of such interventions as mining, quarrying, building, ploughing, planting, and harvesting. Landscape is where I live, what I look at, what I draw, and what I stitch.

I am currently exploring silk-screen prints and various methods of discharging color. The initial surface choice affects these processes immensely. Here, the organic softness of the discharged cloth is the perfect complement to the hard-edge, printed image, although the very similar colors were arrived at by very different methods.

BARBARA BUSHEY

ANN ARBOR, MICHIGAN

Reflections

Hand-dyed polyester fabrics, silk-screening (pigments), bleach discharge with resists; machine stitched; 12 x 21 inches (30.5 x 53.3 cm).

271

1999

ANN HARWELL

WENDELL, NORTH CAROLINA

J. C. Raulston Arboretum

Cotton fabric with each piece cut from
individually designed plastic templates that
are positioned as appropriate to the pattern
in the cloth; machine pieced and hand
quilted; 57 x 57 inches (144.8 x 144.8 cm).

*A rainy June walk in the arboretum: down green-walled paths, over
stepping stones to a water garden, hopping among the fish, frogs, and
toads...past sculptures that evoke a sensual, spiritual freedom to a huge
wicker dome entwined by red flowering vines and lorded over by raucous
birds. Under your feet is a tiled floor depicting trees with interlaced limbs.*

MARJORIE HOELTZEL

ST. LOUIS, MISSOURI

Cacophony

Silk necktie fabric; machine
pieced and hand quilted; 55 x
55 inches (139.7 x 139.7 cm).

*On the wall of my studio there is pinned a quotation from Proust: "Be
regular and orderly in your life, so that you may be violent and original
in your work." I had been madly and obsessively slashing, stitching, and
constructing this piece during a rather disruptive period when I realized
that the grid and quilting of the Log Cabin block formation exemplifies
that order and regularity. The rest...well, the rest speaks for itself.*

JOHN W. LEFELHOCZ

ATHENS, OHIO

Money for Nothing

Sugar packets, nylon window screening, dental floss (mint flavored), green paper, and plastic flies;
73 x 33 inches (185.4 x 83.8 cm).

Money is a strange force to be dealt with, and this force is in us rather than in the tactile paper and coins. Here's where I tell you what this piece is supposed to mean…Well, not really…I hope that you reach your own conclusions. I just make it, I don't define it. If I could define it, I wouldn't have to make it.

ANNE WORINGER

PARIS, FRANCE

Le Labyrinthe de Merlin

Antique linen and hemp, hand spun and hand woven during the 19th century in France and hand dyed by the artist; hand/machine pieced, appliquéd, and top stitched; 62 x 60 inches (157.5 x 152.4 cm).

My first creative quilt in 1985 was a very tame, geometric labyrinth... and my last quilt is still a labyrinth, but now it has reached a free dynamic and spontaneous folly. Why this fascination? Does the labyrinth represent a journey of initiation? A mysterious image slow to decipher? Or a magic positive-negative interplay? Another magic is added by my hand-dyed antique linen attesting to the touching work of our ancestors.

LINDA R. MACDONALD

WILLITS, CALIFORNIA

Town News

Cotton fabric and batting; fabric
is airbrushed, dyed, painted
and hand quilted; 40 x 30
inches (101.6 x 76.2 cm).

*I live in a small town and every week the whole town reads the police log in the news-
paper. It's a source of great entertainment. We read mainly about minor crimes, looking
for people we know yet hoping we won't find our own or our family's names in there.
While we are so myopic about the trivial pastimes of our fellow townies, I wonder
if something truly amazing happened, such as spaceships landing on our mountain
range, whether we would even notice. The items in the police log have happened in
our town; we do have a hidden economy in the hills; and this is a self-portrait of me
wearing my goldfish earrings and a surface designed T-shirt that has since worn out.*

HEIDE STOLL-WEBER

FRANKFURT, GERMANY

Relief

Hand-dyed cotton from the artist's
dye studio; machine pieced and
machine quilted; 74 x 52 inches
(188.0 x 132.1 cm).

*Like all my work, this quilt is a study in color and light. I start
laying out most of my composition on a flannel-covered wall
and keep adding details while I'm piecing. The whole process
is very satisfying: it's like painting with hand-dyed fabrics.*

JUDY MCDERMOTT

THORNLEIGH, NEW SOUTH WALES, AUSTRALIA

A Real Pretend Wagga For Paul Klee

Wool/acrylic and wool fabrics; machine pieced and hand quilted with hand-dyed silk thread; 48 x 32 inches (121.9 x 81.3 cm).

This quilt is all about color. What to do with the ferocious orange from the op-shop? Add greens, as did Klee in his color studies. The yellow "makes the orange sing," says Johannes Itten, author of The Art of Colour. *A wagga is a traditional Australian quilt or bush blanket made from wheat bags, old clothes, or found scrap materials. Many are roughly cobbled together, although my favorite is "sewn" with wire.*

SHERRI WOOD

CARRBORO, NORTH CAROLINA

The Empty Tomb

Various fabrics and found objects including velvet, polyesters, organza, glass beads, photo transfers and mirrors; hand and machine stitched and quilted; 96 x 90 inches (243.8 x 228.6 cm). Private collection.

The void as the epicenter of God's creative activity...
out of the tomb/womb comes transformation.

URSULA BAUMUNG

STUTENSEE, GERMANY

Obsessed

Commercial fabrics; machine
stitched; 47 x 61 inches
(119.4 x 154.9 cm).

*Scraps on my table and my new sewing machine in the midst.
Trying out my new toy, putting together the scraps around me
without thinking about what I am doing, sewing for hours just
for fun...what an adventure! When looking at the result of my
obsession the next morning, I suddenly realized I had created
something unique the night before—the birth of this work.*

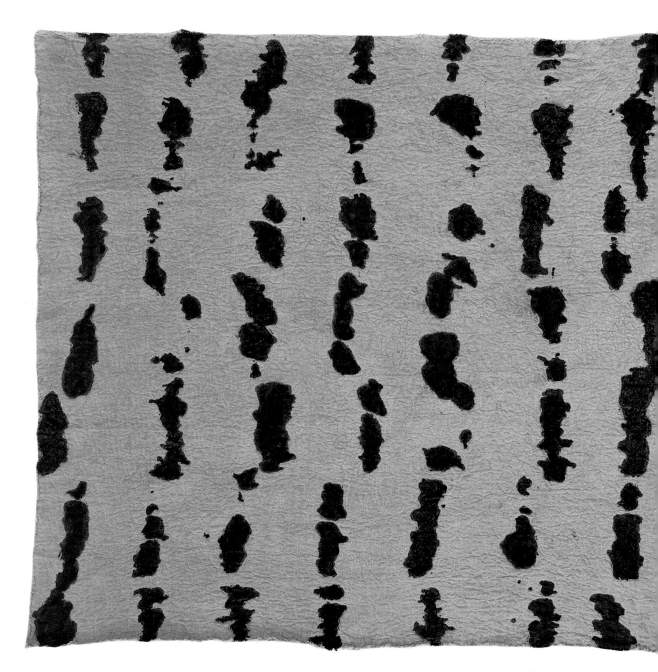

SUZAN FRIEDLAND

SAN FRANCISCO, CALIFORNIA

Binary Zen

Hand-dyed linen, monoprinting;
machine quilted; 108 x 56 inches
(274.3 x 142.2 cm).

This piece is from a series, Skillful Means/Binary Zen, *that explores monoprinting on linen. I wanted to use a simple technique that would convey a meditative quality in the midst of turmoil. The 0s and 1s represent the complexities of life in the digital age. The term "skillful means" is often used by Buddhists to describe various methods of teaching; here it refers to the attempt to discover simplicity in seemingly complex patterns. This particular piece represents emptying, from a solid pattern of 1s to an all encompassing 0.*

JEANNE LYONS BUTLER

HUNTINGTON, NEW YORK

Rapture

Silk, cotton, and polyester fabrics;
machine appliquéd and quilted;
41 x 55 inches (104.1 x 139.7 cm).

*Space that encompasses endless views. White. Something shows
through; it is not clear; is simple; is winter. Veiled, yet crisp. A
path; to who knows where? Space you can breathe; is cool. It lifts.*

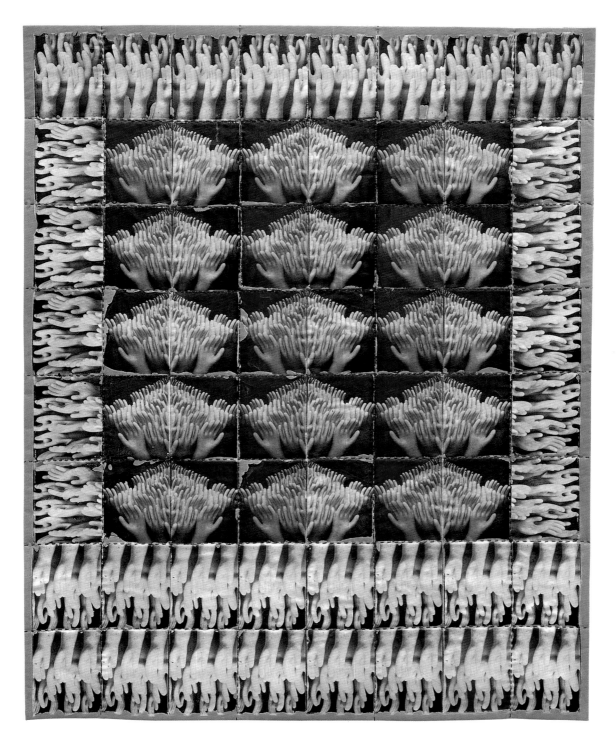

MELISSA HOLZINGER

ARLINGTON, WASHINGTON

Hands

Cotton cloth treated with textile paint
and Polaroid transfers; hand stitched;
24 x 32 inches (61.0 x 81.3 cm).

Hands *is a whole cloth quilt that has been block printed with
Polaroid film. It is part of a series of work called* Object Cloth.

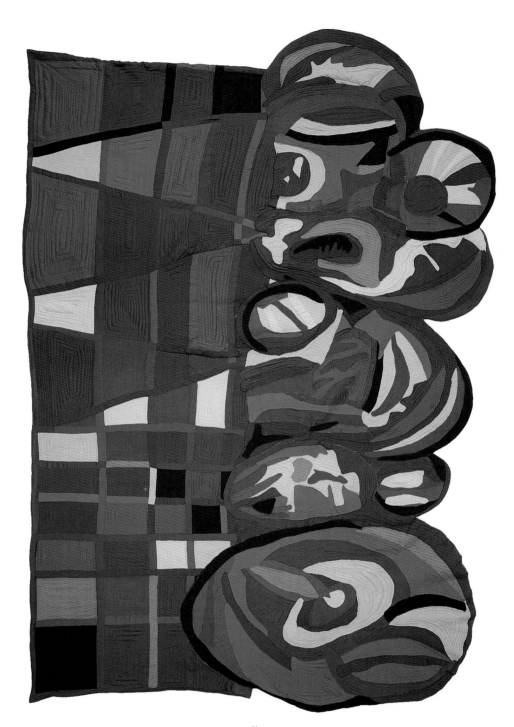

CVETKA HOJNIK-DOROJEVIČ

LENDAVA, SLOVENIA

Harmony

100 percent cotton fabrics; direct
appliqué, machine stitched;
64 x 104 inches (162.6 x 264.2 cm)

*Shapes and structure give new character to the quilting picture.
Vibrant feminine character (represented by the curving and
circular shapes) joins in harmony with the more serious
masculine character (represented by the square shapes).*

LINDA GASS

LOS ALTOS, CALIFORNIA

After the Gold Rush

Silk crepe de chine hand painted using acid dyes, water-based resist, salt, and alcohol techniques; machine quilted with monofilament and rayon threads; 26 x 21 inches (66.0 x 53.3 cm).

I grew up in California and have spent countless hours exploring the beauty of its mountains and deserts. In this quilt I have tried to beautify an unnatural landscape through a play of color and texture on silk. The landscape is I-5, a major transportation artery, crossing from the California Aqueduct, the man-made river that moves water from north to south and irrigates farm fields in what once was a desert. This is the second mining of California and hence the name of the quilt. (Inspired by a photograph by Ray Atkeson, courtesy of the Ray Atkeson Image Archive.)

1999

LIBBY LEHMAN

HOUSTON, TEXAS

Drop Zone

Hand-dyed and commercial cottons,
sheers, and decorative threads;
reverse appliqué, sheer appliqué,
machine embroidery, bobbin
drawing, machine quilting;
63 x 63 inches (160.0 x 160.0 cm).

*When I make a quilt, I play with many elements: fabric,
design, color, light, and threads. I delight in working
without a net—no preplanning or drawing ahead of
time. This keeps the quilt in progress alive and kicking.*

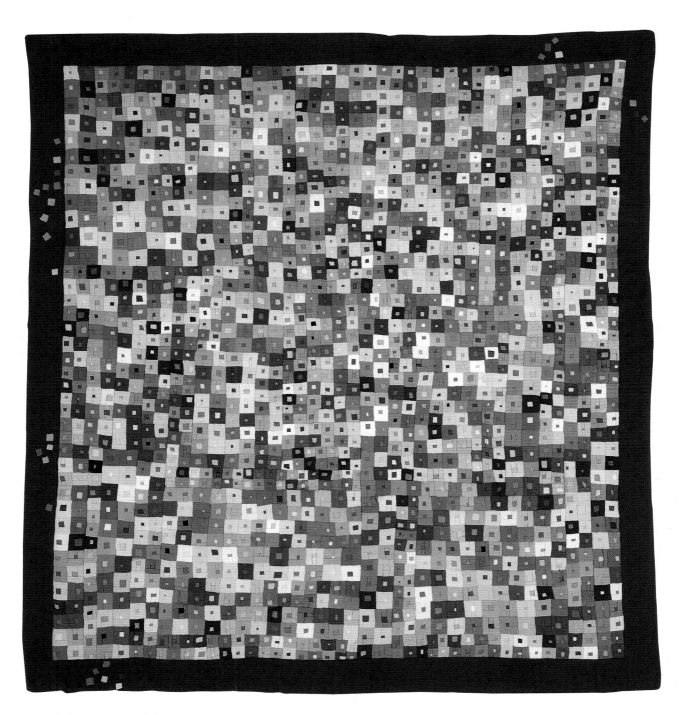

BEATRICE LANTER

NIEDERLENZ, SWITZERLAND

Colours in Disorder

Commercial fabrics including cotton, blends, silk, and wool; pieced and appliquéd by machine and hand; hand quilted; 35 x 38 inches (88.9 x 96.5 cm).

Colors have always been very important for me, and patchwork is a good way to play with them. I try to express my feelings and ideas with colors and simple forms.

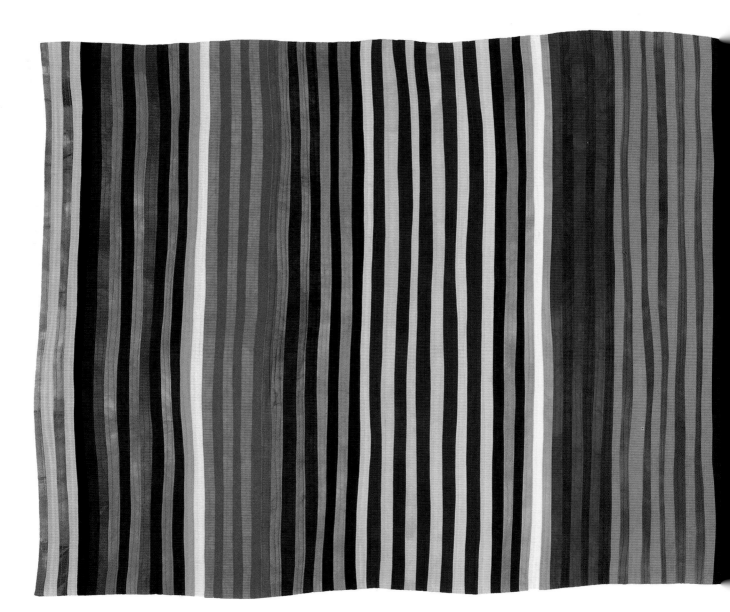

ELEANOR A. MCCAIN

SHALIMAR, FLORIDA

Color Study 2

Commercial and hand-dyed cottons; machine pieced and quilted; 87 x 35 inches (221.0 x 88.9 cm).

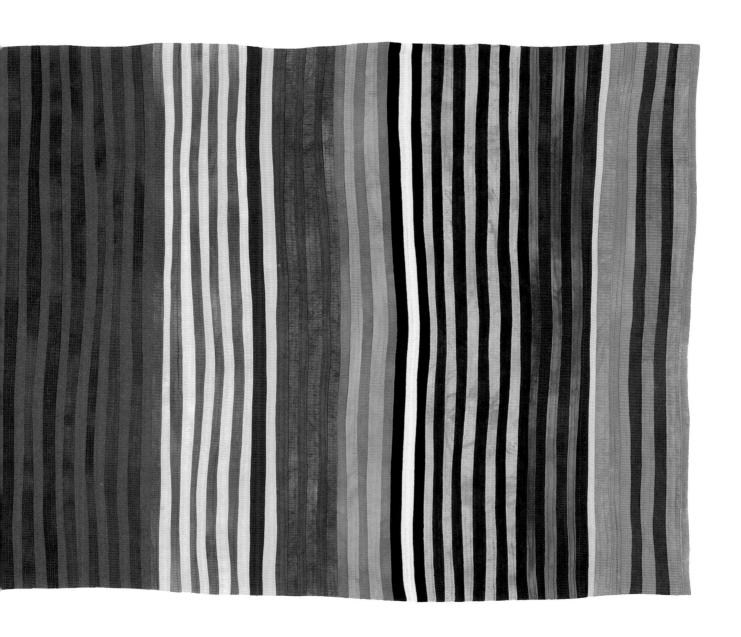

Quilting provides a creative outlet that is grounded in family, community, and common experience, while offering unlimited problem solving, experimentation, and aesthetic range. I choose fabrics for their sensuality, tactile intimacy, familiarity, and tradition. Fabric has qualities of texture, light absorption, and reflection unmatched by any other medium. This quilt is an exploration of color interrelationships and line.

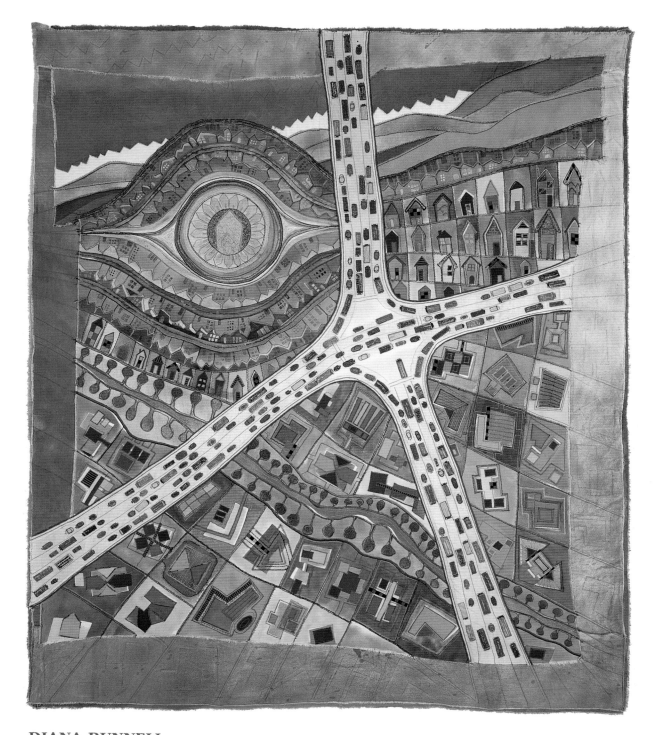

DIANA BUNNELL

BOULDER, COLORADO

An Eye on Boulder

Airbrushed canvas; fused,
machine quilted, embroidered,
and appliquéd; 60 x 71 inches
(152.4 x 180.3 cm).

*During my 40 years in Boulder, Colorado, I have seen many changes in the
environment precipitated by growth. There is much competition for space in
this small valley. Although our green belt policy has preserved many natural
areas (including both banks of the creek that traverses the city), still the building
continues, the traffic grows. I watch from the golden sanctuary of my home
which dominates the landscape and is the center of the universe in my mind's eye.*

AUG·74

MARIE WOHADLO

CHICAGO, ILLINOIS

The Patchy Memory of Roy G. Biv

Cotton and blend fabrics and metallic and monofilament thread; cyanotype printing, machine pieced, appliquéd, and quilted; 36 x 35 inches (91.4 x 88.9 cm).

Life's commonalities are fleshed out in my work, which is often inspired by family photo albums. I transmute snapshots into compositions of patchwork, appliqué, and embroidery. This process strips photography of its heavy pretense to a specific reality into something more tactile and iconographic. Beyond the appearance of immediacy and inherent suggestion of naiveté, my quilt work is sandwiched with satire, commentary, inquiry, and humor. Is it naive to believe that art can be tied to everyday experiences?

ANN SCHROEDER

JAMAICA PLAIN, MASSACHUSETTS

Natural Forces #3

Cotton fabrics; machine pieced
and machine quilted; 53 x 58
inches (134.6 x 147.3 cm).

My goal in this quilt was to get as much variety in rhythm and color as possible, while limiting the palette to only four fabrics. It is the third in a series of quilts inspired by the natural world, the elemental forces, growth, and regeneration.

EMILY PARSON

ST. CHARLES, ILLINOIS

A Sunny Day in April

Hand-dyed and commercial cottons; machine appliquéd and machine quilted; 83 x 62 inches (210.8 x 157.5 cm).

Last year, my husband and I bought our first house. Because we bought the house in the winter, we were unaware of the wonderful gardens planted by the previous owners. Spring was full of surprises, as hundreds of green shoots popped their heads through the snow. The profusion of tulips, combined with the happiness I was feeling in my new home, gave me a wonderful new enthusiasm for my work.

1999

FRAN SKILES

PLANTATION, FLORIDA

Blue Fish

Cotton duck fabric and woven hemp
treated with oil stick, acrylic, and
fabric paint; photo silk-screen, color
copy transfer, machine stitching;
52 x 68 inches (132.1 x 172.7 cm).

*My work evolves intuitively as I draw from the images of
my personal photography. Accidents are incorporated and
appreciated in the form of creases and torn areas. I hope to
create an internal landscape which captures the essence of nature.*

ODETTE TOLKSDORF

DURBAN, KWAZULU-NATAL, SOUTH AFRICA

Some Heaven Some Earth No.1

Commercially and hand-dyed cotton, cotton blend, and silk fabrics; machine pieced and machine quilted; 43 x 80 inches (109.2 x 203.2 cm).

Three ideas came together as my starting point: first, the desire to explore the use of sinuous, curved lines (rather than shape); second, thoughts of integration; and third, the desire to create an impression of landscape. The design is a metaphor of my hopes for South Africa. In the upper area, narrow wavy lines enter in isolated groups with a sense of uncertainty. As they move lower down, they gradually start integrating with the other elements until they form a cohesive unity.

GUDRUN BECHET

DUDELANGE, LUXEMBOURG

Wolfwomen

Hand-dyed cotton, airbrushed, stamped,
and drawn; hand and machine pieced
and appliquéd, hand quilted; 54 x 58
inches (137.2 x 147.3 cm).

Listening to our inner Wolfwomen, *we experience wisdom
and intuition. Inspired by a book by Clarissa Pinkola Estés.*

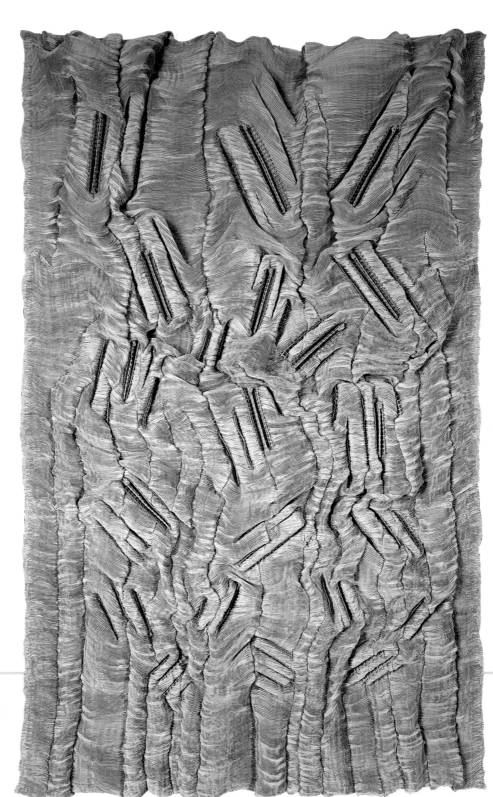

In my recent work I have been exploring ways of making the inner (batting) layer more evident. The idea for the forms in this piece developed after watching a film about pillow lava forming underwater from fissures in the contorted sea floor.

ARDYTH DAVIS

RESTON, VIRGINIA

Wrapped Grid/Blue

Hand painted and pleated silk, shaped rug canvas; shaped and tied with silk threads; 28 x 49 inches (71.1 x 124.5 cm).

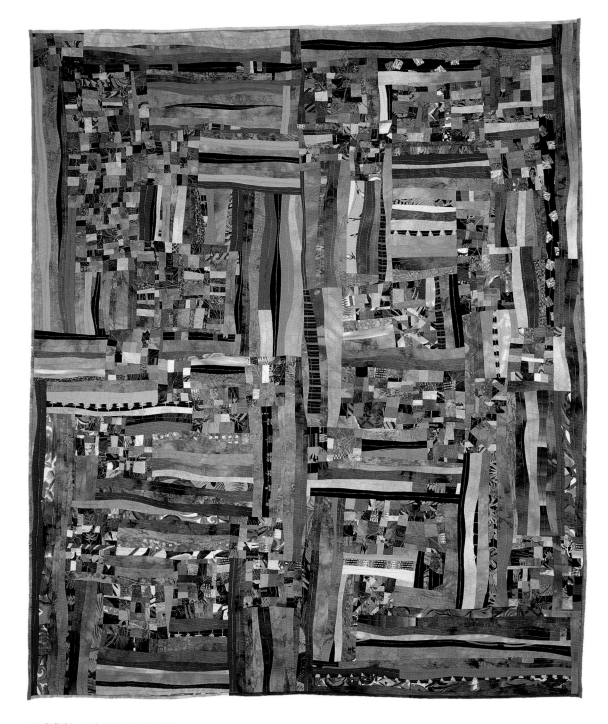

JUTTA FARRINGER

CONSTANTIA, CAPE TOWN, SOUTH AFRICA

In the Smoky Mountains

Cotton fabric and batting; machine pieced and quilted; 71 x 90 inches (180.3 x 228.6 cm).

This quilt was inspired by a trip through the Smoky Mountains and the beautiful diffused colors of those mountains. The quilting design was taken from the shrubs and trees growing in the area.

ODILE TEXIER

SAINT-AUNES, FRANCE

Persiennes

Silk and cotton fabrics; machine
pieced using the paper piecing
method and machine quilted;
45 x 63 inches (114.3 x 160.0 cm).

*I am fascinated by geometric lines, light, colors, and
fabrics. Silk is my favorite fabric, as it shines and lives
at the same time. I was born in Lyon, France—the capital
of silk—and silk inspired me to create* Persiennes.
*(*Persiennes *means Venetian shutters in French.) The
quilt reminds me of the times in my childhood when
I enjoyed the light coming through my room's shutters.*

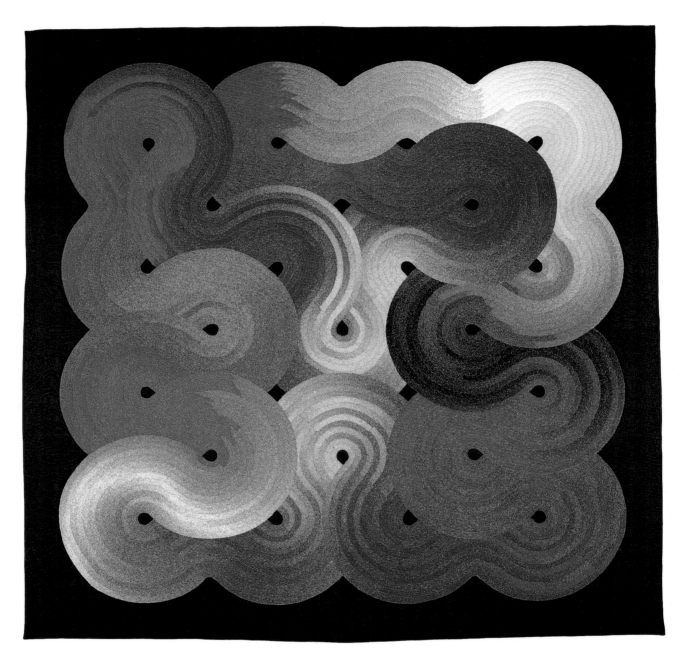

ETSUKO TAKAHASHI

YOKOHAMA, JAPAN

Waves #4

Cotton fabrics; machine pieced,
appliquéd, and quilted; 77 x 77
inches (195.6 x 195.6 cm).

*This work is an outcome of a sudden flash of inspiration which
struck me while trying to find out how these fabrics could be
used to make this design more effective. These waves are like life.
Sometimes it's bright and delightful, sometimes gloomy and difficult.
But hope always shines again; it reflects my life as a quilter.*

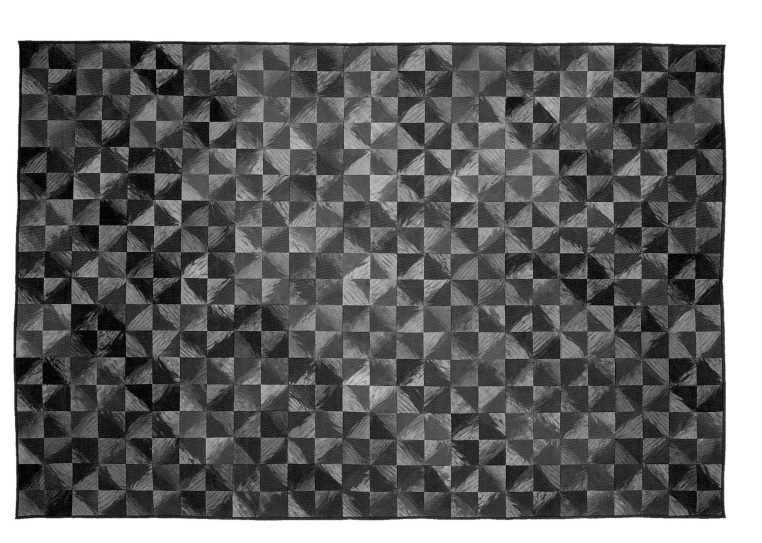

DEBRA LUNN AND MICHAEL MROWKA

LANCASTER, OHIO

Grandmothers' Influence

100 percent cotton fabric shibori dyed in
Procion dyes with multiple immersions;
machine pieced and quilted; 88 x 62
inches (223.5 x 157.5 cm).

*This quilt is in honor of our grandmothers, who, in their respective
ways, taught us the beginnings of our art. Debra's grandmother
taught her to sew four-patch quilts as a child, while Michael's
grandmother taught him jewelry making and gem cutting
at an early age. We thank them both for their vision.*

1999

In the dream, the only way down the stairwell was by a strip ladder. As I nervously edged out onto the slipping, knotted-cloth assemblage, I noticed that the only way to proceed was to grab another strip and tie it on.

TERRIE HANCOCK

CINCINNATI, OHIO

The Struggle

Silk (metallic and other) and cotton fabrics, cotton embroidery thread; left, 42 x 80 inches (106.7 x 203.2 cm); right, 48 x 98 inches (121.9 x 248.9 cm).

1999

TIM HARDING

STILLWATER, MINNESOTA

Swimmers

Silk and cotton duck fabrics;
reverse appliqué, layered,
stitched, cut, restitched, and
cut again; 80 x 60 inches
(203.2 x 152.4 cm).

In an effort to unify form with content, the representation of two underwater swimmers in a pool is partially obscured—but also revealed—by my reverse appliqué method. This accomplishes an abstracted, broken-up image somewhat like the refraction of light that occurs in water. I use an iridescent silk which is reflective, like water. The surface texture is a broken-up wave pattern such as you might see in a pool. A slight use of perspective is accomplished by a subtle foreshortening of the torsos and elongation of the arms. Light/shadow and figure/ground relationships are also used to create the illusion of depth.

RUTH EISSFELDT

ESSEN, GERMANY

Atlantis

Commercial and hand-dyed
cotton fabrics; machine pieced
and machine quilted; 59 x 59
inches (149.9 x 149.9 cm).

*The legend of Atlantis maintains that this fictional island
once existed before sinking into the Atlantic Ocean. We all
dream about someday discovering a beautiful island or a lost
paradise. I, too, am always looking for my private Atlantis,
and it is an ardent desire that will never be fulfilled.*

VIRGINIA A. M. ABRAMS

HOCKESSIN, DELAWARE

Pond Life

Hand-dyed cotton broadcloth;
improvisationally pieced and
machine quilted; 56 x 35 inches
(142.3 x 88.9 cm).

*Color and abstract forms are what drive my work. The inspiration for
this work was a beautiful piece of hand-dyed fabric with areas that
appeared to glow with light. In the background of the piece, I built up
various levels of greens (representing plants) and blues (representing
water currents) to give depth to the work. In the foreground, I added
bright yellow greens and fuchsia to give the feeling of springtime.*

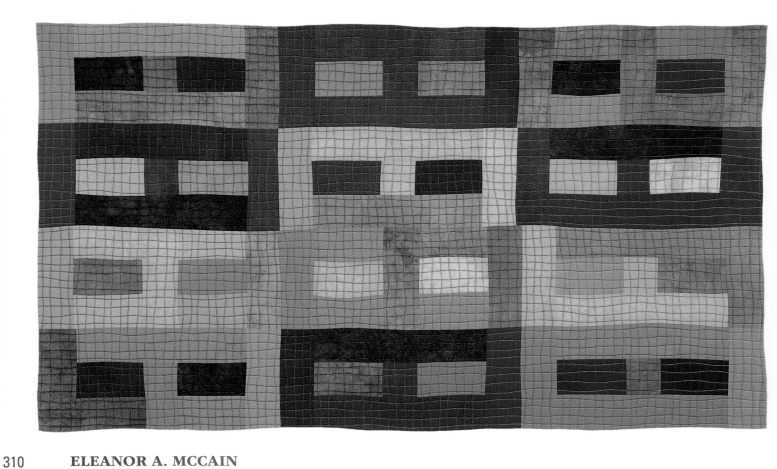

ELEANOR A. MCCAIN

SHALIMAR, FLORIDA

Blue/Green/ Yellow Rectangles

Cotton fabrics, hand dyed by the artist and by others; machine pieced and quilted; 106 x 60 inches (269.2 x 152.4 cm).

I am interested in the interaction of color, shape, and line. This quilt is a three-color study of object/ground relationships. The overlay of the quilt grid and its interplay with color shapes are the focus of this exploration.

ANNE SMITH

WARRINGTON, CHESHIRE, ENGLAND

Via Matt Fields

Hand-painted and hand-dyed cotton fabric; machine pieced and embroidered, hand quilted; 55 x 60 inches (139.7 x 152.4 cm).

Matt Fields is a place to stop and lean your elbows on the gate, to listen and take stock, and perhaps find a different route to the place you think you want to go—before moving on.

NOËL M. RUESSMANN

STROUDSBURG, PENNSYLVANIA

Autumn Leaves Triptych

Silk and linen fabrics; hand quilted and hand embellished with painted cotton and linen leaves; 61 x 76 inches (154.9 x 193 cm).

It is late autumn at dusk. Here and there an individual leaf captures the day's final slanting light and is briefly illuminated. The burnished gold is contrasted by the deep purple of the shadows. The oriental influence in my work is apparent—the three hanging panels are meant to suggest a kimono.

JUTTA FARRINGER

CONSTANTIA, CAPE TOWN, SOUTH AFRICA

Reisefieber
(Anticipating the Journey)

Hand-dyed and commercial cottons;
machine pieced and machine quilted;
44 x 65 inches (111.8 x 165.1 cm).

This quilt is part of a series called Journeys *that is about journeys of exploration. Investigating the motif-driven design in this piece is also a part of this exploration.*

CARYL BRYER FALLERT

OSWEGO, ILLINOIS

Feather Study #14

Hand-dyed and hand-painted
cotton fabrics; machine pieced
and machine quilted; 56 x 56
inches (142.3 x 142.3 cm).

This quilt is one of a series inspired by a close-up of a fantasy feather that evolved from a series of hundreds of drawings on this theme. The illusion of light in this quilt was created by using fabric dyed in gradations of color and value. These gradations intersect in the plumes of the feathers to create areas of emerging and submerging contrast and luminosity.

YASUKO SAITO

TOKYO, JAPAN

Movement #6

Cotton and silk fabrics (some of which have been painted); machine pieced and machine quilted; 75 x 75 inches (190.5 x 190.5 cm).

The petals, opening timidly from the bud, are gradually blossoming into a big flower. Breathing in the fresh air under the brilliant sunlight, the newly born flower is gaining its vivid color and, at last, showing us its energy—its will to live.

My recent work is about the distortion of light. This piece is inspired by the idea of light refracted through a prism that generates alternating colors and patterns. I wanted to create a some- what transparent hanging that could be viewed from both sides to create depth and patterning shifts as the viewer moves. This piece has a transient dynamic similar to the dappled patterns of sunlight penetrating the leafy canopy of a forest.

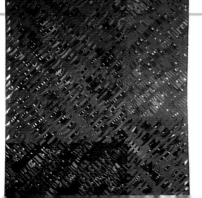

TIM HARDING

STILLWATER, MINNESOTA

Prism Quilt

Manipulated layers of silk with reverse appliqué process cut through quilted layers to reveal others behind the surface (including a sheer silk organza sublayer); front and back hung between spacer bars to allow an open air layer and sheer sublayers to be randomly visible throughout; 60 x 71 inches (152.4 x 180.3 cm).

REVERSE VIEW

2001

ROBBI JOY EKLOW

GRAYSLAKE, ILLINOIS

King of Cups

Hand-dyed cotton and variegated
rayon thread; fused appliqué and
free-motion machine quilting;
57 x 72 inches (144.8 x 182.9 cm).

*This quilt is named after the tarot card called the "king
of cups," and there are 14 vessels or cups in this quilt.
I love ambiguity: Is the central image an orange with
a handle or a teacup with a slice of orange? I hope the
viewer has as much fun looking at it as I did making it.*

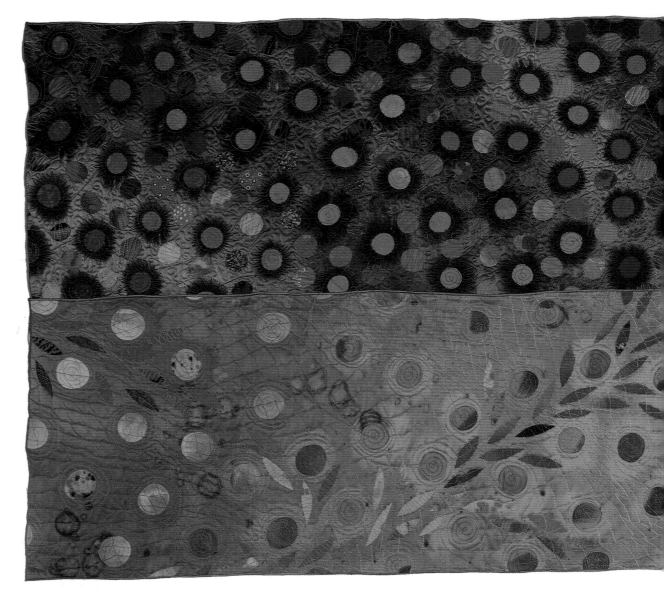

SUE BENNER

DALLAS, TEXAS

Skin Deep II

Commercial and hand-dyed
silk and polyester fabrics; fused
and machine quilted; 83 x 34
inches (210.8 x 86.4 cm).

Skin Deep II *continues my exploration of watery environments with musings about the skins of imagined fish, amphibians, and other mysterious creatures. A quilt can be a covering, and a quilt can have a type of skin.*

ANGELA MOLL

SANTA BARBARA, CALIFORNIA

Calligraphy I

Cotton fabric painted with
fiber-reactive dyes; machine
pieced and quilted; 54 x 32
inches (137.1 x 81.3 cm).

*The force of the calligraphic mark, the trace of the individual gesture
holding the movement, and the energy of the hand fascinate me. In
this piece I have intuitively extended and cropped the gesture, focusing
its energy in a terse statement. This quilt is the first in an ongoing
series centered on the power of calligraphy as a personal mark.*

ALISON MUIR

SYDNEY, AUSTRALIA

Short Poppies
Are Valuable Too

Hand-dyed and commercial silk,
lamé and blended fabrics; direct
appliqué with fusing and stitches,
machine quilted; 39 x 54 inches
(99.1 x 137.2 cm).

*This work was made in response to a movement in Australia
known as "Refabricating the Future." It offers an alternative to the
present in which short and tall poppies work together harmoniously
to produce a nurturing, caring, valued, and productive future for all.*

JUDY HOOWORTH

TERREY HILLS, NEW SOUTH WALES,
AUSTRALIA

Life Force

Torn fabrics, stitched in layers
to canvas; machine stitched
and machine quilted; 57 x 54
inches (144.8 x 137.2 cm).

*The combination of yellows and reds always excites me. They are
the colors of life—energy and passion, fire and blood, cheese and
tomatoes, happiness and sin, buttercups and roses, illumination
and atonement, bananas and apples, sunshine and sunsets....*

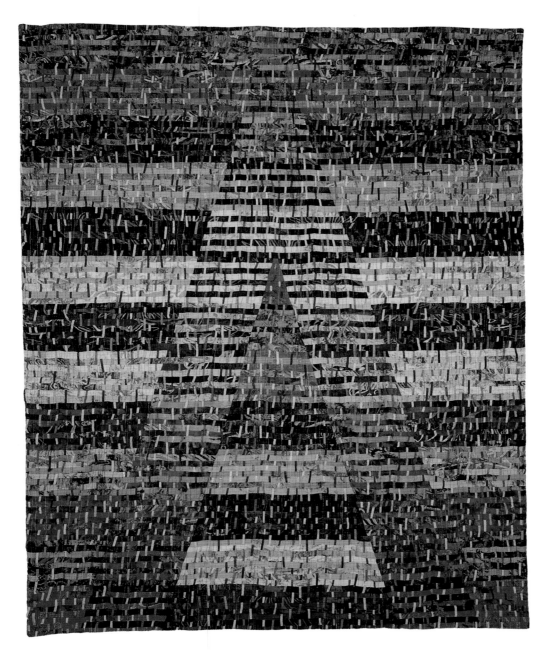

KANTI JOCELYN

KANAGAWA, JAPAN

Celebration

Commercial rayon fabric that has been hand painted, stitched to the foundation, and woven with hand-painted strips of silk ribbon; machine quilted; 41 x 51 inches (104.1 x 129.5 cm).

Prior to creating quilts, I was a weaver. I'm still fascinated by this process and wanted to create the illusion of woven cloth in this quilt. The triangle is a symbol of the atriune nature of existence—a celebration of life.

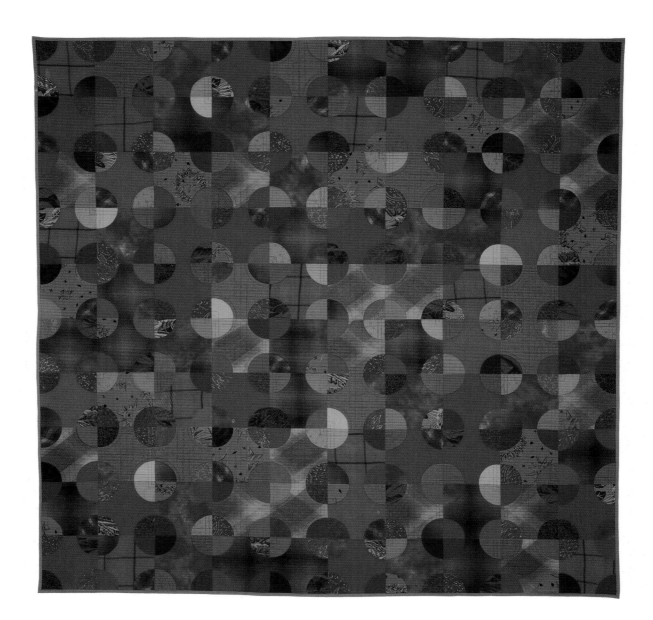

32

REBECCA ROHRKASTE

BERKELEY, CALIFORNIA

Full Circle

Commercial cottons; machine
pieced and machine quilted;
80 x 80 inches (203.2 x 203.2 cm).
Private collection.

I was spurred to undertake an immersion in red through a friend's commission for a quilt. This quilt is about color, repetition, contrast, and playing my intuition against the basic geometric structure of a good old traditional quilt design. Even though it is nonobjective and abstract, it is full of personal history, symbolism, and emotional experience.

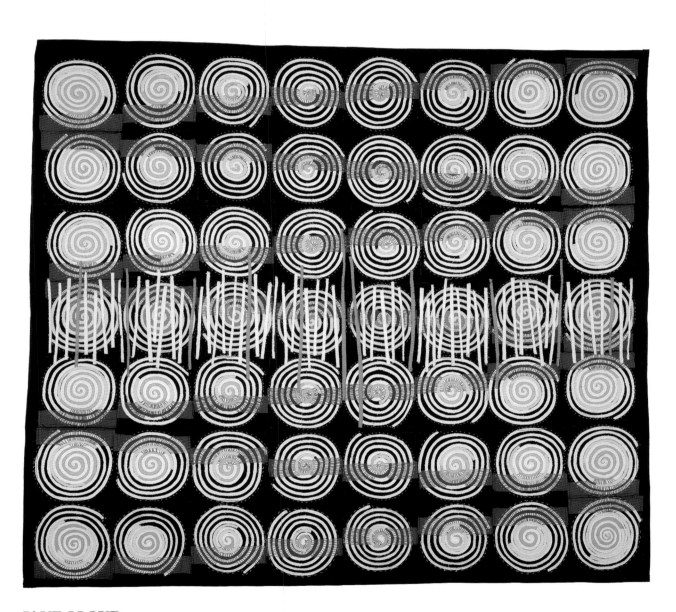

JANE LLOYD

BALLYMENA, COUNTY ANTRIM,
NORTHERN IRELAND

Spiral Shock

Cottons and blends; machine
pieced, hand and machine
embroidered; 37 x 33 inches
(94 x 83.8 cm).

*The spiral is a simple shape that evokes the past and appears on ancient
stones near my home. I am totally absorbed and fascinated by this shape
on the stones. This is one of a series of spiral quilts that I'm making.*

325

ELLEN OPPENHEIMER

OAKLAND, CALIFORNIA

FG Block AB

Hand-printed and dyed fabrics;
machine pieced and quilted;
60 x 75 inches (152.4 x 190.5 cm).

This piece was inspired by the long study of a concrete block. My design process begins with computer drawings that allow me to experiment with many different colors and layering possibilities, but these images are quite different from the results I achieve with silk-screens, fabrics, and inks. FG stands for "flying geese," which refers to the repeated triangles. AB stands for "Ari's bed," because I originally intended this quilt for my son Ari's bed.

SHARON HEIDINGSFELDER

LITTLE ROCK, ARKANSAS

Pennsylvania 6-5000, Please

100 percent cotton fabric; machine pieced and machine quilted; 56 x 63 inches (142.2 x 160 cm).

This piece is the first of a series that involves a block with an unusual shape. The angles were difficult to calculate, and I was pleased when all of the pieces fit together.

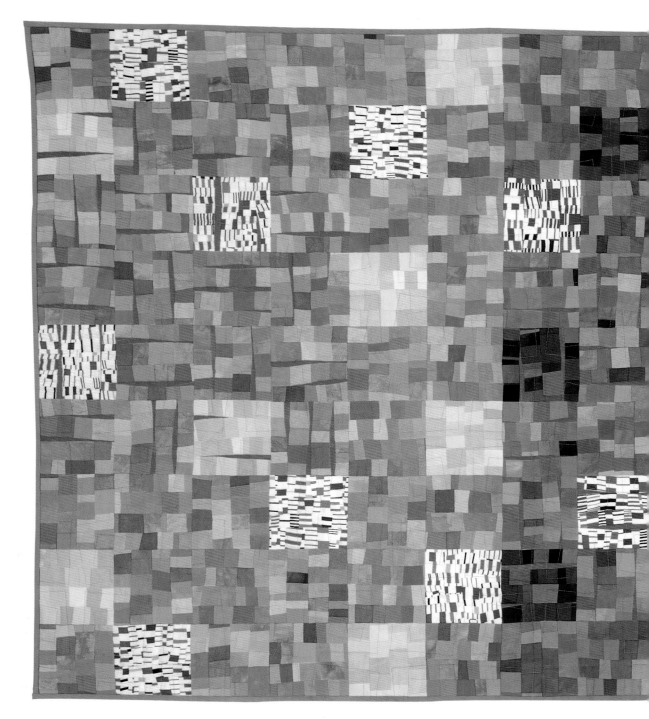

RUTH GARRISON

TEMPE, ARIZONA

Floating I

Cotton fabrics (some hand dyed
and screen-printed); machine
pieced and machine quilted;
83 x 41 inches (210.8 x 104.1 cm).

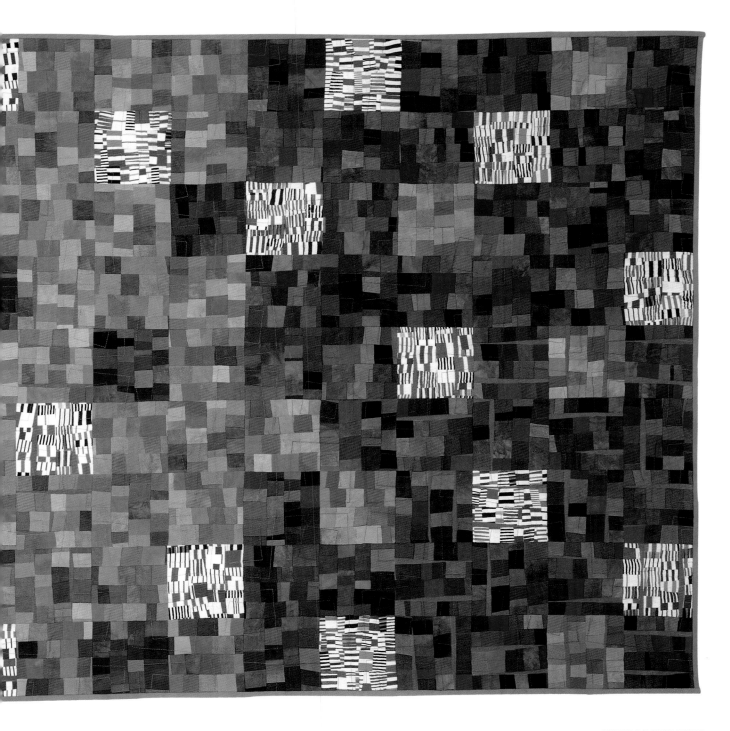

Two sets of strip-pieced fabrics that are different in character
are brought together in this piece. The high contrast allows the
frenzied strips to float above a calm sea of blue-green solids.

COLLEEN WISE

PUYALLUP, WASHINGTON

Solar Energy

Commercial and hand-dyed
cottons; machine pieced, hand
appliquéd and machine quilted;
41 x 41 inches (104.1 x 104.1 cm).

Quilting is essentially a two-dimensional medium. My goal is to add the third dimension. I want the viewer to look into my pieces and feel detached, floating, slightly disoriented, and disconnected from gravity. Solar Energy is one piece in a series involving celestial events. Enjoy your little trip into space!

ANNE MCKENZIE NICKOLSON

INDIANAPOLIS, INDIANA

Falling

Cotton fabrics; hand appliquéd
through all layers; 46 x 68 inches
(116.8 x 172.7 cm).

This piece was inspired by Paul Gauguin's painting titled
The Flageolet Player on the Cliff. *My goal was to abstract
the dynamic lines in the painting, which converge and
then fall. The layering of stripes, the grid structure, and the
color contrasts create a system of tensions that add to the
complexity of the work and the feeling of movement. The
production of this piece was assisted by the Indiana Arts
Commission and the National Endowment for the Arts.*

2001

CAROL TAYLOR

PITTSFORD, NEW YORK

Vibrations

Hand-dyed cotton sateen fabrics by Heide Stoll-Weber, Judy Robertson, Regina Goodman, and the artist; improvisationally cut, machine pieced, and free-motion machine quilted; 56 x 67 inches (142.2 x 170.2 cm).

Vibrations from the striking of a gong move outward in repeating patterns— just as my creative decisions for one quilt affect my future work. In a similar way, the vibrations in this piece emanate from the lightest areas and echo outward with darkening values and diminishing sizes. Each quarter circle motif is an original—individually cut and pieced—with four combined into a fractured gong. A square framework contains each gong; similarly, I contain or limit the challenges I assign myself. Free-motion quilted circles heighten the illusion of resonating tones throughout the quilt.

NELDA WARKENTIN

ANCHORAGE, ALASKA

Tropic of Cancer

Multiple layers of acrylic-painted silk organza on top of a quilted cotton and linen base; machine pieced and quilted; 48 x 60 inches (121.9 x 152.4 cm).

This quilt is the third in a series that emphasizes line and pattern, but also the uniqueness of the quilt medium. The seam lines provide a strong design element, while multiple layers of transparent silk give the work depth and add a painterly quality. Multicolored, free-form quilt stitches add interest and movement.

2001

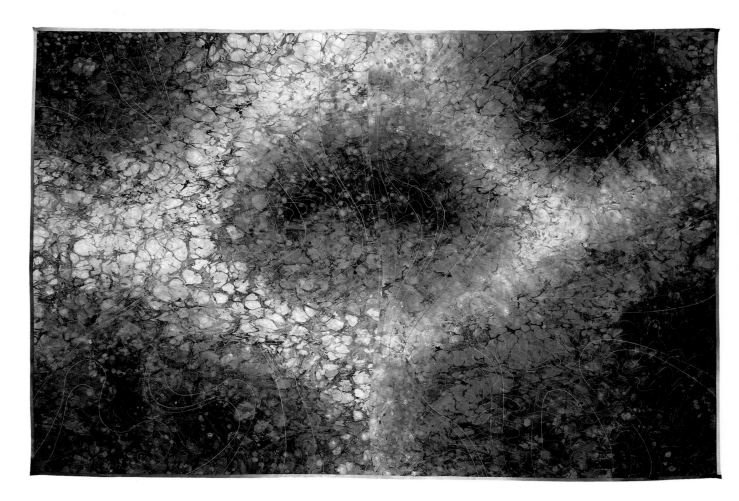

SHARON MEARES COMMINS

LOS ANGELES, CALIFORNIA

Wind and Wave III

Dye-painted cotton sateen which has been discharged, spattered, and monotyped with textile paints; free-motion machine quilting with hand-dyed silk, cotton and rayon threads; 76 x 50 inches (193.1 x 127 cm).

Patterns of light and air flowing across water echo patterns of emotions flowing across life.

EMILY RICHARDSON

33

PHILADELPHIA, PENNSYLVANIA

Cloud Forest

Silk fabric embellished with
acrylic paint and embroidery;
hand appliquéd and hand
stitched; 56 x 42 inches
(142.2 x 106.7 cm).

*When I look at a scene in nature, I watch the changes going on around
me—the visual elements, their movement, the light that defines them,
and the atmosphere that surrounds them. These changes, along with
my own shifting point of view, lead to the components of my work.
In* Cloud Forest, *I used layers of painted sheer fabrics to evoke this
shifting sense of a place where the trees and the sky have an exchange.*

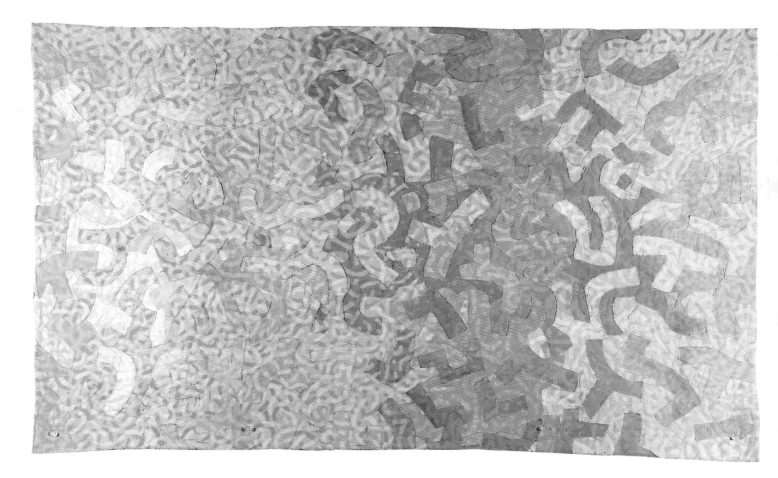

ANN M. ADAMS

SAN ANTONIO, TEXAS

Chroma Zones VII: Kuba Chroma

Silk and linen fabrics that have been hand dyed, silk-screened, and discharged; machine pieced and appliquéd, machine quilted; 53 x 32 inches (134.6 x 80 cm).

My Chroma Zone *quilt series is based on a block that includes 10 geometric shapes that have been modified by substituting curves for right angles. The resulting curved templates are very similar to shapes found in African textiles from the Kuba Kingdom in Zaire. They seem to convey a message and suggest living things. The fabric is mottled with printed calligraphic forms that appear to relate to the figures. Through this series I am experimenting with figure-ground relationships and illusions as well as an expanded palette.*

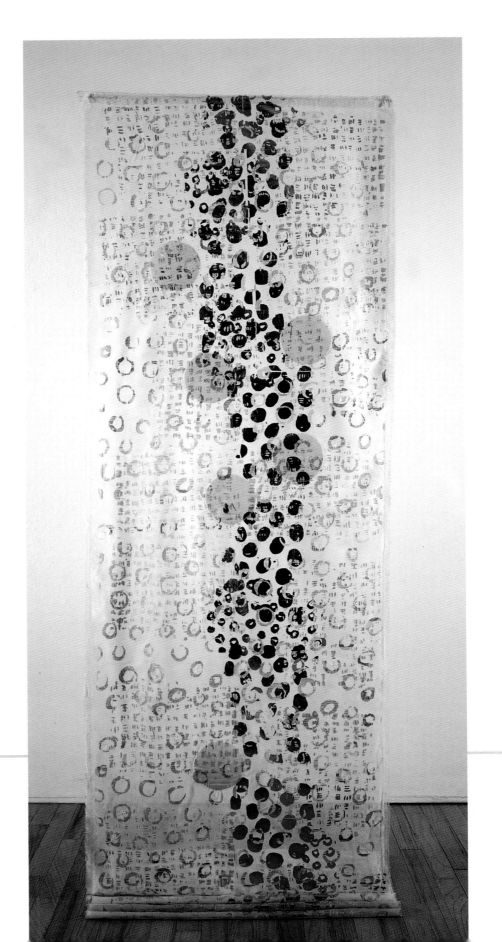

I continue to explore the visual surface as a means of investigating spirituality. This piece alludes to the seven chakras and was inspired by the contemplation of my energetic being—my physical self as it relates to my mental self. When I challenge myself to move beyond what I've already done and know, the physical and the mental combine in exhilarating and surprising ways.

JANE DUNNEWOLD

SAN ANTONIO, TEXAS

Meditation Seven

Cotton batting and sheer polyester fabric that has been patterned with screen printing textile paint as well as laminated newspaper and gold leafing; hand quilted; 28 x 108 inches (71.1 x 274.3 cm) as installed.

CONNIE SCHEELE

HOUSTON, TEXAS

Where the Grass Grows Tall

Hand-dyed cottons; machine pieced and
hand quilted with silk threads; 83 x 37 inches
(210.8 x 94 cm). Private collection.

*The tall grasses in the shallow areas of the northwestern
Wisconsin lakes are so peaceful and beautiful. These areas
continue to inspire my work. To emphasize the height of the
grasses, I made the quilt long horizontally and short vertically.*

JUDITH CONTENT

PALO ALTO, CALIFORNIA

Tempest

100 percent black Thai silk that has been hand patterned with discharged dye and a variety of Japanese arashi shibori techniques; machine pieced and machine quilted; 52 x 87 inches (132.1 x 221 cm).

I think of my work as abstract interpretations of stone, sky, fire, and water. My current work is inspired by the windswept, fog-enveloped Northern California coastal marshes. I am fascinated by the play of light and shadow as the fog descends or dissipates in the sunlight. Tempest was inspired by the winds and waves of storms that sweep in across the Pacific in winter, obscured by fog until they're upon you.

LONNI ROSSI

WYNNEWOOD, PENNSYLVANIA

Too Close to Home

Cotton fabrics hand painted and patterned by the artist through a variety of techniques, including stenciling, typography, and offset typesetting; machine pieced, appliquéd, embroidered, and quilted; 60 x 65 inches (152.4 x 165.1cm).

My work comes from feelings within. Examining them closely, these feelings find form, meaning, and sometimes resolution within the work. A comment, a poem, and a personal relationship were the inspiration/catalyst for this piece.

LAURA CONNERS

CRAWFORDSVILLE, INDIANA

Ground Cloth

Rust print on cotton fabrics
with overprinting, dyeing, and
discharging techniques; machine
pieced and quilted; 72 x 50 inches
(182.9 x 127 cm).

*The surface qualities of aged and weathered materials intrigue me—such
as the rust stain left from a nail in exposed wood, or layers of chipped and
crackled paint on an old chair. In Ground Cloth I have created patterns and
marks by exposing fabric to rusted metal surfaces before using overprinting,
dyeing, and discharging techniques to build up rich surfaces. The imagery
on these fabrics can be unpredictable, and the random nature of this working
style requires an intuitive approach and an innovative response. The work
reflects a kind of spontaneity and freshness that are uniquely my own.*

MARY ANN SCARBOROUGH

HOLLEY, NEW YORK

Visible Solitude

Silk fabric (hand dyed by Renee
B. Gentz), hand appliquéd to
muslin, hand embroidered and
embellished with glass beads;
hand quilted; 65 x 65 inches
(165.1 x 165.1 cm).

I walk along the Erie Canal every morning.
The changing light, reflections, and colors are
a daily lesson in combinations and possibilities.

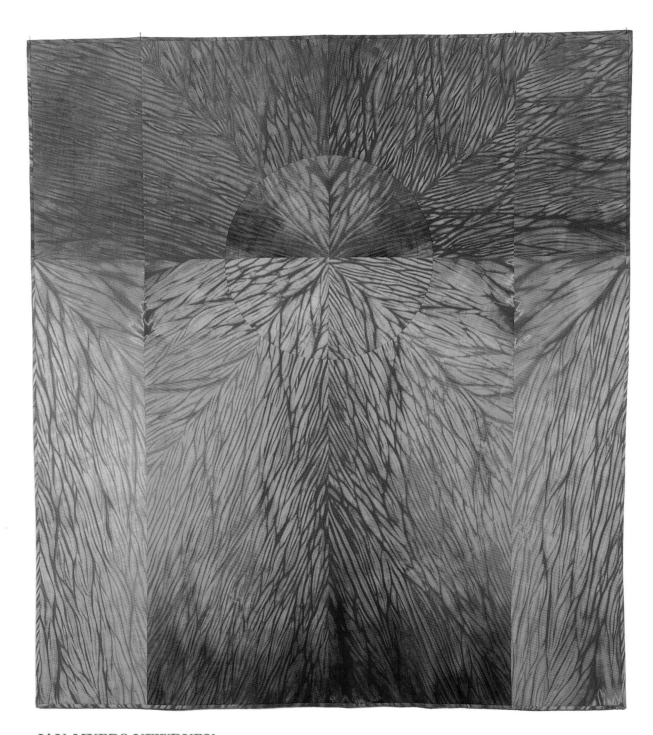

JAN MYERS-NEWBURY

PITTSBURGH, PENNSYLVANIA

Icarus

Cotton muslin fabric hand dyed
using arashi shibori technique;
machine pieced and machine
quilted; 55 x 65 inches (139.7 x
165.1 cm).

*For the past eight years, I have been creating quilts by "forming
relationships" among patterned fabrics. In most cases, these
relationships are the indistinct patterns created by arashi shibori.
Often the piece begins with a fabric that has a particularly demanding
"voice" that I try to add to as I orchestrate the interplay. The story
of Icarus is spiritual and universal—it is about the value of striving
upward, even if it is for the ultimately unattainable.*

BOB ADAMS

LAFAYETTE, INDIANA

Circular Images No. 4

Fabric that has been hand dyed, discharged and dye painted; whole cloth
construction, machine embroidered with
polyneon thread, and machine quilted;
55 x 32 inches (139.7 x 81.3 cm).

*My pieces range from boldly simple to intricate. In this series,
I used thread as a major element in the design of the pieces.
The threads were applied entirely by free-motion machine stitching.*

34

JANET STEADMAN

CLINTON, WASHINGTON

I Love a Mystery

Commercial and hand-dyed
cotton fabrics; machine pieced
and machine quilted; 58 x 50
inches (147.3 x 127 cm).

*Sometimes I escape life's troublesome realities by retreating into my
studio and letting my hands, rather than my conscious mind, create
a quilt. When this quilt was done, I saw images that brought back
memories of an old 1940s radio show called* I Love a Mystery.
*It is easier for me to deal with the cleverness of a whodunit mystery
than the mysterious conundrums of the modern world.*

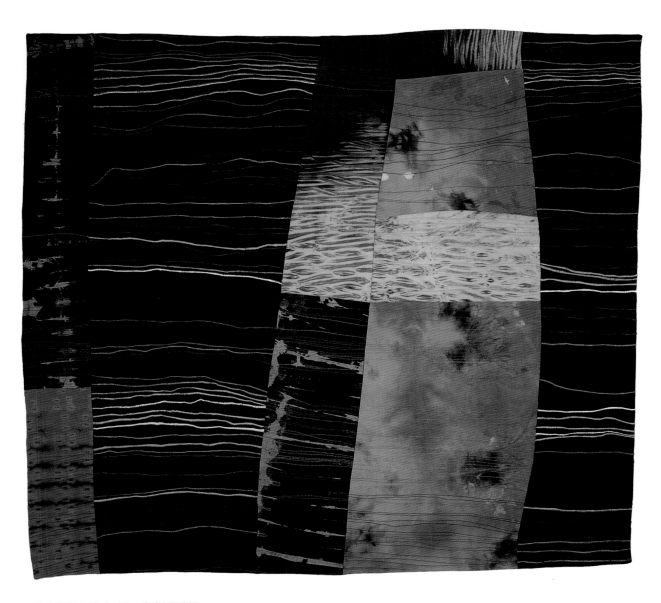

BARBARA D. COHEN

DENVER, COLORADO

Elegant Legacy

Cotton and linen fabrics that have been hand dyed using a discharge process; machine pieced, quilted and embroidered; 44 x 40 inches (118 x 101.6 cm).

Elegant Legacy is the result of an exercise that I undertook to trust my intuitive ability as a visual artist. I had produced an ample supply of discharge-dyed fabrics with the hope of assembling pieces in an artful manner to highlight values and textures. After studying the resulting composition, I feel certain that, through me, my elegant female ancestors are showing their influence.

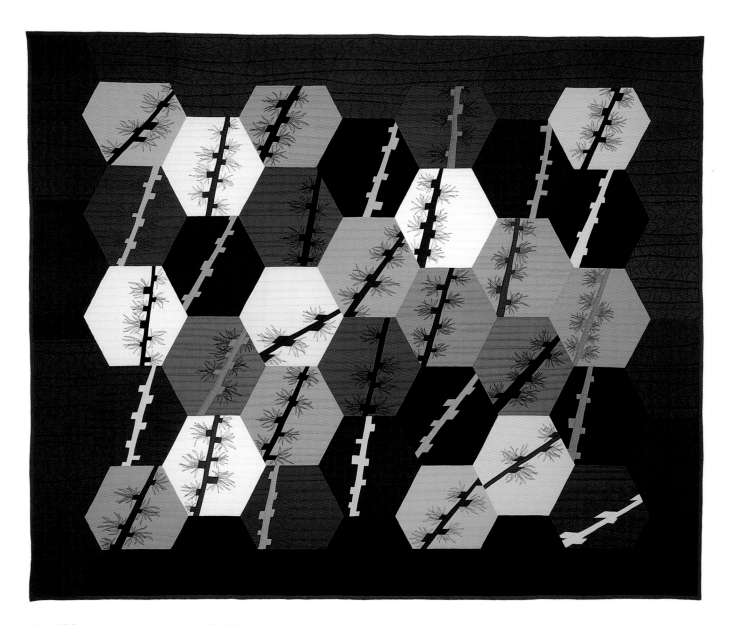

HEATHER WALDRON TEWELL

ANACORTES, WASHINGTON

Larch in Spring

Cotton fabrics, pieced by improvisational and precision methods;
machine quilted; 77 x 66 inches
(195.6 x 167.6 cm).

A larch is a deciduous conifer. In fall, needles drop, leaving an irregular rhythm of nubs on each branch. In spring, needles burst forth in pom-poms, bathing the tree in chartreuse. A friend, recognizing that I am inspired by incidental details from nature, brought me a larch branch from her hike in the woods. Not being able to get the bare branch out of my visual memory, I began to construct a quilt.

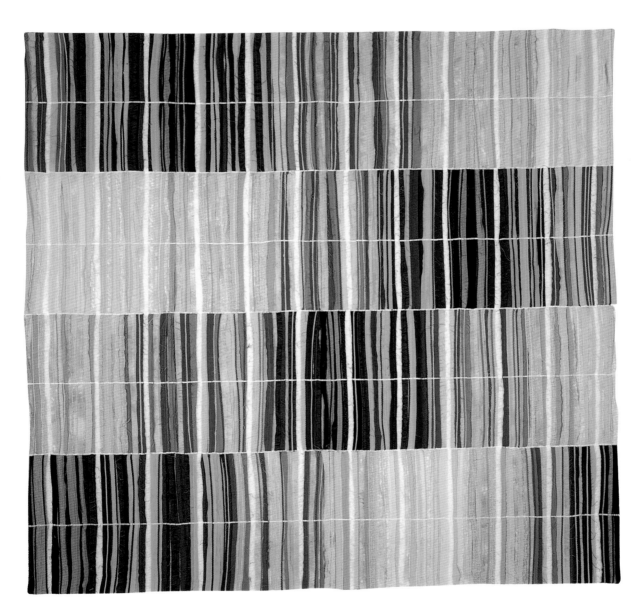

2001

CECILE TRENTINI

ZURICH, SWITZERLAND

Fragile Peace of Mind

Cotton fabrics; machine pieced,
appliquéd and machine quilted;
55 x 56 inches (139.7 x 142.2 cm).

*The calm, ordered white grid contrasts with the vibrating, lively strips
of colored fabric. The grid holds the vivid surface together, but at the same
time, the strips also surround and protect the frail uncovered lines of
cotton batting. These two elements interact and create a fragile balance.
The overall impression may be one of peace, but how long will it last?*

DALE FLEMING

WALNUT CREEK, CALIFORNIA

Corporate Attire

Silk ties and other silk fabrics; machine pieced and machine quilted; 46 x 62 inches (116.8 x 157.5 cm).

The impetus for this quilt was my husband's decision to discard a number of silk ties after he had cleaned out his closet. These ties with their rich colors, wonderful textures, and intricate designs just begged to be used. This quilt flows from a single square into a design-as-you-go quilt that plays with color, texture, value, and shape.

NANCY CROW

BALTIMORE, OHIO

Constructions #33

Hand-dyed cotton fabric; machine
pieced and hand quilted; 65 x 60
inches (165.1 x 152.4 cm).

I have made 40 quilts for a series called Constructions.
*All of them have been influenced by the renovation of a huge
timber-frame barn built in 1884. The proportions of the interior
timbers and boards are so exquisite that I am energized to
work intuitively to capture their dynamic proportions.*

35

2001

LIZ AXFORD

HOUSTON, TEXAS

Within / Without 6

Cotton fabrics treated with shibori and other mechanical resist patterning techniques; machine pieced and machine quilted; 70 x 49 inches (177.8 x 124.5 cm).

In 1993, my husband and I moved to a classic 1950s home with walls of glass on the front that look out to a courtyard enclosed by a curved and perforated block wall. Within/Without 6 depicts the wall at its most dramatic—backlit by the setting sun near the time of the summer solstice.

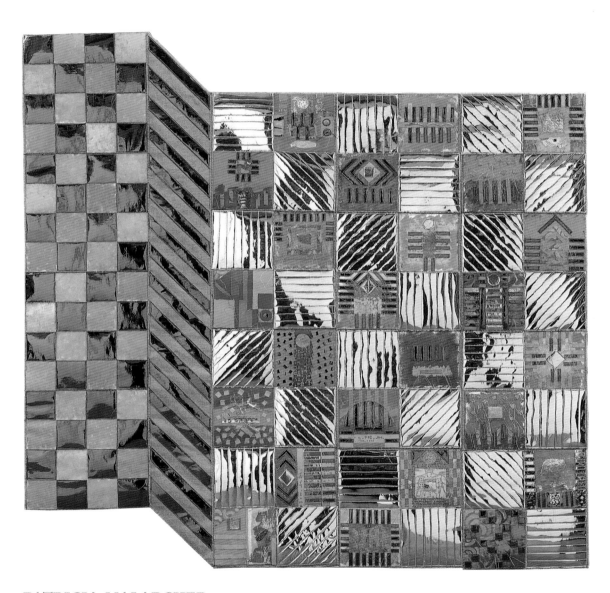

PATRICIA MALARCHER

ENGLEWOOD, NEW JERSEY

Checkpoint

Linen and cotton canvas, mylar, paint, found materials; machine-sewn appliqué collage, screen printing, hand-sewn construction. 54 x 54 inches (137.2 x 137.2 cm).

My work is inspired by textiles that are used in ritual and celebration as architectural embellishment, vesture, or ceremonial accessories. Geometric patterning, pieced construction, collage, and appliquéd Mylar provide an expressive vocabulary as well as a means of solving formal problems. The inclusion of found and ready-made elements, as well as images from popular culture, encodes the work with contemporary references. The use of Mylar, which responds to ambient light, adds to overall complexity of the surface.

353

2001

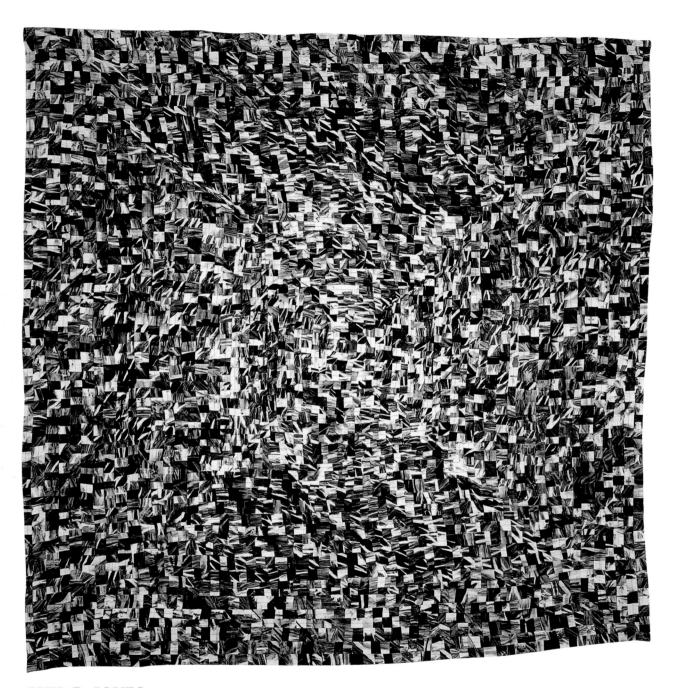

354 **PHIL D. JONES**

TOPEKA, KANSAS

Redeye

Discharged shibori and discharged
overdyed shibori cotton fabrics;
machine pieced and machine quilted; 74 x 76 inches (188 x 193 cm).

*I love transforming raw materials into objects of beauty and contemplation.
I alter cloth through the processes of discharging, dyeing, cutting, pressing, and
stitching. At some point, the materials come together to form something greater
than the sum of the pieces. At that moment, I ask myself: Is this what I imagined?
Does it embody the spirit and energy I envisioned? Did I get out of the way
and allow this work to bloom? This is how the process works for me.*

BEATRIZ GRAYSON

WINCHESTER, MASSACHUSETTS

Fences in the Dunes

Cotton fabrics (some hand printed in the Caribbean Andros Islands); machine pieced, appliquéd, and quilted; 51 x 35 inches (129.5 x 88.9 cm).

All of my quilts reflect my loves and interests from both the past and the present. Sometimes they express my feelings of delight in surroundings, as does this quilt. I love the look of retaining fences along our local beaches that have been bent by ocean winds. I am fascinated by the straight lines of the wooden posts against undulating sand dunes that signal the interaction of man and nature.

ELIZABETH BRIMELOW

MACCLESFIELD, CHESHIRE, ENGLAND

Maravu

Silk fabrics that have been direct and reverse appliquéd; hand and machine stitched, hand tied; 60 x 60 inches (152.4 x 152.4 cm).

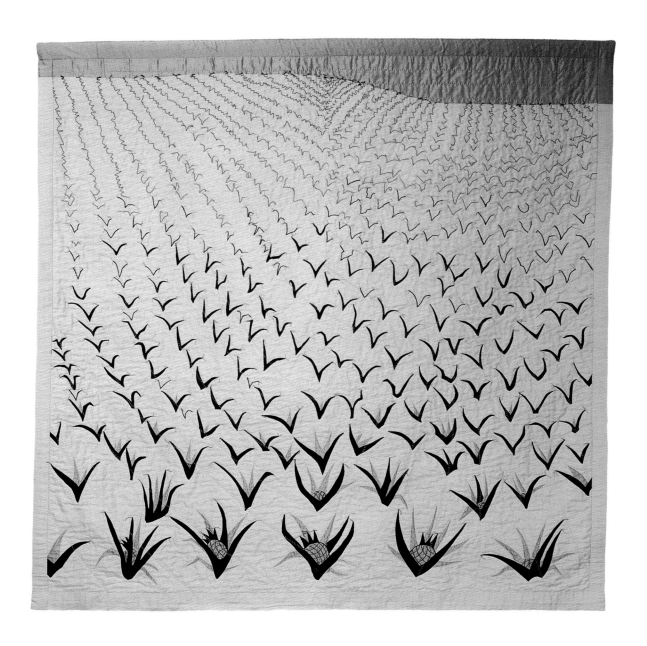

This piece was inspired by the first time I saw pineapples growing in Maravu in Fiji.
My work is influenced by the landscape and man's mark on it. I am interested in the
marks that are made in the process of plowing, planting, and harvesting as well as
the history that has shaped fields, woods, paths, and open spaces. Through my hands,
I have a story to tell, and this connects me to other times, places, and cultures.

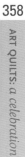

ERIKA CARTER

BELLEVUE, WASHINGTON

Perspective

Hand-painted cotton and silk organza; machine pieced, hand appliquéd, machine and hand quilted; 38 x 59 inches (96.5 x 149.9 cm).

My return to recognizable tree imagery reflects my interest in both the inner and outer selves and the ensuing dialogue between the two. Perspective *symbolizes how differently two people can view the same subject with similarities and differences in perspective.*

HUI-LING YU

SAN DIEGO, CALIFORNIA

Floating 1

Rayon and cotton fabrics patterned
with fiber-reactive dyes and block
prints; whole cloth construction,
hand quilted; 56 x 44 inches
(142.2 x 111.8 cm).

My work conveys the primitive feelings evoked by my inner world.
These feelings then transform into inspiration for the structures in
my work. These include leaves, cocoons, and seed pods. My imagery
evolves primarily from nature. Personal emotion is combined with
a study of the relationships among colors and shapes.

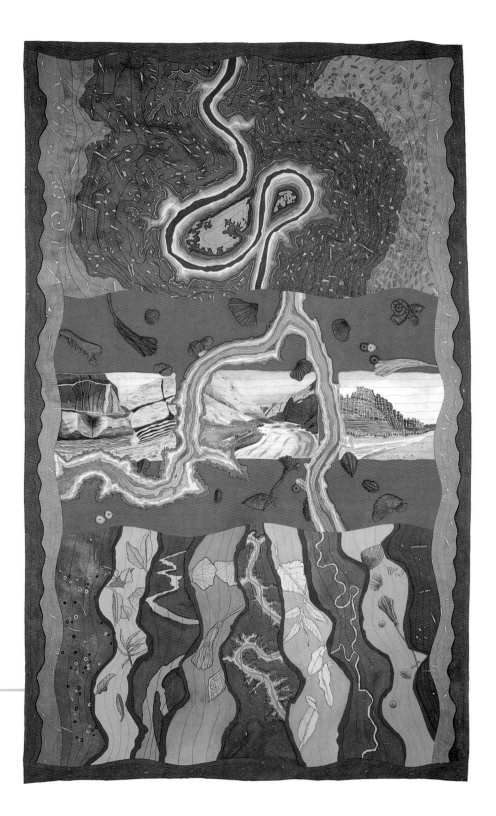

This quilt was inspired by a rafting trip on the Colorado River through Canyonlands National Park in Utah and a hiking trip in the Grand Canyon. Another source of inspiration was a gift from a friend—a piece of rock from Utah containing bright orange fossilized shells. The quilt reflects my interest in landscape, nature, geology, maps, patterning, a sense of place and searching, and the restorative powers of nature and art.

DONNA JUNE KATZ

CHICAGO, ILLINOIS

Current

Hand-painted fabric; machine pieced and machine quilted; 29 x 50 inches (73.7 x 127 cm).

LIBBY LEHMAN

HOUSTON, TEXAS

Windfall

Various fabrics, including hand-dyed and commercial cottons, organza, rayon, and metallic decorative threads; "potluck" appliqué, direct appliqué, bobbin drawing, machine embroidery, and machine quilting; 87 x 87 inches (221 x 221 cm).

Can anything be more beautiful than nature's designs? I have been fascinated lately with the shape of leaves—the flow of the curves, the endless color variations, and the unique individual shapes that imprint themselves on this quilt. Windfall *is a tribute to Mother Nature in all her glory.*

VELDA E. NEWMAN

NEVADA CITY, CALIFORNIA

BASS: In Your Dreams!

Hand-dyed and hand-painted cotton fabrics embellished with metallic fabric and threads as well as paint, foil, and ink; hand and machine pieced, hand appliquéd, and hand quilted; 86 x 79 inches (218.4 x 200.7 cm).

Nature's colors and patterns are the essence of my designs. My approach to quilt design is similar to a painter's—I use color, composition, and scale to capture the spirit of nature through the medium of textiles. Many classic works of art depict nature on a scale smaller than life, but I take life and amplify it. I believe that the greatest emotional and aesthetic impact of my works come from their larger-than-life scale.

ROSEMARY HOFFENBERG

WRENTHAM, MASSACHUSETTS

Broad Strokes

Cotton fabrics that have been hand dyed, painted, and printed with blocks and screens; machine pieced and machine quilted; 62 x 65 inches (157.5 x 165.1 cm).

Circular forms are fundamental to our universe—atoms and plants, cells and bubbles, eyes and wheels. Circles often appear to be perfect, such as the earth or the moon. Broad Strokes is my metaphor for this simple but meaningful and complex shape.

2001

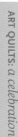

BARBARA J. SCHNEIDER

MCHENRY, ILLINOIS

Reflections, Burano, Italy, Variation 1

Hand-dyed and commercial cotton fabrics; fused and appliquéd, machine stitched; 32 x 47 inches (81.3 x 119.4 cm).

Over the years, I've taken a lot of photos in Italy, trying to capture the particular beauty of the light, color, and patterns that make it a special place for me. This quilt is one of a series of photos that I've tranformed into a tactile medium. I like the abstract nature of this photo quilt because you see the patterns created by the reflections first, and then you realize what the image is.

MARILYN HENRION

NEW YORK, NEW YORK

Byzantium X
(Strange Attractors)

Cotton fabrics; hand pieced and
hand quilted; 56 x 42 inches
(142.2 x 106.7 cm).

In this work and the others in my Byzantium Series, *I explore the arch—an
intriguing architectural form that appears to flirt with the ambiguities of two-
and three-dimensional space. Inspired by Byzantine architecture, the arch is
also symbolic of the passageway created as we exit one millennium and enter
another. The following passage from Alfred Lord Tennyson's poem* Ulysses
provides the viewer with a clue to my inspiration and intent in this series:

I am part of all that I have met,
Yet all experience is an arch
Wherethrough gleams that untravelled world.

DENISE LINET

CENTER HARBOR, NEW HAMPSHIRE

Untold Stories

Hand-dyed cotton fabrics
(some with photo transfers);
machine pieced, hand and
machine quilted; 40 x 40
inches (101.6 x 101.6 cm).

*Daily, I see around me, a myriad of
untold stories waiting to be heard—
Old stone walls, broken fences, and
abandoned barns.
They are the silent reminders of the
fragile and complex relationship
between man and nature.
Man struggles to tame and control.*

*Nature is patient and, in time—
Walls, fallen, are covered with ivy,
Fence posts lean, with rusted wire askew,
Birds fly in and out of the gaping eyes
of an abandoned building.
Fingers of barbed wire wind gently
around a young sapling as time
tightens its grip.*

LINDA LEVIN

WAYLAND, MASSACHUSETTS

Walking the Dogs/Summer

Cotton fabrics treated with dyes, oil pastels,
and colored pencils; machine pieced, direct and
reverse appliquéd, machine embroidered, and
machine quilted; 64 x 49 inches (162.6 x 124.5 cm).
Private collection.

*This piece is one of a series seeking to evoke
the excitement of the changing seasons and
the very changeable New England weather.*

MAYA SCHÖNENBERGER

MIAMI, FLORIDA

Urban Sprawl II
(In Memory of Sidney)

Cottons and blends (some of which
have been hand painted and embellished
with various yarns, threads, and found
objects); machine pieced, machine
and hand appliquéd, machine quilted;
68 x 55 inches (172.7 x 139.7 cm).

*This piece is the second of a series of work in which
I explore our relationship with nature. In South Florida,
urban sprawl grows like an uncontrolled brush fire,
leaving behind large concrete and asphalt-covered areas.*

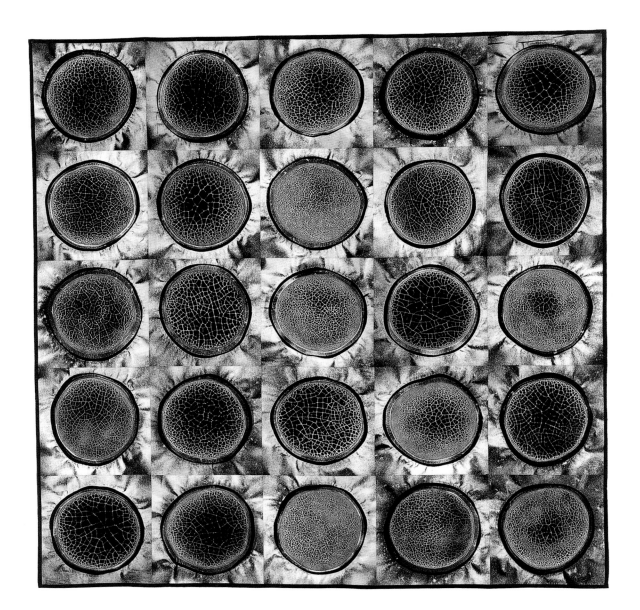

DEBRA LUNN AND MICHAEL MROWKA

LANCASTER, OHIO

Illumination

100 percent cotton fabric patterned with bleach and potato dextrin starch resist; machine pieced and machine quilted; 62 x 62 inches (157.5 x 157.5 cm).

Our goal is for our works to have their own energy and presence. We achieve this by allowing the "sweet spot" (the perfect combination of process, fabric, and technique) to have its own voice. We are fascinated by the fractal marks created by our process and their dimensional quality, which imitates both the micro- and macrocosmic aspects of nature. The machine quilting is done to enhance the dimensional feeling of the image and to suggest living force fields.

LAUREN ROSENBLUM

FOREST HILLS, NEW YORK

Journey

Cotton fabric that has been patterned with fiber-reactive dyes, discharge paste, silk-screens, and paint; machine pieced and hand quilted; 32 x 41 inches (81.3 x 104.1 cm).

We each have our own unique journey in life. We react to experiences and challenges in order to sculpt our characters and establish our values. Some journeys are treacherous, others are subtle. Our interpretation and reaction take us another step on our journey. Some welcome their lessons, others repel or avoid them due to fear or complacency. Regardless of the attempt at avoidance, the lessons will resurface and manifest themselves repeatedly, persisting and frustrating us.

ANN REED

WITHAMSVILLE, OHIO

Lost Mariner

100 percent cotton fabrics and cotton batting; machine pieced, paper pieced, hand appliquéd, machine quilted and hand beaded; 35 x 35 inches (88.9 x 88.9 cm).

This piece was the result of a challenge to use a certain fabric. I didn't care for the fabric, so it became a challenge to make something that I liked from it. I feel confined with preplanning a piece, so I planned only the mariner's compasses. The rest of the design was a result of what the piece called for. I ended up using the "challenge fabric" to frame the piece.

ANNE WORINGER

PARIS, FRANCE

Les Mains Négatives

Linen from the 19th century that has
been hand dyed and fused; machine
appliquéd and machine quilted; 56 x
50 inches (142.2 x 127 cm).

The title of this work comes from a poem entitled
Negative Hands *by Marguerite Duras, a French
novelist and film producer. In the poem, Duras
refers to the open-hand prints made by primitive
people on the walls of archaeological sites.*

My work focuses on landscape art and textile techniques found in Eastern and Western traditions. American quilting and Japanese shibori techniques are joined to create the quiet stream surrounded by New England pussy willows and Asian plum blossoms.

CAROL ANNE GROTRIAN

CAMBRIDGE, MASSACHUSETTS

Harbingers of Spring

Cotton fabrics that have been hand dyed with indigo through shibori techniques of pole wrapping, stitching, and pleating; hand and machine pieced, hand appliquéd, hand quilted; 23 x 51 inches (58.4 x 129.5 cm).

PAT KROTH

VERONA, WISCONSIN

Revisiting Jackson

Hand-dyed and commercial fabrics
embellished with a variety of materials,
including buttons, cording, rickrack,
lace, coins, stamps, paper clips, safety
pins, candy wrappers, toys, and other
found objects; fused and machine
appliquéd, stapled and machine quilted; 104 x 65 inches (264.2 x 165.1 cm).

*I have created a series of fiber-fragment quilts by working in a
fairly random and spontaneous manner. I'm constantly reminded
of the simple beauty of found objects, recycled materials, and
castoffs. From my background in abstract painting, I recently
remembered how much I enjoy Jackson Pollock's work. Now
I feel as though I'm truly painting with fabric and thread.*

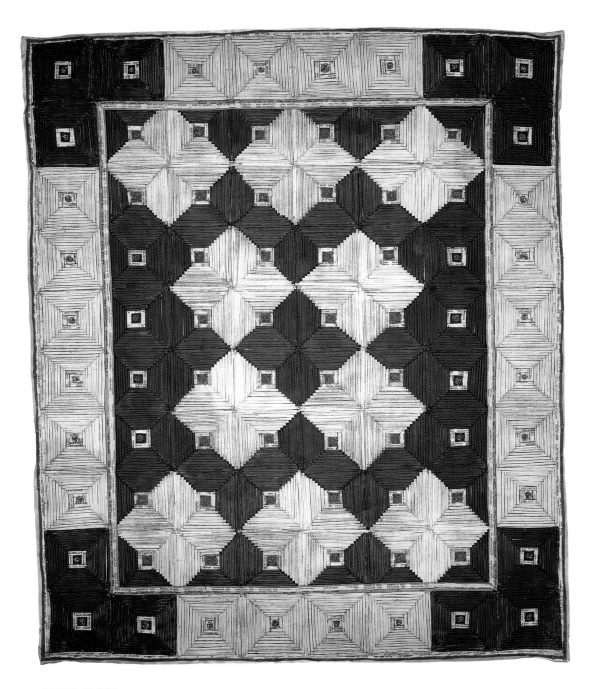

AMY ORR

PHILADELPHIA, PENNSYLVANIA

Twist Tied Log Cabin

3,500+ twist ties hand colored on each edge; cross-stitched into 80 log cabin squares, beaded in center, and assembled for the face layer; 34 x 41 inches (86.4 x 104.1 cm).

I spend hours making order from scraps and disposable artifacts. This work process is a ritual folly that distances the pace and transforms the waste of modern life. This piece pays homage to the traditional domestic arts, and it, as well as life, should be viewed with humor.

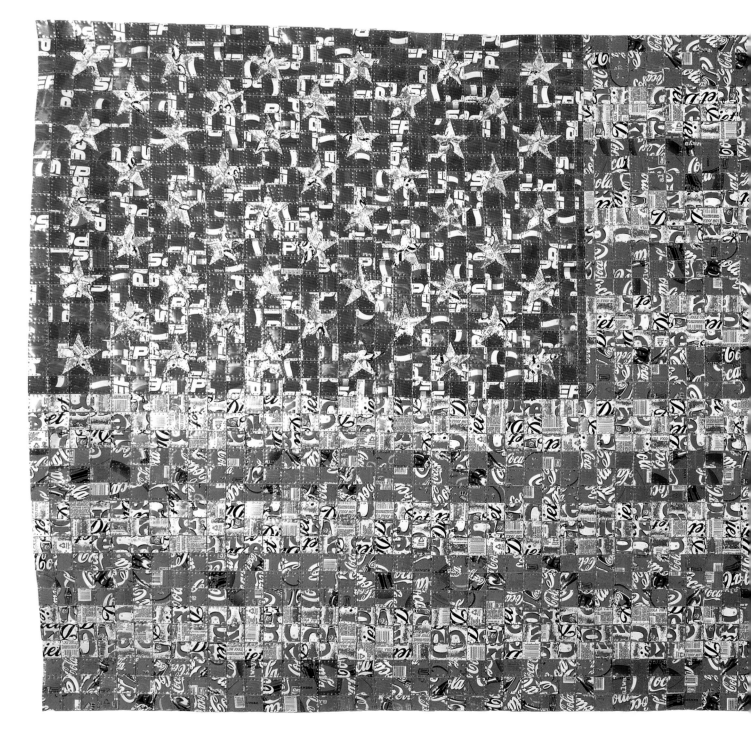

JANIE MATTHEWS

DARLINGTON, AUSTRALIA

American Icon

Cotton fabric with recycled aluminum
soda cans; hand appliquéd and hand
quilted; 86 x 45 inches (218.4 x 114.3 cm).

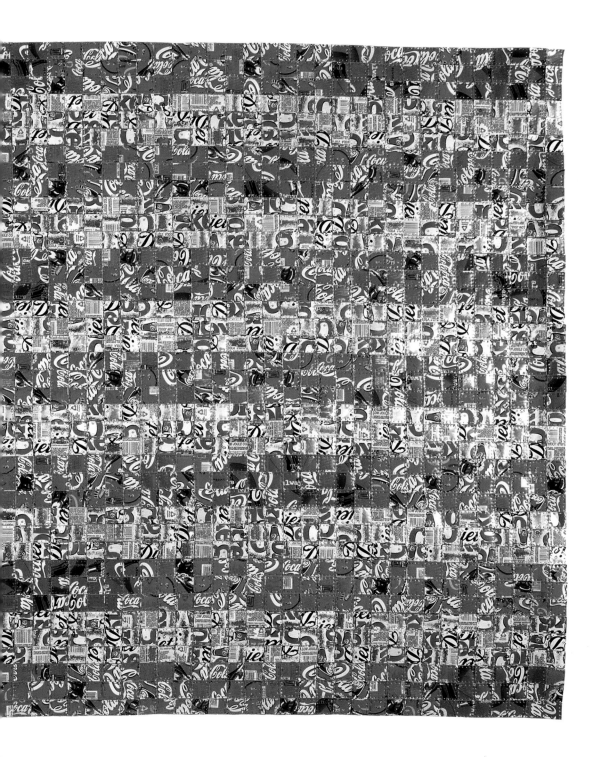

We live in a time of global influences, where huge corporations have worldwide profiles. We are seeing an Americanization of other cultures through the products these corporations produce. By recycling product packaging in a traditional quilt format, I have aimed to create work which has some evidence of the time, effort, and value of something made by hand in the face of runaway consumerism.

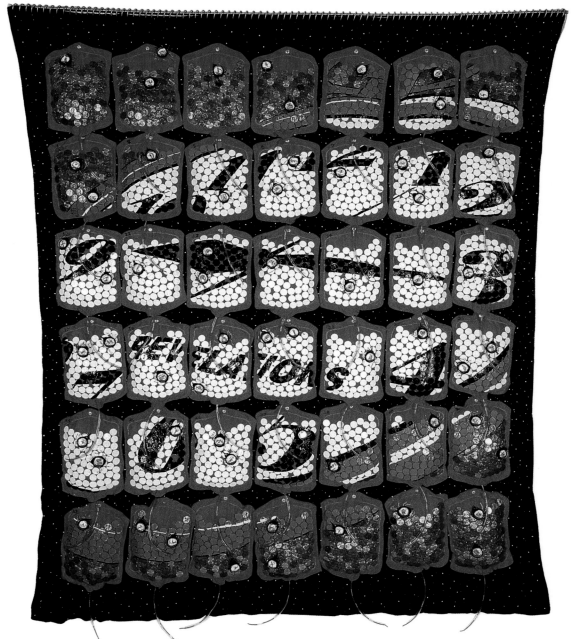

JOHN W. LEFELHOCZ

ATHENS, OHIO

Pennies from Heaven/
Make Your Ticks Count

Various fabrics and found objects, including
pennies, velvet, satin, mesh, glass beads,
clear plastic tubing, toy watches, copper
wire; hand and machine stitched, hand
painted; 58 x 69 inches (147.3 x 175.3 cm).

*"Time is the coin of your life. It is the only coin you have,
and only you can determine how it will be spent.
Be careful lest you let other people spend it for you."*

—*Carl Sandburg*

Is it time for a change? —*J.w.L.*

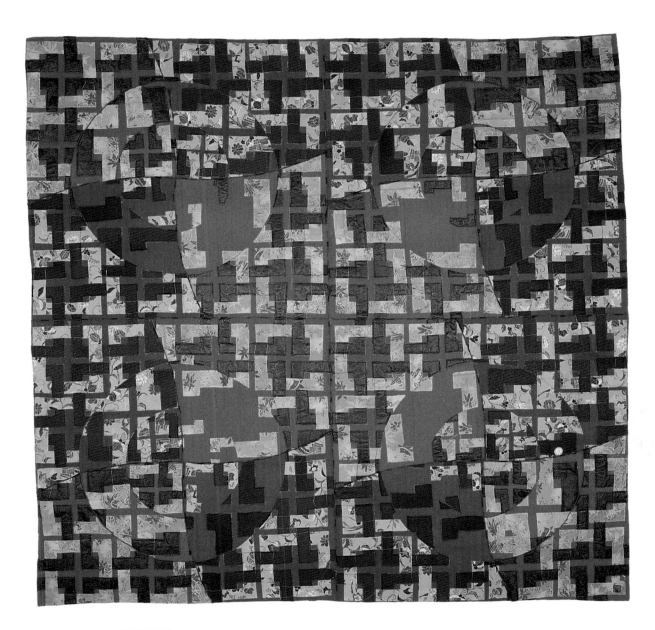

HARUE KONISHI

TOKYO, JAPAN

Syo #2

Antique silk fabric; machine
pieced and machine appliquéd;
63 x 63 inches (106 x 106 cm).

*This work was inspired by a particular piece of antique silk
fabric. After I decided on the design that I wanted to use, I
began the pleasant process of arranging the pieces. In the future,
I would like to continue making quilts by refining the simplest
patterns to create visually appealing works for my audience.*

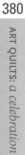

TAFI BROWN

ALSTEAD, NEW HAMPSHIRE

Sengakuji Temple Gables

Hand-dyed and cyanotype-printed cottons;
machine pieced and quilted; 44 x 44 inches
(118 x 118 cm).

*This piece was inspired by a couple of early morning walks around
the Sengakuji Temple in Tokyo during the time I spent there in 1998
as a Fulbright memorial scholar. The strong color and design express
my responses to the intensity of the light, time, and season there.*

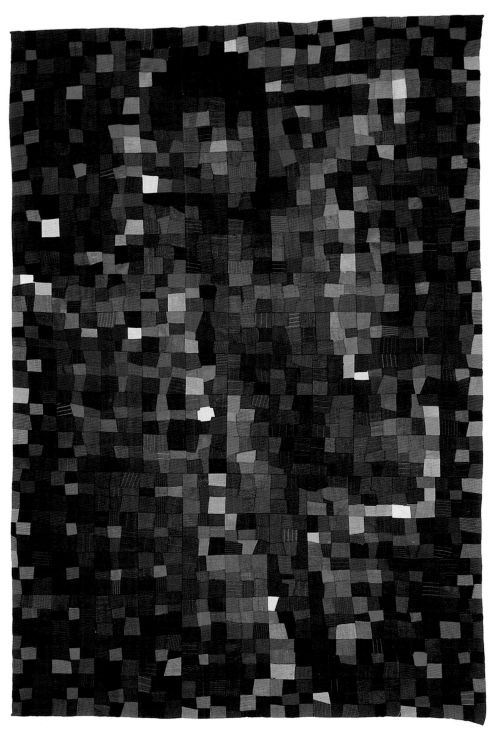

SCOTT ALLEN ELLEGOOD

SAN FRANCISCO, CALIFORNIA

Workman's Quilt

Overdyed men's suiting material; machine pieced and appliquéd, hand tied; 52 x 82 inches (132.1 x 208.3 cm).

Because my work is about memory and loss, I like to impose a sense of a real history, use, and wear on my materials. Up close, this image loses its clarity, and one sees that the "distant perfection" is actually flawed. As memories fade, the "repairs" serve to capture a moment and preserve it. The roughness of the holes and repaired frayed edges are intended as a visual marker for the essence of time. They are an attempt to retain an emotion associated with the past.

2001

KATHERINE K. ALLEN

FT. LAUDERDALE, FLORIDA

Figures 8

Commercial cottons and painted cotton, silk and raw canvas; machine appliquéd, embroidered, and quilted; 60 x 38 inches (152.4 x 96.5 cm).

The figures in this piece are pictograms—symbols that suggest ideas, sensations, or states of being—created as similar, interchangeable units to suggest the mobility of memories. As each of us assembles and edits life's narrative, we create a subjective emotional cinema through which we continually reinterpret and redefine ourselves. Figures 8 portrays a visual slice of this process of translating being into recollecting and experiencing into knowing.

MR. AND MRS. SAMUEL LYONS MOSS (Isabelle Harris) WITH THEIR CHILDREN,
ERNEST GOODMAN AND ELLA AMELIA, AND SLAVE BOY
By Augustin Edouart
Courtesy of the American Jewish Historical Society

LOUISE SILK AND LESLIE A. GOLOMB

PITTSBURGH, PENNSYLVANIA

Middle Matzah

Silk-screened and embroidered
commercial cotton; whole cloth
construction, hand quilted;
40 x 35 inches (101.6 x 88.9 cm).

Each spring, Jews celebrate the holiday of Passover with a traditional seder meal. At the seder we remember the time that Jews were enslaved in Egypt. During the seder and the eight days of Passover, we eat matzah, a traditional flat bread. The matzah reminds us that the Jews left Egypt so quickly that their bread didn't have enough time to rise. This quilt, printed on matzah-like fabric, confronts the question asked by the youngest person at the seder table: "Why is this night different from all other nights?" The answer is our quest to understand the issues of race and bondage.

LORI LUPE PELISH

NISKAYUNA, NEW YORK

A Break from the Storm

Commercial cottons; machine appliquéd,
embroidered, and quilted; 70 x 41 inches
(177.8 x 104.1 cm).

*I have been working on a series of images that deal with emotions within the
family. The challenges and difficulties that can surround even a young child's
life can be overwhelming. This theme is explored in this piece. The mother
and son are caught in a moment of time. They have turned their backs on
the storm, while ignoring the debris, to experience a moment of pure joy.*

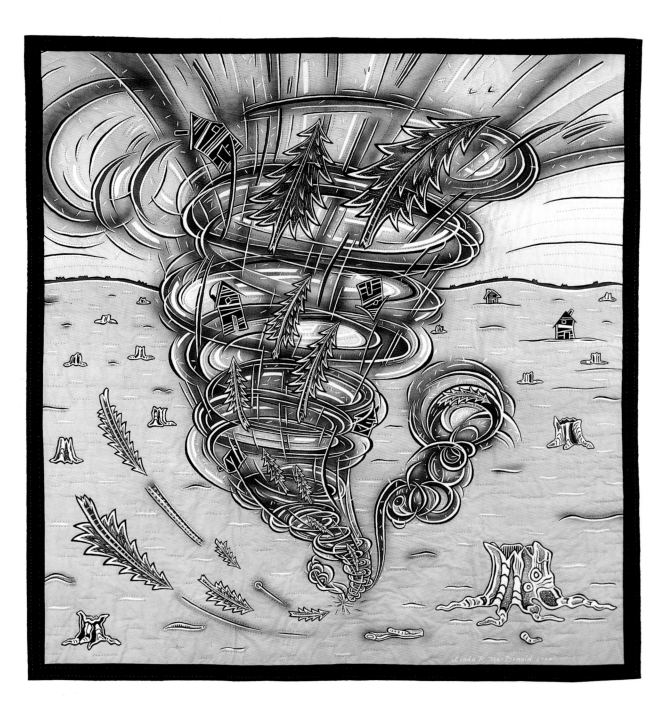

LINDA MACDONALD

WILLITS, CALIFORNIA

Into the Tornado

Cotton broadcloth that has been
dyed, airbrushed, and brush painted
with fiber-reactive dyes; whole cloth
construction, hand quilted; 44 x 48
inches (111.8 x 121.9 cm).

*I'm working on a series of quilts and drawings concerning
what happens to trees—in northern California, it is quite an
issue because they are disappearing. Do they dance away, fly,
burn up, travel to Europe, or what? These trees have gone
up through the funnel in a rare California tornado.*

INGE MARDAL AND STEEN HOUGS

CHANTILLY, FRANCE

Contour Highway

Cotton and rayon; machine quilted;
56 x 41 inches (142.2 x 104.1 cm).

This composition of images was created in the state between sleep and awareness. The subdued appearance of the work symbolizes the materials of which dreams are made, whereas the busy and strangely populated motif reflects the day that lies ahead.

GERRY CHASE

SEATTLE, WASHINGTON

Time Piece: Millennium

Commercial and hand-dyed cotton patterned
with ink, computer-generated images, paint,
and found objects; pieced and appliquéd with
hand and machine stitches, machine quilted;
33 x 38 inches (83.8 x 96.5 cm).

This piece is a part of a series of five time-related works:
Nonce, Dusk, Monday, Summer, *and finally, this grand
measure of time,* Millennium—*the stroke of midnight
when the old milliennium changes to the new.*

ROBIN SCHWALB

BROOKLYN, NEW YORK

Heroic Optimism

Photo silk-screened, stenciled, overdyed, and commercially available cotton fabrics; painted polyester, machine pieced; hand appliquéd and reverse appliquéd, hand quilted; 60 x 82 inches (152.4 x 208.3 cm).

This is the third in a series of quilts inspired by a 1996 trip to Russia. Much residue, both physical and figurative, remains after the fall of communism. A quote from David K. Shipler's book Russia: Broken Idols, Solemn Dreams *plays out across ripped wall posters on the crumbling facades, contrasting the party line of a social realist cityscape with the rich interior lives of its inhabitants.*

MARCIA STEIN

SAN FRANCISCO, CALIFORNIA

All Dressed Up
with No Place to Go

Commercial cottons, tulle; machine
pieced, appliquéd, embroidered and
quilted; 67 x 47 inches (170.2 x 119.4 cm).

*This piece is part of a series of work based on photographs
that I took in Santa Fe, New Mexico, and the south of
France. These two lovely Provençal ladies would no doubt
prefer a night on the town to being cooped up in a shop
window—but such is the life of a French mannequin.*

MIRIAM NATHAN-ROBERTS

BERKELEY, CALIFORNIA

Wine with Lichtenstein

Commercial and hand-dyed cottons (some of which have been painted, air-brushed and discharged with potato dextrin resist); machine pieced, appliquéd, embroidered and quilted; 42 x 62 inches (106.7 x 157.5 cm).

This piece could be subtitled "a toast to the new millennium." Since all human endeavors build on what has gone before, this quilt references the history of Western art: the Greek column; still life; cubism and Picasso; Roy Lichtenstein and the Pop Art Movement. It was made in honor of the quilt artists of the new millenium—something on which to build.

B. J. ADAMS
WASHINGTON, D.C.

A Seasonal Spectrum

Painted canvas and dupioni silk; machine pieced, appliquéd, and embroidered; 56 x 21 inches (142.3 x 53.4 cm).

393

Nature's color studio works overtime, reflecting the seasons. Work done in my studio tends to duplicate this bounty of colors. The trees in this piece are created with freehand machine embroidery on a dissolvable stabilizer. All other images are first drawn in colored pencil on paper before being reproduced in thread on a dissolvable stabilizer.

2001

394

DENISE BURGE

CINCINNATI, OHIO

The Sower

Commercial fabrics, yarn, and beads; hand and machine pieced, direct and reverse appliquéd, fused, hand embroidered, hand and machine quilted; 62 x 83 inches (157.5 x 210.8 cm).

This piece is part of a series about the women in my family. The images are derived from a combination of history/myth and personal memory. Sometimes the woman in this series appears as storyteller, at other times she presents herself through the metaphor of a tree or mountain. In The Sower, *my grandmother appears as a blue jay wearing pink panties—a fierce bird with a strident, passionate call. She was a woman who half-resided in her garden, wresting vegetation from the sun-dried red clay of North Carolina.*

SUSAN SHIE AND JAMES ACORD

WOOSTER, OHIO

The Cookbook/Hierophant: Card #5 in the Kitchen Tarot

Cotton duck canvas and other cotton fabrics embellished with airbrush paint and found objects (including embroidery floss, buttons, glass bugle beads, ceramic alphabet beads, antique leaded glass beads, antique rhinestone beads, thimble, and a scissors trinket); hand and machine embroidered, hand quilted; 71 x 61 inches (180.3 x 154.9 cm).

This is the fifth in a series of Kitchen Tarot *quilts that began in 1998 with* The Colander/Fool: #0. *We've got 72 quilts to go! This quilt represents the tarot deck's authority figure, high priest, or pope. In the Turtle Moon Test Kitchen, we look at the cookbook, and then go wild with our creations!*

Who wouldn't be tempted to attend a tea party with a voluptuous blonde Venus pouring the tea?

396

WENDY HUHN

DEXTER, OREGON

Temptress with a Teapot

Painted and sanded canvas, screen printing, and mixed media including vintage tablecloth, color laser transfer and inkjet photo transfers, photocopy fabric, horsehair netting, couching with gold braid, beads, and sequins; bound with beads, machine quilted with monofilament; 40 x 70 inches (101.6 x 177.8 cm).

ART QUILTS: *a celebration*

JANE BURCH COCHRAN

2001

RABBIT HASH, KENTUCKY

Paper Plates and Bone China, Some Hand Painted

Various fabrics, paper, paint, beads, buttons, silver leaf, cloth with photocopy transfers, and found objects including vintage Dresden plate pieces, a glove, paper fortunes; machine and hand pieced, hand appliquéd, hand quilted and tied; 52 x 41 inches (132.1 x 104.1 cm).

Combining various materials and textures is one of my favorite parts of making quilts. Vintage quilt pieces, an artist's canvas painted and stenciled with black and white acrylic paint, and a ragged handmade paper inspired this quilt. The title came to me, and I continued a play with words in the piece. Chinese fortunes from cookies were transferred to cloth and then zigzag stitched to the plate. "Bone" was the last word that came to me, so serving dog biscuits seemed appropriate. I added silver leaf to a commercial fabric to complete the setting.

CHERI ARNOLD

COLUMBUS, OHIO

TV Test Pattern: The Center of Chaos

Commercial and hand-dyed cotton fabrics that have been airbrushed, appliquéd, fused, embroidered, and beaded by hand and machine; machine quilted; 52 x 52 inches (132 x 132 cm).

Here's how to get started in mosaic artwork: Begin with a cat (such as mine) with a serious yen for flowers. Throw some blooms in your favorite vase and set them in your newest hiding place. (You know, the one you're sure she won't be able to sniff out this time.) Clearly, you're in denial...but the good news is that you can use all that busted glass and pottery as inspiration for a magnificent mosaic cat memorial such as this one!

MARILYN L. HARRISON

BOCA RATON, FLORIDA

The Kissss
(From the MOM Series)

Cotton broadcloth patterned with paste resist and dyes; whole cloth construction, machine quilted; 16 x 22 inches (40.6 x 55.9 cm).

The first work in my MOM *series, called* Don't Tread on MOM, *opened a wellspring of ideas for autobiographical quilts that is gushing faster than I can translate them into quilts. The snakes in these pieces are covered with flowers, birthstones, and favorite things that symbolize family members. Other objects refer to the theme or title of the quilt. I allow the skin patterns on the snakes to develop spontaneously and am often surprised by their unplanned meanings.*

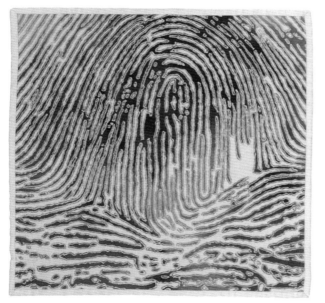

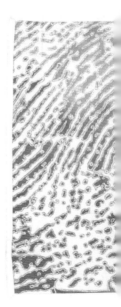

BARBARA W. WATLER

HOLLYWOOD, FLORIDA

Painter's Prints

Cotton fabric that has been hand painted with permanent silk dyes; reverse appliquéd and machine quilted; 77 x 15 inches (195.6 x 38.1 cm).

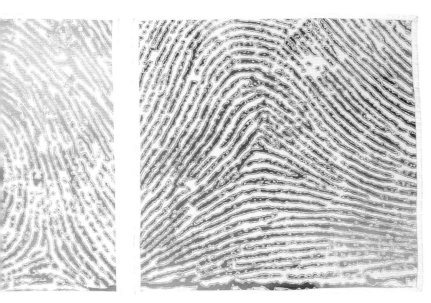

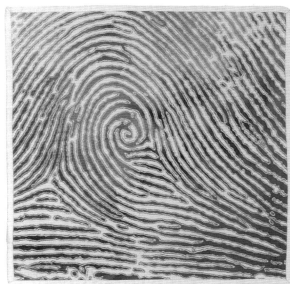

I made this set of five fingerprints on fabric using the palette of colors left from painting a picture. They explore the many differences in graphic design along with those created by genetics, age, life experience, and vocation. The use of color along with the freedom of painting was great fun after using only black and white in 20 fingerprint quilts that began this series.

KATHY DAVIE

DENVER, COLORADO

A High Fiber Tea

Various materials including cotton, silk, velour, lamé, satin, beads, paint, and found objects; hand embroidered, pieced, appliquéd, and beaded; machine pieced, appliquéd, couched, and quilted; 34 x 48 inches (86.4 x 122 cm).

Out of nowhere I had a desire to create a three-dimensional teapot pouring into a free-floating cup. It only seemed proper to place it against a 1950s background and surround it with foods tied together with a braided vine. I like to tell people that it's a "diet" quilt—one that is high in fiber and low in calories!

MARIE WOHADLO

CHICAGO, ILLINOIS

W.O.W.
(Weight of the World)

Silk and cotton fabrics stitched with
polyester thread and treated with my
own "secret" imaging processes;
machine embroidery and machine quilting; 36 x 48 inches (91.4 x 121.9 cm).

*OVER-adjust-advertise-all-amplify-analyze-assess-bill-
burden-caffeinate-cast-commit-complicate-concern-consume-
correct-cultivate-diversifydrive-due-eager-educate-emphasize-
estimate-excite-exert-extend-flow-focus-govern-haul-hype-
inflate-inform-load-look-night-orchestrate-mediate-pass-
pressure-privilege-process-promise-reach-react-refine-regulate-
rely-see-sell-sensitize-sophisticate-spend-simulate-stress-strewn-
suspicious-take-tax-think-tired-use-whelm-work-wrought.*

2003

Inspiration for the patterns used in Cell-U-Lite *came from photographs of cell structures and fabric wastage from other quilt projects. The title came from my constant battle against cellulite. I have never approached quilt making as a quilter; instead, I concentrate on the concept, color, and design of a piece rather than the traditional technique of assemblage. Producing quilts is a natural outlet for exploiting the possibilities of cloth and for providing a dialogue with the viewer.*

BETHAN ASH

CARDIFF, WALES,
UNITED KINGDOM

Cell-U-Lite

Hand-dyed and painted silk, satin and cotton fabrics; machine stitched (after fusing) and machine quilted; 36 x 68 inches (91 x 173 cm).

SUZANNE MACGUINEAS

SAN DIEGO, CALIFORNIA

Lullaby for Luke

Hand-marbled cotton fabrics created by artist; machine pieced, embroidered, and quilted; 41 x 42 inches (104 x 107 cm).

The process of creating the fabric is pure childlike joy. I have only partial control on the outcome of the design when I work with this variation on marbling. I must work very quickly and be ready for the exact moment when I let the fabric make contact with paint that is floating on a thickened liquid support. I try not to think too much, but, rather, to just keep moving in a very spontaneous way.

JANE LLOYD

BALLYMENA, COUNTY ANTRIM, NORTHERN IRELAND

Clockwise Circulation

Indian cotton layered and worked in squares;
machined stitched; 54 x 35 inches (137 x 89 cm).

This is one of a series of spiral quilts. I am interested in the play of colors, and as the spirals are quite thin, the color blends together. Colored stitching adds another textured layer, while the fraying fabric creates more texture.

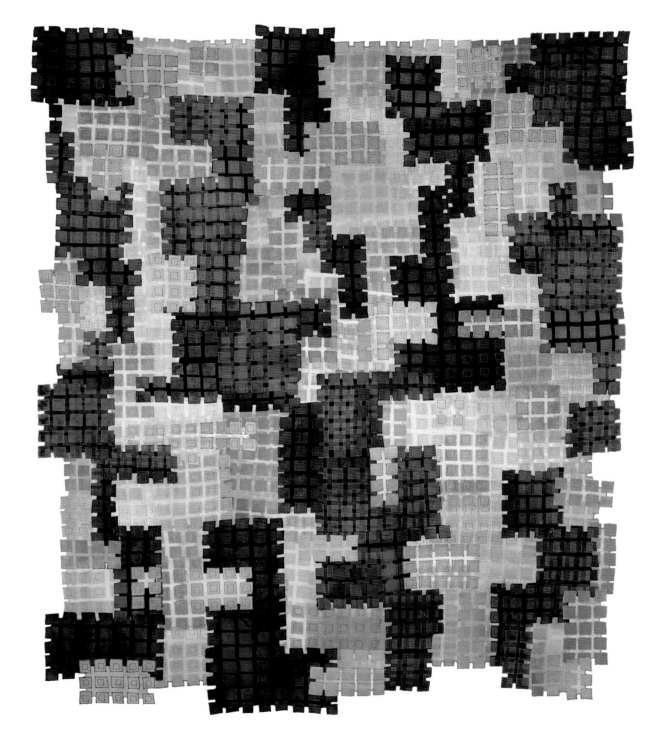

JUDY LANGILLE

OAK PARK, ILLINOIS

Large Puzzle Grid

Fused 100 percent cotton fabrics; painted with dyes and printed with thermofax screens; machine quilted; 49 x 59 inches (124 x 150 cm).

A single square unit is the fundamental element of this grid design. The individual units have formed aggregates of varying sizes, shapes, and contrasting colors, creating depth and a sense of movement. The illusion of jigsaw puzzle pieces floating on top of one another and the irregular edge of the design imply that this is a work in progress, with other pieces yet to be joined.

MAGGIE BATES

ANCHORAGE, ALASKA

Seeds and Pods

Commercial and hand-dyed cottons, paint, metal and glass beads; machine appliquéd and quilted; 28 x 44 inches (71 x 112 cm).

This quilt is my reaction to observing the incredible logic and beauty of the natural world. I did not design the seeds and pods that I interpreted in cloth, but I was amazed by the natural design in these items. For me, art is my way of acknowledging that I have taken notice of something and find it interesting enough to ask someone else to take notice as well.

BETTE USCOTT-WOOLSEY

BALA CYNWYD, PENNSYLVANIA

Quilted II

Hand-dyed painted silk; machine
pieced, fused, embroidered, and
hand quilted; 53 x 55 inches
(135 x 140 cm).

*I believe that my work bridges the gap between traditional needle textile
arts and painting. Working with thread and fabric solves my need to create
works that are beautiful, contemplative, and artistically compelling. I want
to make my art inclusive, exciting, pleasurable, and substantial in content.
I wish to keep traditional techniques alive by reinventing their context,
promoting the value of the process while engaging in strong image making.*

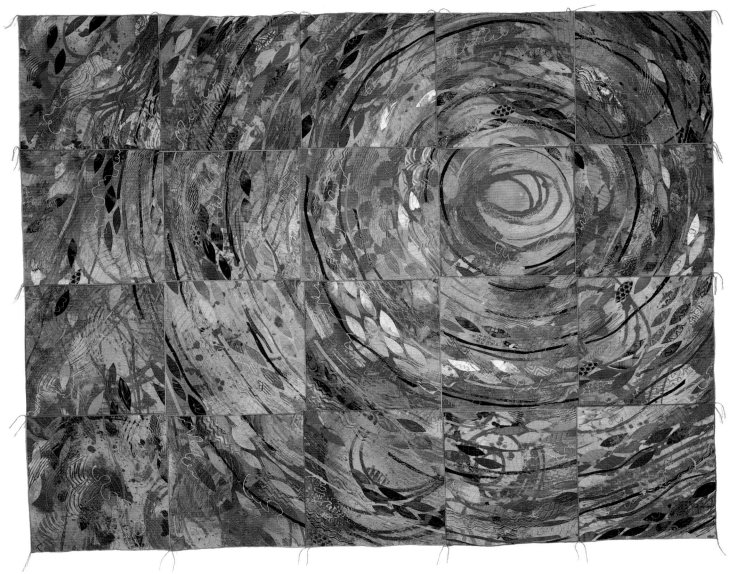

SUE BENNER

DALLAS, TEXAS

Nest III

Dye and paint on silk, monoprinted, fused; machine quilted,
pieced construction; 77 x 62
inches (196 x 157 cm).

*Over the past 12 years I have periodically approached the subject of
motherhood in my work. Last winter my two sons found a nest that
had fallen from a tree in our yard. I put the nest in my studio and
soon my quilts became nests. I see an image of home and center
in this series but others see hurricanes and galaxies. I like that.*

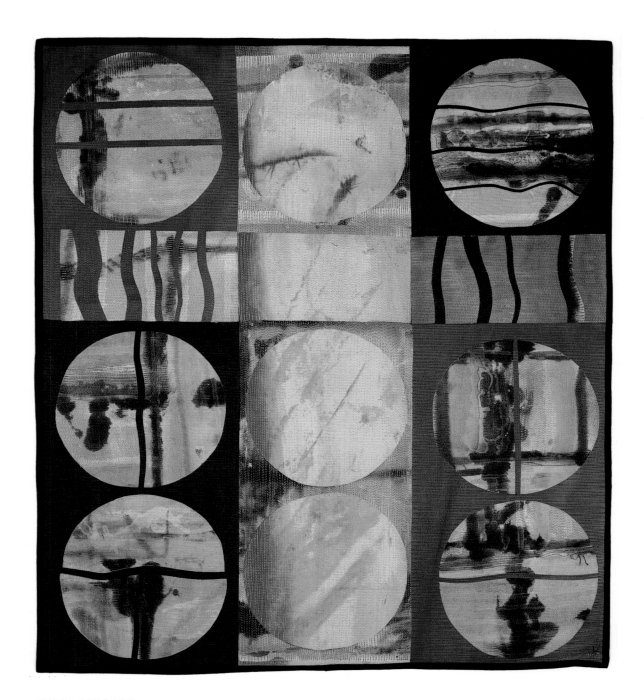

414

BOB ADAMS

LAFAYETTE, INDIANA

Lunar No. 2

100 percent cotton dye painted;
pieced and rough-edged
appliquéd, machine stitched;
32 x 36 inches (81 x 91 cm).

After moving from Colorado to Indiana, I noticed that the rising moon seemed much larger and the play of the clouds made interesting patterns. I did a series of "lunar" pieces from this observation. Through manipulation of the color and images and working with the positive and negative relationships, the moons and surrounding elements fell into place.

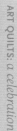

My work is inspired by the use of textiles in ritual and celebration, either as architectural embellishment, vesture, or ceremonial accessories. Geometric patterning, pieced construction, collage, and appliquéd polyester film provide a means of solving formal problems as well as an expressive vocabulary.

PATRICIA MALARCHER

ENGLEWOOD, NEW JERSEY

Crossing

Linen fabric and primed canvas embellished with polyester film, paint, gold leaf, appliqué, and screen-printing; machine and hand stitched; 30 x 53 inches (76 x 135 cm).

415

2003

RACHEL BRUMER

SEATTLE, WASHINGTON

Coral Pollen Pearls

Hand-dyed cotton, silk dupioni
binding, dye sticks, textile paint,
French knots, rubbed, silk-screened;
machine pieced, hand appliquéd,
embroidered, and hand quilted;
60 x 60 inches (152 x 152 cm).

*The concept of imagery from the natural world
comes in part from a quote from Henry David
Thoreau who said, "From the forests and wilderness
come the tonics and barks which brace humankind."*

VALERIE GOODWIN

TALLAHASSEE, FLORIDA

Riverside Settlement

Cotton, silk, and blend materials; machine pieced, direct appliquéd, and fused; 35 x 49 inches (89 x 124 cm).

Quilting as a means of creative expression comes directly to me through my grandmother. As an architect, I combine this heritage with a profound need to find common ground between architectural language and the visual nature of quilting. My work uses a palette of architectural elements and principles such as figure ground relationships, the grid, built form, density, and scale. Riverside Settlement *recalls an ancient network of interior and exterior places along a river's edge.*

LISA CALL

PARKER, COLORADO

Structures #11

Cotton fabric hand dyed by the
artist, cotton batting, cotton
thread; machine pieced and quilted; 72 x 47 inches (183 x 119 cm).

*This quilt is one in a series about stone walls and fences. I am intrigued
by the form, lines, and shapes of these structures. In this work, I was
looking to capture the beauty of the irregular spaces found between
the stones in such walls. The colors of my quilts come either from my
imagination or from nature. This quilt is a combination of spring
colors that were particularly appealing to me on a cold winter day.*

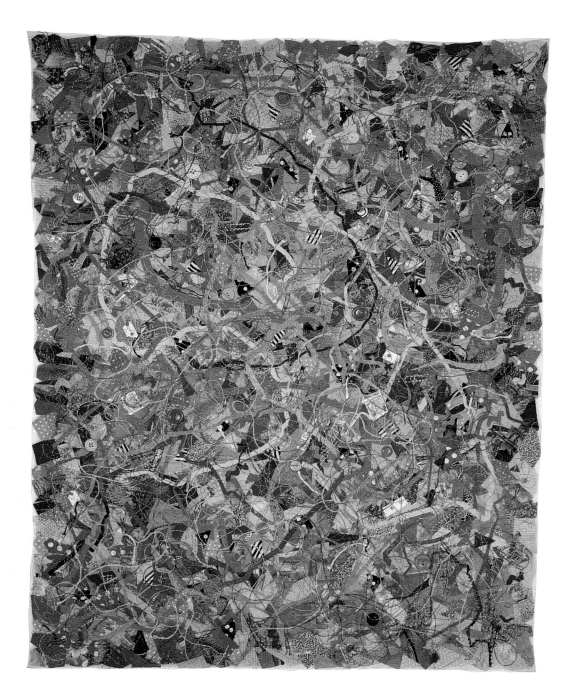

PAT KROTH

VERONA, WISCONSIN

Free For All

Hand-dyed and commercial fabrics embellished with a variety of found objects (candy wrappers, paper clips, buttons, rickrack, cording, computer paper, trapped threads, stamps); fused and machine appliquéd, then machine quilted; 24 x 30 inches (61 x 76 cm).

I try to work spontaneously and quickly, letting the materials and the process take over. Just as the title Free For All *suggests, I was hoping for the spirit of light and playfulness to come bursting forth. This quilt is a celebration of life and joy.*

CHER CARTWRIGHT

WHITE ROCK, BRITISH COLUMBIA, CANADA

Rock, Paper, Scissors

Cotton fabrics hand dyed by the
artist; machine pieced and quilted;
44 x 35 inches (112 x 89 cm).

*In our lives of mass media and instant communication, there is tremendous
emphasis on being attuned to what is currently considered trendy and
sophisticated. Making quilts allows me to escape those concerns and tap
into the part of my personality that is usually buried, and to rejoice in timeless pleasures such as simple shapes, bright colors, and children's games.*

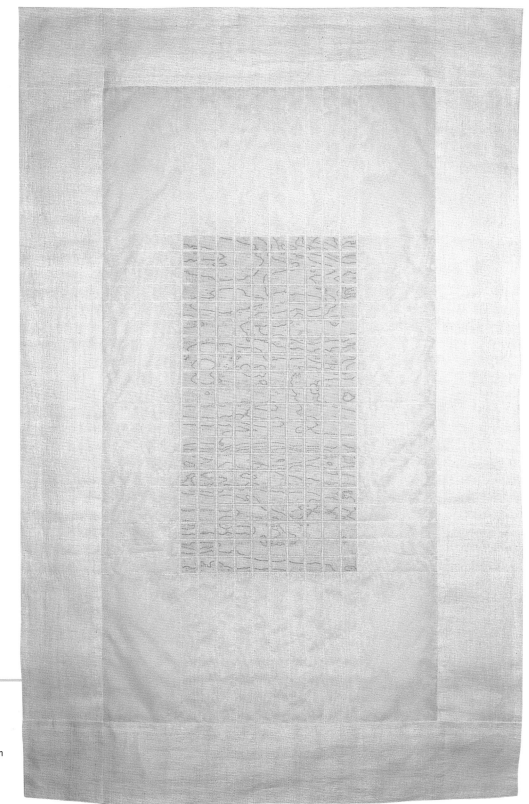

KYOUNG AE CHO

MILWAUKEE, WISCONSIN

Veil III

Maple veneer, cut and marked
with burns, sandwiched between
two layers of silk organza;
secured by hand stitches;
36 x 60 inches (91 x 152 cm).

IRIS AYCOCK

WOODVILLE, ALABAMA

Cedar Rose

Cotton fabric treated with natural plant dyes and leaves; machine quilted; 50 x 50 inches (127 x 127 cm).

This leaf hammering work is my version of an old Cherokee craft. I find leaf forms endlessly fascinating; sometimes the imperfect ones are more interesting than the unblemished specimens. Occasionally I enjoy presenting them in a somewhat traditional setting, paying homage to the quilters of past years who appliquéd fabric leaves on their quilts.

DENISE BURGE

CINCINNATI, OHIO

Maquette

Cotton and synthetic commercial fabrics (some hand dyed);
pieced, appliqued, embroidered;
80 x 75 inches (203 x 191 cm).

*I am now working with the form of the mountain as a part natural,
part manmade construct. Human imprints such as roads, dams, mines,
'nature parks,' etc., result in a mutated tragic entity, modified to fit our
needs and desires. In this image, an unknown hand has constructed a
'mountain' for its home from the detritus of the construction site.*

ANNE WORINGER

PARIS, FRANCE

Lucarne

19th-century linen and hemp hand spun, hand woven, and dyed by the artist; pleated and machine stitched; 45 x 62 inches (114 x 157 cm).

This quilt is from a series that visualizes log cabins made of old damaged boards. Since my country house is in a great forest I have always been fascinated by the old trees: their trunks, roots, branches, twigs, the wood's veins, the bark, and even the logs. I also have a great fondness for primitive wood sculptures when they tend to abstraction.

NORIKO ENDO

NARASHINO, CHIBA, JAPAN

Autumn Walk

Commercial and hand-dyed cotton, rayon, and nylon cut in small pieces and covered with soft tulle; machine quilted; 90 x 48 inches (229 x 122 cm).

This piece is part of a recent series of work that deals with landscapes. I am totally absorbed and fascinated by the beauty of nature's colors. The inspiration for this work was a series of beautiful trees with changing colors along a sidewalk in Tokyo.

KRISTIN TWEED

NORTH FORT MYERS, FLORIDA

#9 Big Head Series— The Rose

Whole cloth quilt made from recycled cotton bed sheets; machine stitched and hand painted; 42 x 45 inches (107 x 114 cm).

I make art quilts that are portraits. Exaggerations and distortions reveal complex emotions and motivations. A secondary stitched portrait appears. Unexpected relationships of lines and shapes produce unplanned complexity, creating additional levels of interest. These double portraits symbolize lives not lived, careers not followed, lovers not married, children not born. Ambiguity, mystery, and a sense of having a life of its own are goals for work in the Big Head Series.

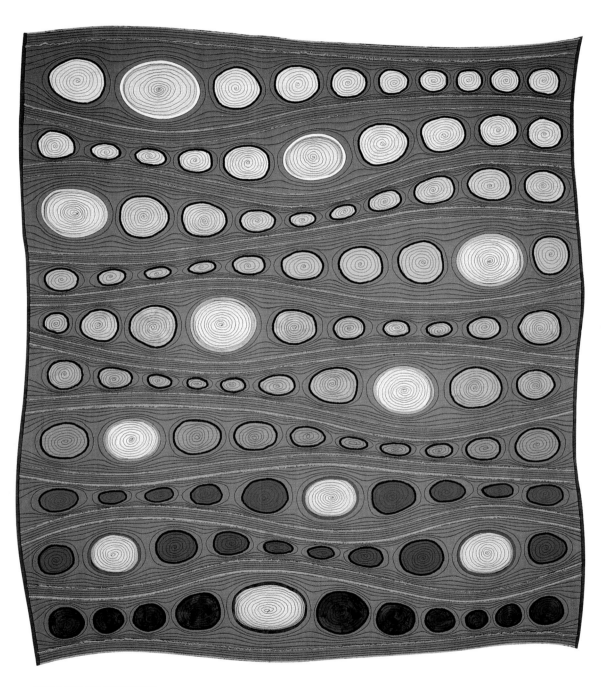

DIANNE FIRTH

TURNER, AUSTRALIAN CAPITAL TERRITORY, AUSTRALIA

One Hundred Stones

Commercial cottons, nylon netting, polyester batting; machine pieced, appliquéd, and quilted; 38 x 43 inches (97 x 109 cm).

Using the idea of placing stones to mark the passing of time, circular shapes (stones) are arranged in this quilt in ten rows of ten to represent Australia's hundred years of federation under the British monarchy in 2001. The transparent stones represent each decade's home for a republic, and the gradation of color represents the fading memory. There are actually 101 stones on the quilt, with the bottom line acknowledging the extra year taken for negotiations in 1900.

DARCY FALK

FLAGSTAFF, ARIZONA

Chair (Divine Vessel Series)

Commercial, hand-dyed, and photocopied cotton, silk, polyester, and rayon fabrics; layered, fused, and stitched; 15 x 18 inches (38 x 46 cm).

Chair *is an illustration of the perfect sitting place in the ideal room, where the sitter is enthralled with pattern and thrilled by color. Dig a little deeper, and* Chair *becomes a rowdy portrait of a sacred vessel, where metaphor is understood and, ultimately, invented.*

Ariel sings

Full fathom five
    thy father lies,
Of his bones are
    coral made;
Those are pearls
    that were his eyes;
Nothing of him
    that doth fade,
But doth suffer
    a sea-change
Into something
    rich and strange.

———

From The Tempest,
    Act I, Scene 2,
    by William Shakespeare

EMILY RICHARDSON

PHILADELPHIA, PENNSYLVANIA

Full Fathom Five

Acrylic paint on linen, silk, and
cotton; hand stitched and quilted; 31 x 61 inches (79 x 155 cm).
Private collection.

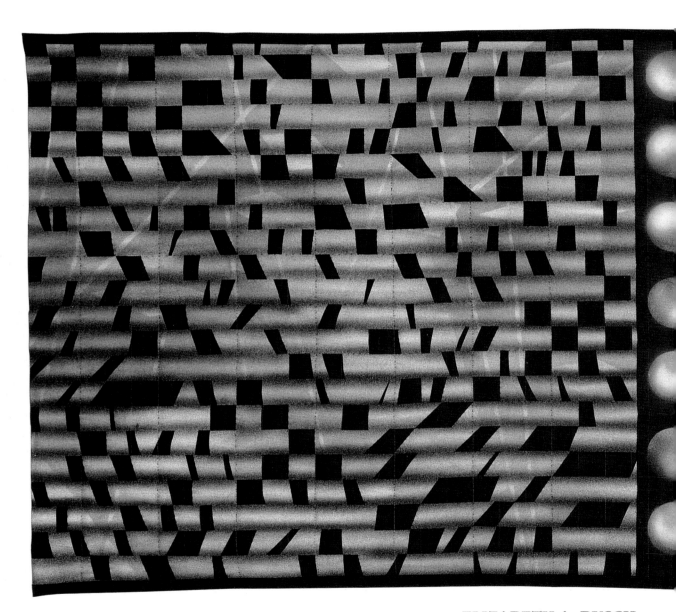

ELIZABETH A. BUSCH

GLENBURN, MAINE

Abundance

Cotton canvas, purchased fabric, acrylic paint, textile paint, hand painted, airbrushed; machine pieced, hand and machine quilted; 54 x 22 inches (137 x 56 cm).

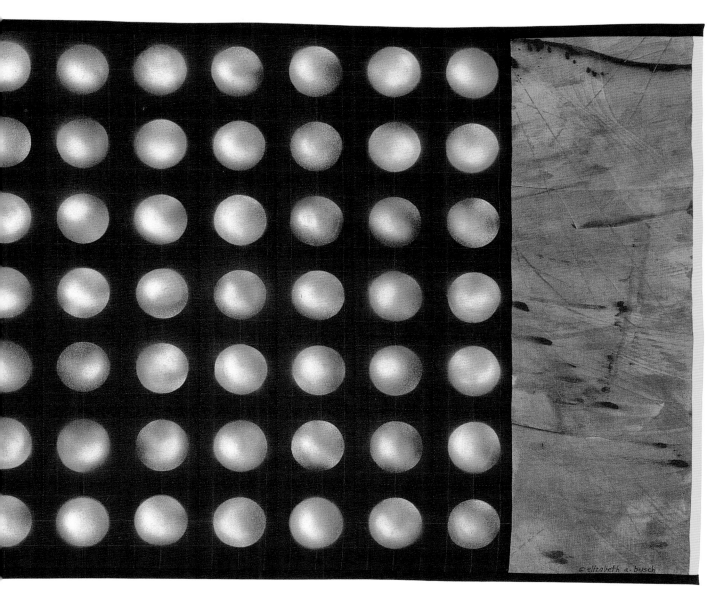

© elizabeth a. busch

Abundance. I cannot keep what I don't give away.
Annie Dillard in The Writing Life *says it all:*
"These things fill from behind, from beneath,
like well water ... Anything you do not give
freely and abundantly becomes lost to you.
You open your safe and find ashes."

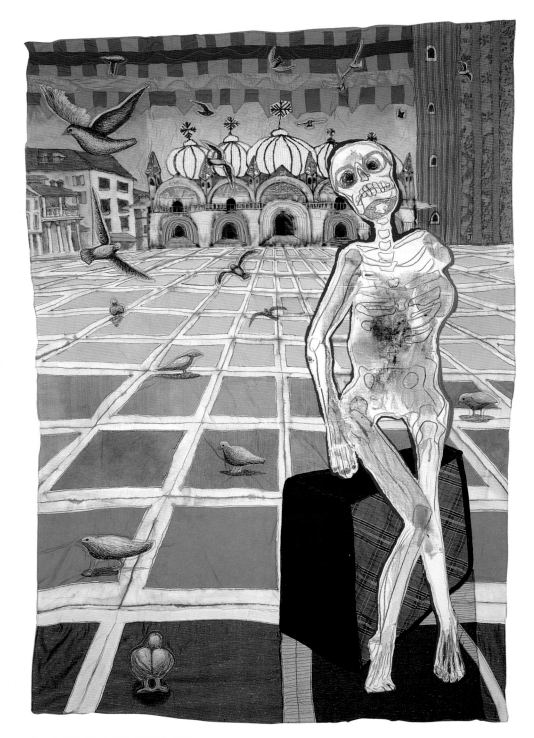

ANNEMARIE ZWACK

ITHACA, NEW YORK

Artist's First Trip to Venice

Printed commercial fabrics hand dyed with
Procion MX dyes and embellished with an
acrylic body print (mine); reverse appliquéd
and piecework; 51 x 78 inches (130 x 198 cm).

*This is an X-ray snapshot of me at a turning point in
my life. You can see "me" right down to the bones. The
birds taking flight represent the soaring feeling in my
heart of standing in the same piazza where so many
artists had tread before me. I used a body print to show
the ghost or afterimage of what the skeleton once was.*

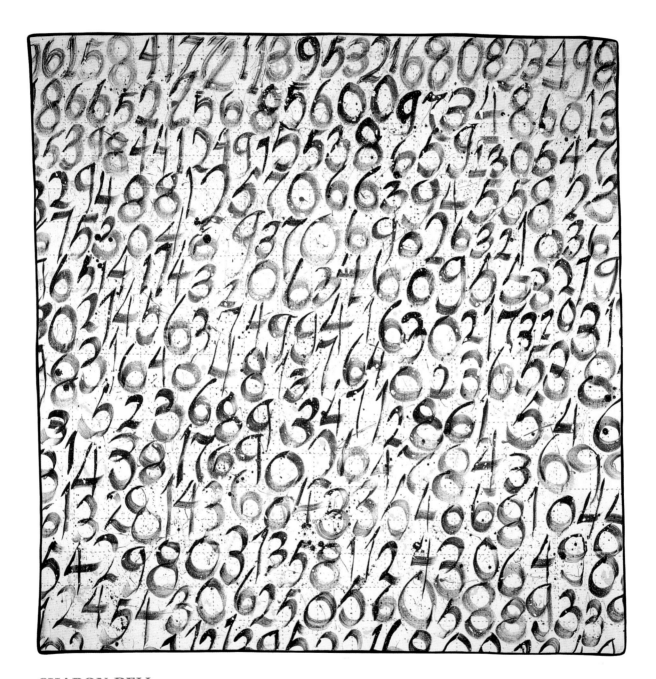

SHARON BELL

SHAKER HEIGHTS, OHIO

Numbers

Whole cloth cotton twill face and commercial cloth overdyed by artist, sumi ink and acrylic paints; hand quilted; 50 x 55 inches (127 x 140 cm).

This is one of a series of seven quilts visually interpreting biblical titles. Each is a whole cloth quilt that uses a dichotomy of controlled quilting techniques: the much freer application of paint or ink, the mix of traditional and contemporary, and, for this quilt, the orderliness of the mathematical universe and the randomness of numbers. The visual symbol of the Book of Numbers *was obvious; the challenge was to make it engaging.*

URSULA KÖNIG

BERN, SWITZERLAND

Cactus

Commercial and hand-dyed cotton fabrics; machine pieced and quilted; 35 x 50 inches (89 x 127 cm).

The cactus' rigidly patterned surface with its ribs, wrinkles, warts, hair, and thorns lies at the center of my interest. The specific colors of these gray-green plants—with their flashing orange-, pink-, and magenta-colored flowers—fascinate me. My feelings, thoughts, and memories influence the creative process so that the piece does not simply reflect nature. It is my aim to bring rhythm and color to a symbiosis.

INGE HUEBER

COLOGNE, GERMANY

Sweet melodies of colors, played in the summer of 2001.

Colour Melody (Summer 2001)

Home-dyed cotton; machine pieced and quilted; 91 x 72 inches (231 x 183 cm).

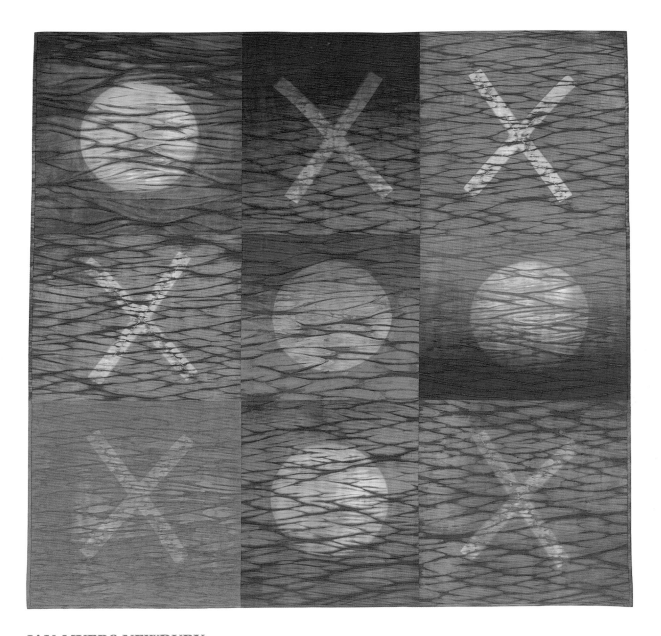

JAN MYERS-NEWBURY

PITTSBURGH, PENNSYLVANIA

Cat's Game

Kona cotton, dyed by the artist
using various forms of mechanical
resist; machine pieced and quilted;
55 x 56 inches (140 x 142 cm).

A Cat's Game is a conclusion in which nobody wins. I am rarely political in my work, but apparently present and proposed military engagements have "ooched" their way into the consciousness of my dye pot. My nine-year-old son offered several compositional suggestions by providing me, at my request, with an array of cat games. My first collaboration!

This quilt is a tribute to our female ancestors who embraced modern production technologies to bring the beauty of hand-crafted arts to many. The natural harmonies of earth and sky contrast and balance the precise geometry of this machine-quilted textile. The bold, vibrant color juxtaposed by delicately veiled quilting lines transforms the warp and weft into a unified whole.

SUSHMA PATEL-BOULD

EAST PALO ALTO, CALIFORNIA

Bauhaus

Cotton fabrics; machine pieced and quilted; 36 x 72 inches (91 x 183 cm).

PATTY HAWKINS

ESTES PARK, COLORADO

Aspen Seasons

Cottons with patterns created
by the artist, free-cut curved and
pieced to imitate tree trunk
vertical shapes; 78 x 34 inches
(198 x 86 cm); two-panel piece.

Colorado's mountain environs and natural colors constantly inspire my fabric dyeing and design. The combination of their white bark, black scarring by elk antlers, and their unique shaking green leaves (called "Colorado gold" in the fall) makes Aspen poplar trees mesmerizing at any season. My hope is Aspen Seasons brings you peace and tranquility.

MARILYN HENRION

NEW YORK, NEW YORK

Night Thoughts # 2

Silk, cotton, and metallic fabrics;
hand pieced and quilted; 51 x 53
inches (130 x 134 cm).

*Transcending the impersonal objectivity of geometric abstraction
through the sensuousness of materials, my works reveal a blend
of reason and passion, reflecting my nature. I find inspiration in
diverse sources, including the complexity of Indian miniatures, the
mystery of Russian icons, the lush intensity of Matisse paintings,
and the elegance of kesa robes worn by Japanese monks.*

JOAN SCHULZE

SUNNYVALE, CALIFORNIA

Concert Hall

Silk, cotton, and paper; monoprinting,
photocopy and glue transfer processes,
pieced, machine stitched, and quilted;
50 x 50 inches (127 x 127 cm). Collection
of The Oakland Museum of California.

Concert Hall is a place where people dressed in tuxedos stand around waiting for the music to begin. Perhaps it has already begun.

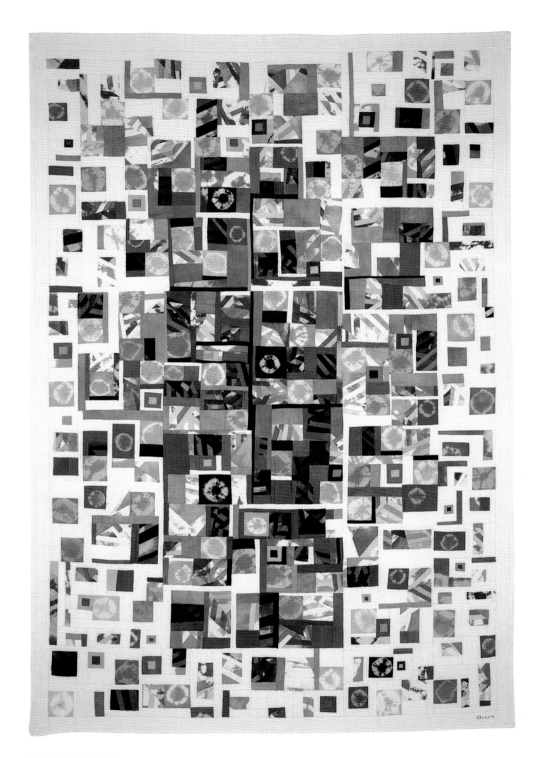

444

MI SIK KIM

NONSAN CITY, KOREA

The Years Lost

Commercial and hand-dyed
cottons; machine pieced and
hand quilted; 49 x 73 inches
(124 x 185 cm).

*I feel that my memories, both painful and joyful,
change as time passes; sometimes they remain,
sometimes they fade away. Memories are like stitching
and sewing: when many small pieces join together to
make a larger one, they transform into something new.*

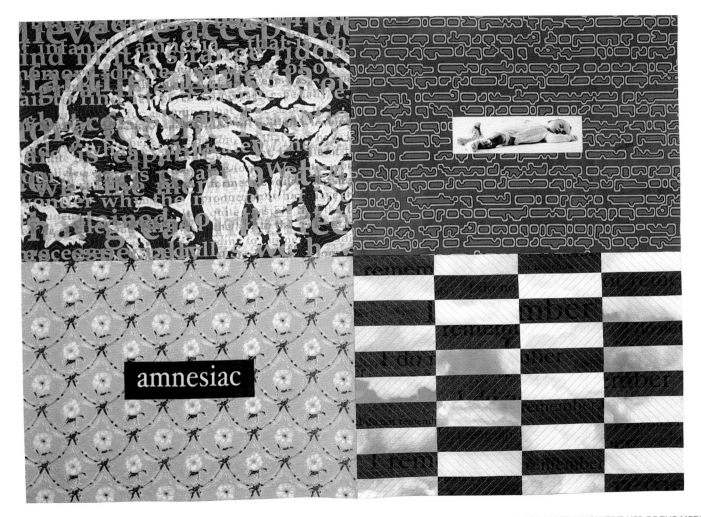

MICHAEL JAMES

LINCOLN, NEBRASKA

A Strange Riddle

100 percent cotton surface
embellished with digitally developed and printed images using
Photoshop and CAD software
and a Mimaki textile printer;
machine pieced and quilted;
76 x 57 inches (193 x 145 cm).

*A 1949 photograph taken by my father when I was five months old and an
essay by Freud on the mystery of infantile amnesia were the triggers for this quilt.
The child's neurological immaturity would seem to prevent the "reading" of visual
patterns, such as the genteel floral wallpaper of that first room, but can we be sure?
While I don't have any memories of that first bedroom, I am fascinated by pattern
of all kinds, and believe that fascination has deeply embedded roots.*

2003

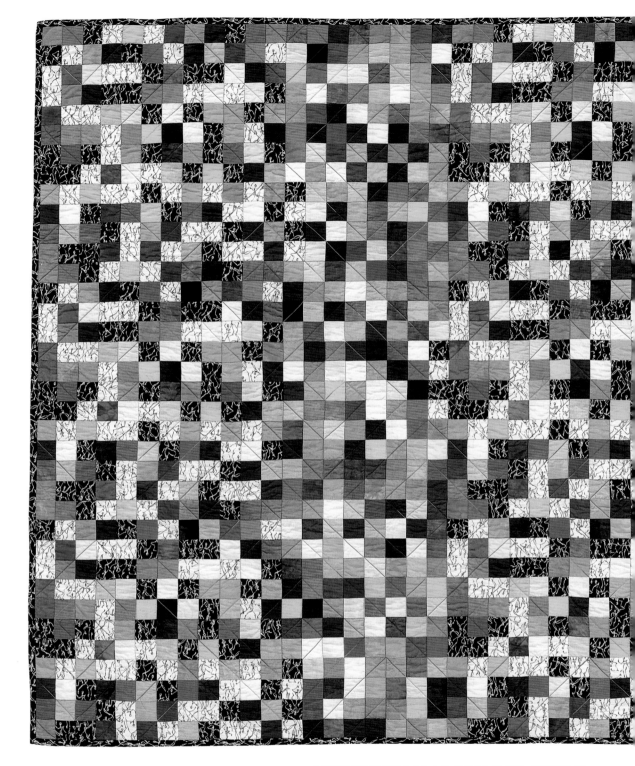

MEINY VERMAAS-VAN DER HEIDE

TEMPE, ARIZONA

Earth Quilt #106: Lines XVIII

Commercial and hand-dyed cotton fabrics (made as a group effort in a two-day workshop with Heide Stoll-Weber in Germany); machine pieced and quilted; 66 x 46 inches (168 x 117 cm). Sashiko topstitching pattern from the book *Sashiko* by Mary S. Parker, adapted by the artist.

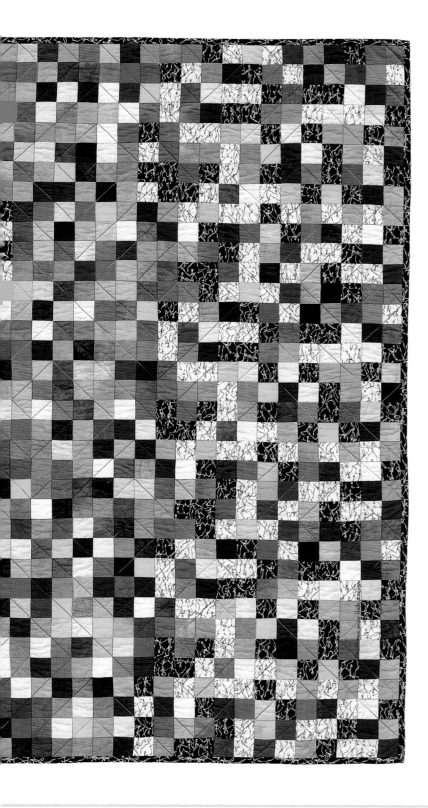

447

My quilts are known for their strong graphics, minimalist appeal,
and the color magic of visual illusions. My trademark wrinkled
heirloom appearance within the quilt surface and the crisp edge
of the binding juxtaposed with the influence of Mondrian and
the Dutch style reveals my fascination with midcentury modern
as well as op art, making my quilts contemporary classics.

MARIE L. JENSEN

TACOMA, WASHINGTON

Global Warming

Raw canvas embellished with
fabric paint and photo transfers;
machine pieced and appliquéd;
25 x 40 inches (64 x 102).

*Inspired by a local radio station's ecology report,
this is a somewhat light approach to a serious
concern. Just as the flood of rising waters from
melting ice caps threatens our environment, the
deluge of daily responsibilities and information
makes me feel like I'm only treading water.*

The dish soap bottle sits under the sink in the dark cupboard, like a hermit. The lace appliqué pattern down the middle of the bridal train found by Lucky (Susan) suggested the form of the dish soap bottle, so off we went to Card #9 out of 78 Kitchen Tarot cards!!!! Lucky wrote lots of little diary stories while slowly stitching: "Finding the Carnival Glass Butterdish with Pat," "Sharing the Diamond Ring with Gretchen," and "Getting Hattie's Knee Operation."

SUSAN SHIE & JAMES ACORD

WOOSTER, OHIO

The Dish Soap/ Hermit: Card #9 in the Kitchen Tarot

Recycled bridal train and dish towels, cotton and satin fabrics, assorted trims, shrink art drawings, shisha mirrors; appliquéd, airbrushed, hand painted, hand quilted and embroidered; 34 x 59 inches (86 x 150 cm).

449

2003

JUDITH RUSH

BEXLEY, OHIO

Wheat Fields in Egypt #1

Hand-dyed cotton; machine pieced
and quilted; 31 x 33 inches (79 x 84 cm).

*Artists in ancient Egypt lived in a world of fascinating and brilliant colors.
I had a unique opportunity to visit Egypt, and my Egyptian companions
provided extraordinary insight and guidance as we traveled to many
different types of sites. The overwhelming feeling of awe I felt left me with
sweaty palms that ran the colors from my sketchbook. This piece is one
of my efforts to communicate that feeling of trembling excitement.*

The organic qualities of a hand-stitched line sewn with a single thread are represented by machine-stitched segments of machine-woven fabric, and make reference to the colors and lines of a wheat field. Australian farmers have been called the best in the world, but farming is tough in this country, and each year when our farmers sow a crop in this drought-prone environment, they take a leap of faith. I salute their dreams and their courage with this quilt.

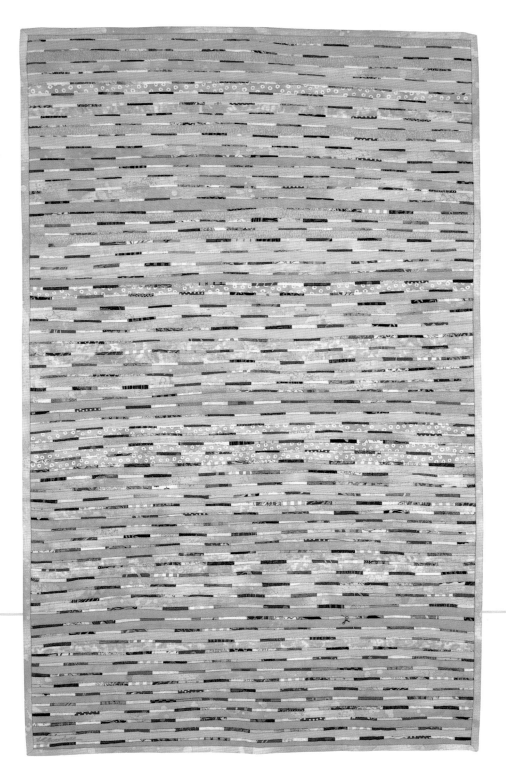

MARGERY GOODALL

MOUNT LAWLEY,
WESTERN AUSTRALIA,
AUSTRALIA

Summer: Harvest #2

Cotton, cotton blend, lamé blend, and rayon fabrics; machine pieced and quilted; 19 x 30 inches (48 x 76 cm).

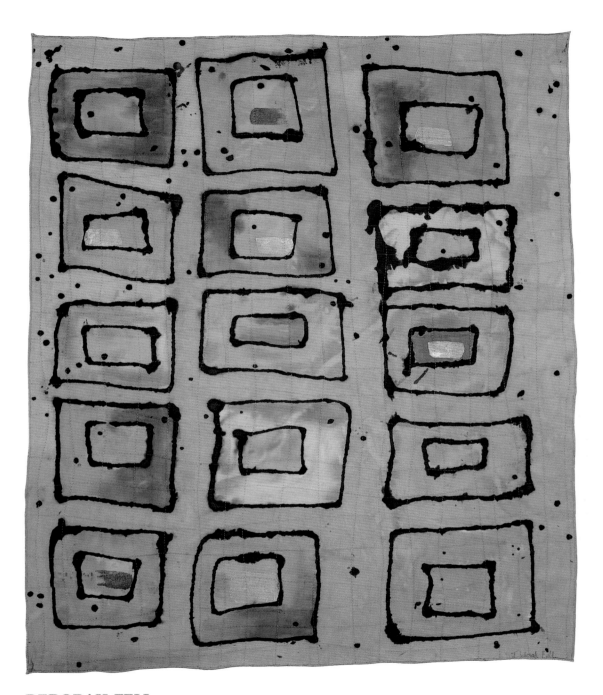

452

DEBORAH FELL

URBANA, ILLINOIS

Painted Squares

Whole cloth quilt, dye-painted
and stamped by artist; machine
quilted; 35 x 42 inches (89 x 107).

This quilt is the third in the series of the Tuesday's Child/Rebuilding *pieces. Continuing with the theme of destruction and rebuilding, this piece is very simple. Many in the country believe they have been changed because of the September 11, 2001, terrorist events, and I am no exception. My previous work was somewhat representational, but things are not so clear to me now and my work reflects this in a more abstract form.*

ELLIN LARIMER

NORDLAND, WASHINGTON

Verdant Counterpoint

Hand-dyed (by the artist) pima and kona cottons and several commercially dyed cottons; machine pieced and quilted; 54 x 70 inches (137 x 178 cm).

I am inspired by our northwest woods and ground covers and have tried to express that feeling with curved lines and shapes. Counterpoint seemed an appropriate title because I was combining the motifs into a single harmonic texture. I wanted a rhythmic quality in my work, and my quilting continued this feeling.

2003

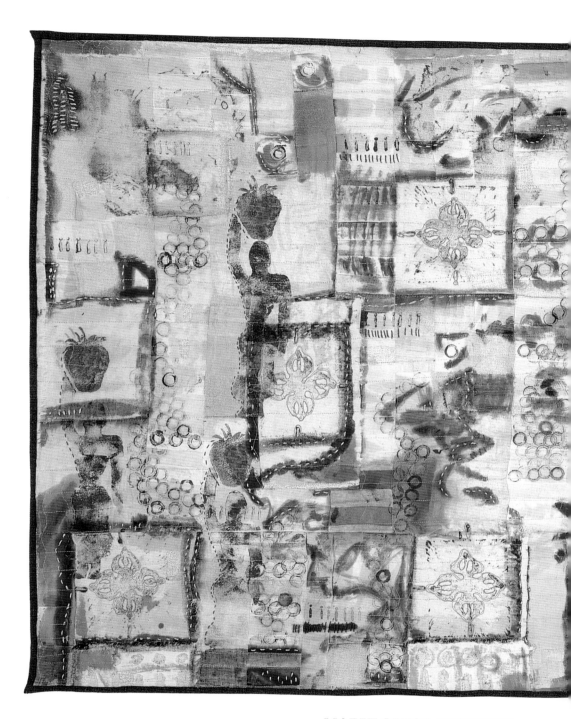

MARYLOUISE LEARNED

BOULDER, COLORADO

Sign and Symbol

Pieced cotton, silk, gauze, and canvas;
dye painted, monoprinted, stamped,
hand stitched, machine and free-motion
quilted; 62 x 33 inches (157 x 84 cm).

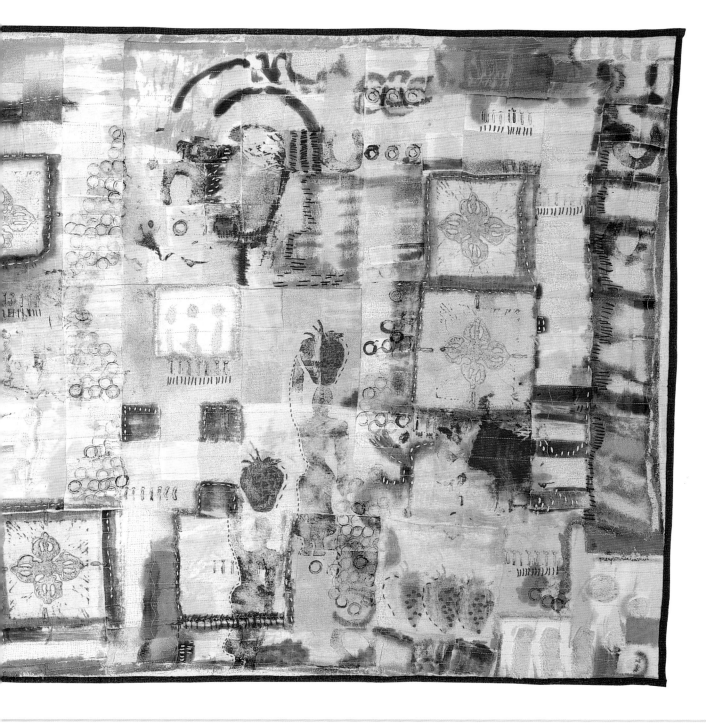

There is always some connection to the traditional arts, done primarily by women, in my work. It is my link to history, to my ancestors, and to the feminine principles of nurture, nature, and enjoyment. Each piece is a birth of some sort. Whether its duration is long or short, there comes a time to say good-bye and clear the decks for the next arrival. My visual day-to-day life and music serve as metaphors for this process.

LESLIE GABRIËLSE

ROTTERDAM, NETHERLANDS

Lion Fish

Various fabrics, hand appliquéd
with yarn and thread, embellished
with acrylic paint; 86 x 68 inches
(218 x 173 cm).

*This is the first of three works using ocean life as a subject. The lion fish inspired
me with its color variations, tentacle shapes, and delicate movements. The fish
became the dominant subject, with various layers of textures as the background.*

PATRICIA AUTENRIETH

HYATTSVILLE, MARYLAND

Picnic

Cotton, blends, linen; screen printing, hand appliqué, English paper piecing, machine quilting; 49 x 52 inches (124 x 132 cm).

Everyday forms and materials, autobiographical elements, art historical references, and traditional quilting designs always seem to collide in my work. I sometimes feel that I act as artistic valet, looking for places for all these things to park.

458   **DINAH SARGEANT**

NEWHALL, CALIFORNIA

Link

100 percent cotton fabric hand painted by the artist; hand and machine appliquéd, machine-pieced background, hand and machine quilted; 84 x 78 inches (213 x 198 cm).

One night two owls flew overhead. Oblivious to me, they clicked and glided together in their own world. I walked in mine, feeling privileged for the glimpse of theirs, and then, recognized our connection.

JUDITH CONTENT

PALO ALTO, CALIFORNIA

Desert Pools

100 percent black Thai silk that
has been pleated, discharged,
and Arashi shibori dyed;
machine quilted and pieced;
68 x 67 inches (173 x 170 cm).

*Desert pools are evolutionary wonders of time and isolation—
temporary vessels of ancient soil filled by winter rains, each tiny
refuge cradling plant and animal life uniquely its own. A sanctuary for aquatic plants and animals, wildflowers, and migratory
birds, desert pools are a source of life extending far into the surrounding landscape. This piece was inspired by the ephemeral
beauty of these miniature oases and celebrates their preservation.*

ERIKA CARTER

BELLEVUE, WASHINGTON

Nest IX: Generations

Discharged cotton (bleach, stopped
with anti-chlor); machine pieced and
quilted; 38 x 48 inches (97 x 122 cm).

Nest IX: Generations *continues my* Nest *series that was
initiated when my daughter left home for college. With the
September 11 bombings, the concept of "home" as expressed
through the metaphor "nest" became much more significant and
global. This series calls attention to temporality, resiliency,
growth, the combination of fragility and strength, and, in this
piece especially, family relationships and what gets passed along.*

LINDA LEVIN

WAYLAND, MASSACHUSETTS

Central Park West/Winter I

Cotton and other fabrics, Procion dyed; machine stitched; 44 x 55 inches (112 x 140 cm).

My quilts are made with fabrics I dye myself to achieve a spontaneity purchased fabrics don't provide. I try to capture not a specific scene, but an atmosphere, a mood, or a moment.

461

2003

Time imprinted on an ancient dry landscape, shaped by wind and water...layers of fossils revealing fragments of life long past...fabric folded, scrunched, and stained with leaves and bark...repetitive hand stitches conveying a sense of time and labor...

PAMELA FITZSIMMONS

MOUNT VINCENT,
NEW SOUTH WALES, AUSTRALIA

Fossil Bed #2

Wool and silk, dyed with eucalyptus leaves; machine pieced, hand stitched with silk thread; 29 x 52 inches (74 x 132 cm).

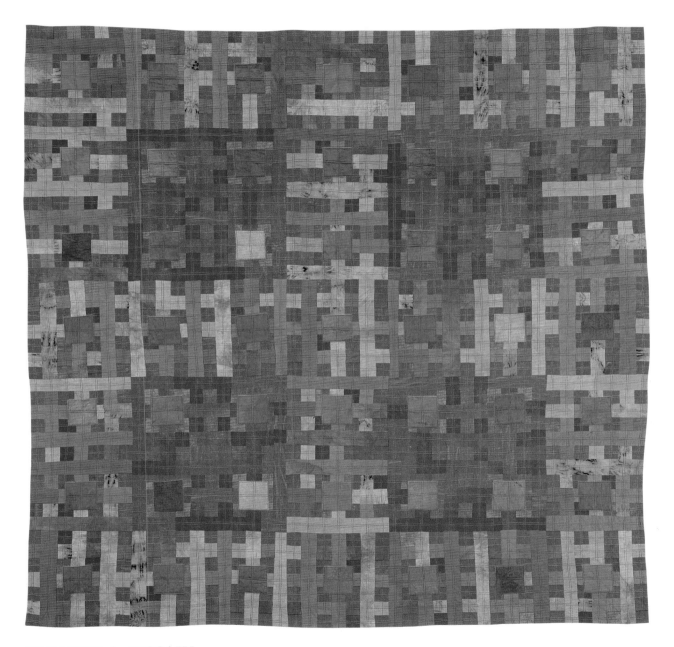

ELEANOR A. MCCAIN

SHALIMAR, FLORIDA

Crab

Hand-dyed cotton fabric (by
the artist and others); machine
pieced and quilted; 90 x 90
inches (229 x 229 cm).

Quilting is grounded in American history, family, community, and common experience. Art quilts are a living document of cultural history, expressing artistic, emotional, and spiritual values, particularly those of women. I use quilts to transpose function and symbol, art and craft, and to express ideas about creativity and community. Crab *uses the colors found on the shell of the female Florida blue crab,* Callinectes sapidus. *The grid structure is a format for exploration of color and spatial relationships.*

BARBARA W. WATLER

HOLLYWOOD, FLORIDA

Spiral Leaf

Cotton fabric; machine satin
stitched and reverse appliquéd;
69 x 38 inches (175 x 97 cm).

465

Leaves, like fingerprints, have "one-of-a-kind" designs. The organic labyrinth created by this coleus leaf is a spiral pathway, leading the eye on a spiritual journey through islands of black and white to an inner destination.

MIRIAM NATHAN-ROBERTS

BERKELEY, CALIFORNIA

Cortland Street Subway Station

Digitally designed and digitally printed on cotton sateen with fiber reactive dyes; machine quilted; 42 x 49 inches (107 x 124 cm).

In November of 2001 I spent a week in New York and visited Ground Zero to pay my respects. In the past, I had taken the subway to the Twin Towers as a tourist destination. Now Cortland Street Station, a stop for the World Trade Center, is completely closed. As I traveled underground, I imagined that people might have been entombed at Cortland Street. Passing through the subway system, dirt and markings on station walls caught my attention.

LINDA MACDONALD

WILLITS, CALIFORNIA

Wildlife Sanctuaries

Cotton broadcloth, airbrushed,
hand painted; hand quilted;
45 x 34 inches (114 x 86 cm).

*Northern California is converting its forest land to vineyards, suburbs,
and plush vacation retreats. These changes affect the wildlife to a large,
usually negative degree. There is hope, though: migration routes from one
shrinking habitat to another and underpasses for roads and freeways are
being considered in state highway and development plans. In the worst
sense, the animals in this piece show how small their natural habitats
may become by having only a small sanctuary to live in.*

LUDMILLA USPENSKAYA

AWARD OF EXCELLENCE

NEW YORK, NEW YORK

Recharge

Silk and cotton fabrics hand
painted by artist, wax resist, collage; machine and hand quilted;
56 x 74 inches (142 x 188 cm).

What once was hot
Eventually gets cold.
What once was full
Eventually gets empty.
It is up to you to "Recharge" it.

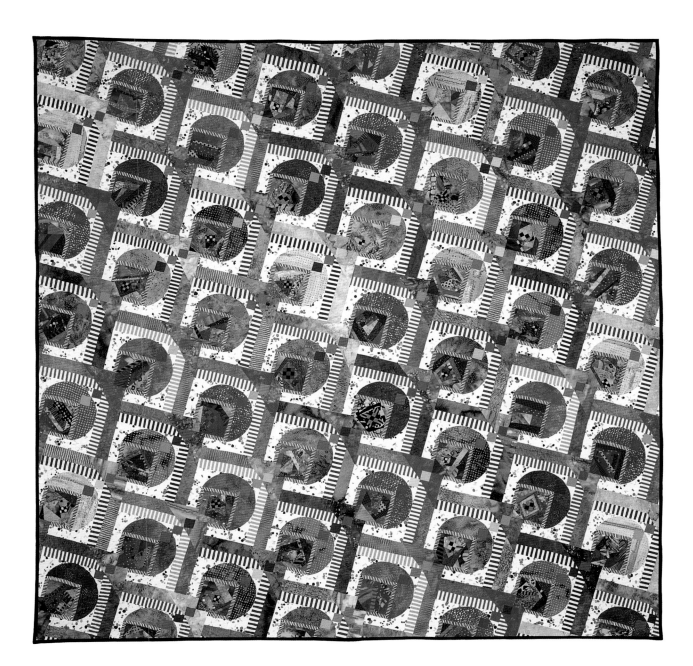

SHARON HEIDINGSFELDER

LITTLE ROCK, ARKANSAS

Grab your pierogies...it's circus time!

Popcorn, Peanuts, and Cracker Jacks!

Cotton, commercially printed fabric, some printed
fabric by artist; repeat block design machine pieced
and quilted; 73 x 74 inches (185 x 188 cm).

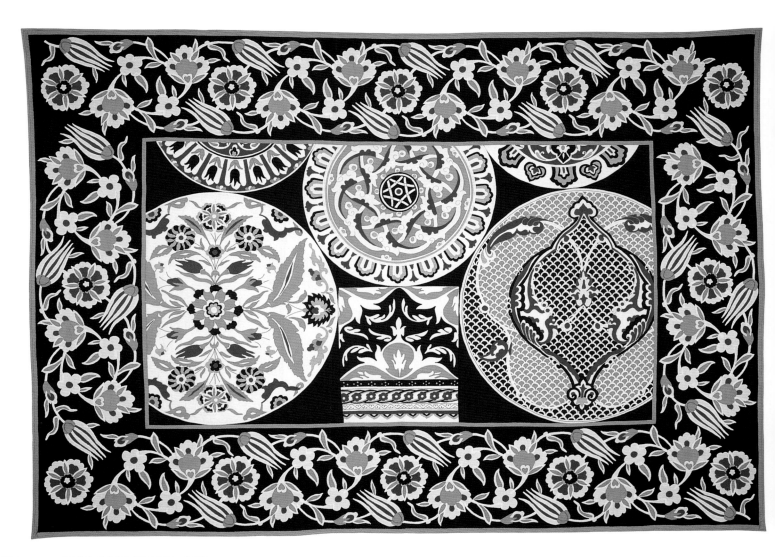

HIROMI HAYASHI

NAGASAKI, JAPAN

Arabesque Plates

Cotton fabrics; pieced, appliquéd,
embroidered, and quilted by hand;
102 x 72 inches (259 x 183 cm).

*I finish every detail of my work completely by hand sewing, using a
traditional technique, as I respect heritage and tradition. I love handwork,
and would like to devote as much of my time as possible to making quilts.*

PATRICIA MINK

ANN ARBOR, MICHIGAN

Concrete Abstraction

Inkjet pigments printed onto various fabrics (silk, cotton, blends, disposable face cloths); fusible appliqué, machine quilted, and embroidered; 28 x 36 inches (71 x 91 cm).

Layers are the focus of my work in several ways: as components of physical structure, as elements of process, and as complex metaphor. Concrete Abstraction was created from photographic images of several different walls, collaged together. The different patterns and textures that occur in aging walls as a result of construction, deterioration, and reconstruction set up interesting visual relationships and contrasts, especially when reproduced in softer materials.

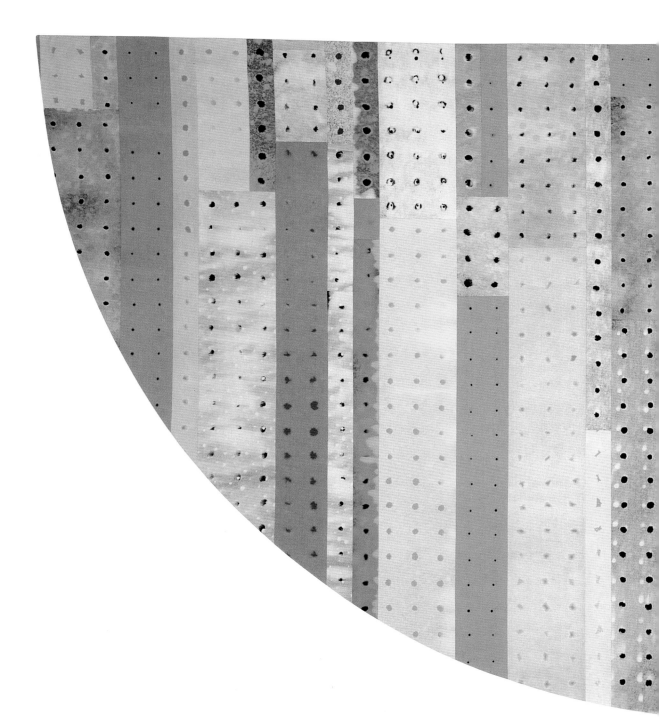

MARTHA WARSHAW

CINCINNATI, OHIO

Cope: Scattering

New and recycled fabrics; bleached
and/or inked; machine pieced and hand
tied; 107 x 54 inches (272 x 137 cm).

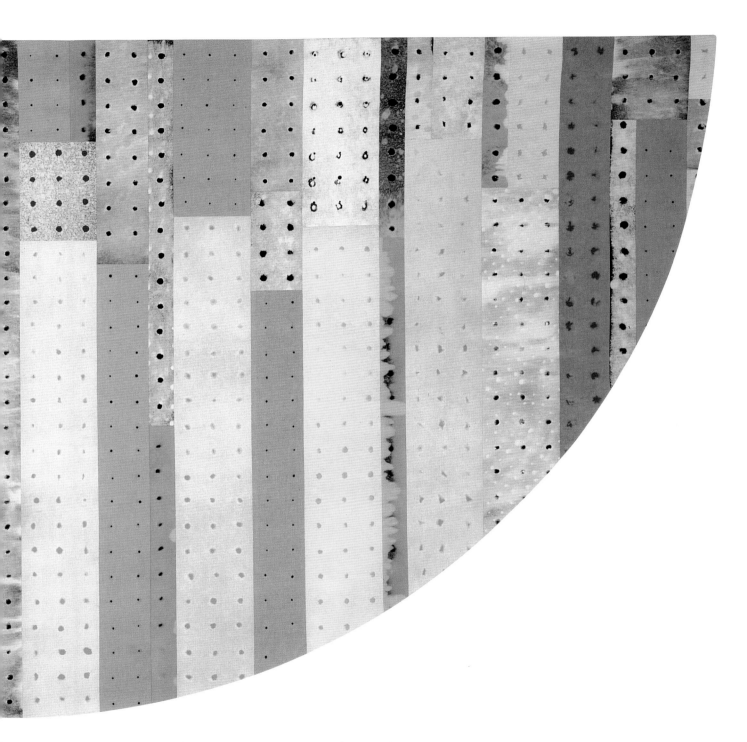

In the summer of 2001, I viewed a number of antique ecclesiastical copes (capes) on display in European museums. One 14th-century cope, worn out after centuries of use, had been cut up and used in three new vestments. In the 19th century, those three vestments were taken apart and the original cope was reassembled. In the 20th century, what remained of the cope was stitched to velvet for display.

DOMINIE NASH

BETHESDA, MARYLAND

Stills from a Life 4

Cotton and silk, hand dyed,
drawn, and printed by the artist;
machine appliquéd and quilted;
61 x 60 inches (155 x 152 cm).

*It's surprising to look at familiar objects in a new context, such as when
setting up a still-life composition. Often the homeliest or most ordinary
things have the most interesting shapes and patterns when abstracted and
made to interact with each other. The challenge of exploring and developing
these relationships into a satisfying arrangement, and then translating it into
fabric on a two-dimensional plane, keeps me interested in pursuing this series.*

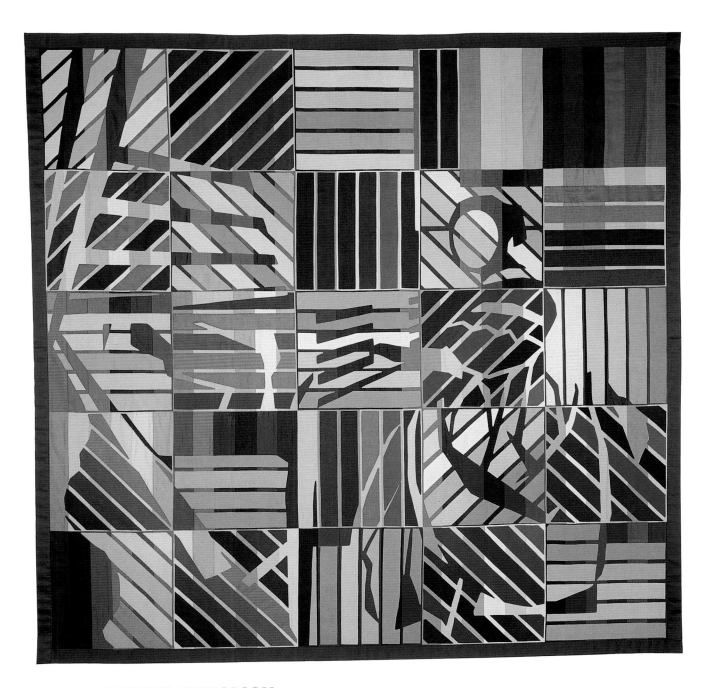

ANNE McKENZIE NICKOLSON

INDIANAPOLIS, INDIANA

Woman Still Seated

Commercially dyed cotton;
machine pieced, hand appliquéd
through all layers; 57 x 57 inches
(145 x 145 cm).

This work was inspired by Jan Vermeer's A Lady Seated at the
Virginal. *I was especially interested in the painting's structure and
luminosity, which I tried to capture in my quilt. Viewing paintings
is an important activity for me, and I am especially moved by the
persistent power of Vermeer's paintings. It is because the 17th-century
painting "still" affects me (and others) that the woman is "still seated."*

JEN SWEARINGTON

ASHEVILLE, NORTH CAROLINA

Good Humor

Pieced bed sheets, layers of gesso, shellac; charcoal and grease pencil drawing, screen printing, free-motion embroidery, and quilting; 24 x 34 inches (61 x 81 cm).

On my wonder ride of everyday experiences, I race and rummage through memories of living in the South, the East Coast, and my Indiana childhood. Good Humor *contains salvaged fragments of my husband's portrait, a photograph shot while passing an ice cream truck, and my own left hand. I record anecdotes in cryptic disarray, saturating the surface of the most intimate fabric of the home: the sheets on the bed. Tucked in, my personal history unfolds.*

ORNA ROGLIT

RAMAT-HASHARON, ISRAEL

Traces III

Hand-printed and dyed cotton
(by the artist) and multilayered
torn strips; machine pieced
and quilted; 41 x 55 inches
(104 x 140 cm).

In the beginning GOD created
The heaven that doesn't exist
And the earth willing to touch it,
Pulling strings between them.
With his tenderness touch
He created the Man-to-be
A prayer, a string, for the never exist.

"Traces" A connection between art and reality
It reflects my feelings motion and energy
At different times during life.
My printed fabrics and torn stripes in
continuously repeated
Lines, create the illusion of movement

CAROL OWEN

PITTSBORO, NORTH CAROLINA

Wildflowers

Commercial and hand-painted
cotton, torn and sewn edge strips;
45 x 42 inches (114 x 107 cm).

Wildflowers reflects my love for gardening, working with the exuberance
and raw energy of flowers. Each one is different, yet together they entice
you with a blast of color. I hoped to capture some of that excitement.

JOHN W. LEFELHOCZ

ATHENS, OHIO

Match Schticks

Bonded paper and nylon net embellished with matchsticks, fabric, beads, and knotted rope, all bordered by peach skin over cotton duck; 62 x 73 inches (157 x 185 cm). Corset images provided by Ann Moneypenny of 100 Proof Press.

Striking, isn't it?

Weaving is fine, but sometimes I like to use glue...lots of glue. —J.w.L.

"The ritual of marriage is not simply a social event; it is a crossing of threads in the fabric of fate. Many strands bring the couple and their families together and spin their lives into a fabric that is woven on their children."
—*Portuguese-Jewish Wedding Ceremony*

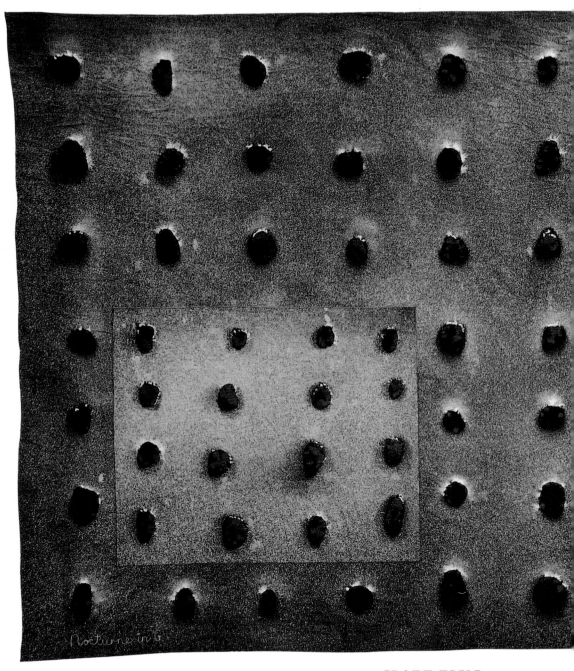

CLARE PLUG

NAPIER, NEW ZEALAND

Nocturne in G

Discharge-dyed cotton; machine
quilted and reverse appliquéd;
74 x 39 inches (188 x 99 cm).

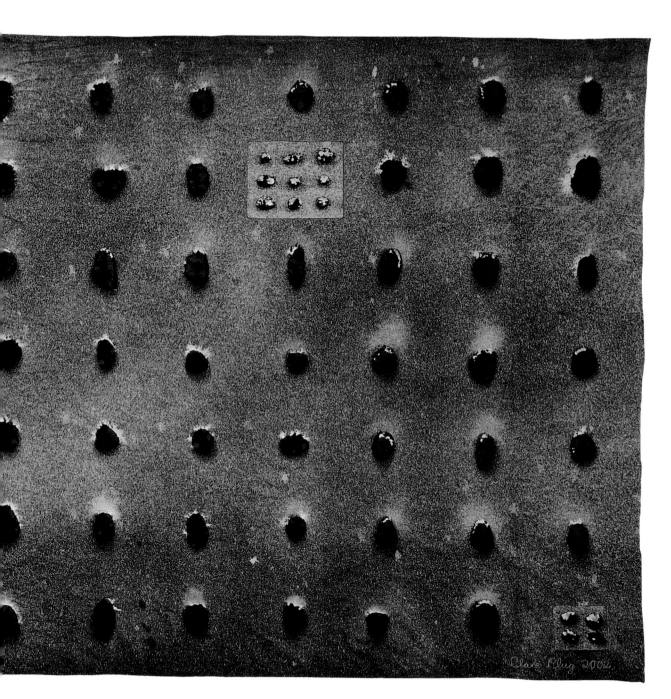

*My current work is created in response to the coastline where
I live: the rhythms, patterns, and textures and its emptiness
and limited color schemes all excite me. The inspiration for this
particular quilt was the graywacke stones that blanket our city
beach combined with the formality of the beachfront gardens.*

2003

SANDI CUMMINGS

MORAGA, CALIFORNIA

Ladies of the Day

Commercial, hand-dyed, and
screen-printed cottons and blends;
machine pieced and quilted;
74 x 66 inches (188 x 168 cm).

*I like to have my photographic images made into halftones
before I print them because it alters the viewer's perception,
making the line between appearance and reality a little hazier.*

KATHLEEN LOOMIS

LOUISVILLE, KENTUCKY

Black I

Selvages from commercial and hand-dyed cottons; machine appliquéd and quilted in one step; 42 x 45 inches (107 x 114 cm).

Fabric always speaks to me, but selvages have a lot more to say than most fabrics! My father is a typographer, so type and graphic arts have been an integral part of my personal life as well as my career in journalism and corporate communication. This is one of a series of alphabet quilts focusing on single letters, executed in different techniques, but always revealing their essential form and beauty.

JANE A. SASSAMAN

CHICAGO, ILLINOIS

Vortex

Cotton fabrics; machine
appliquéd; 42 x 45 inches
(107 x 114 cm).

Vortex is a quilt about energy and movement. Here is a metaphoric whirlpool of planetary thought patterns. A powerful undercurrent scoops up almost everything in its path, but at the same time its excessive force spins off new and opposing currents of awareness.

B. J. ADAMS

WASHINGTON, D.C.

Variations on "B"

Acrylic painted canvas embellished with actual items (bows and buttons) and heat-transferred images; machine embroidered; 42 x 42 inches (107 x 107 cm).

Variations on "B" *is the second in a series using the alphabet as the theme and allowing one wall hanging for each letter. Butterflies, bananas, bows, brushes, buttons, and a baseball become the images for "B." The background was first painted and then pieced to receive the embroidered and heat-transferred subjects. A few bows and buttons were added for texture and depth, and the brushes have paint drifting from their bristles. Why not bones, buckles, or bread?*

2003

CONNIE SCHEELE

HOUSTON, TEXAS

Early Autumn

Monoprinted and dye-painted cotton, silk quilting threads; machine pieced and hand quilted; 65 x 47 inches (165 x 119 cm).

For many years my work has been about things in nature: river rocks, grasses, foliage, etc. Instead of piecing the images together, I have been exploring monoprinting to create the images in the fabric. This piece is about walking through the woods in the early autumn.

INGE MARDAL & STEEN HOUGS

CHANTILLY, FRANCE

Moulting

Hand-painted cotton;
machine quilted; 75 x 56
inches (191 x 142 cm).

*Molting in itself is a fascinating process, but the fact that it allows
us to get this close feel and touch of feathers makes it truly amazing.
Finding the feathers in the birds' own environment adds a bit of reality
for bird-watchers. We have tried to reflect this reality in our quilt.*

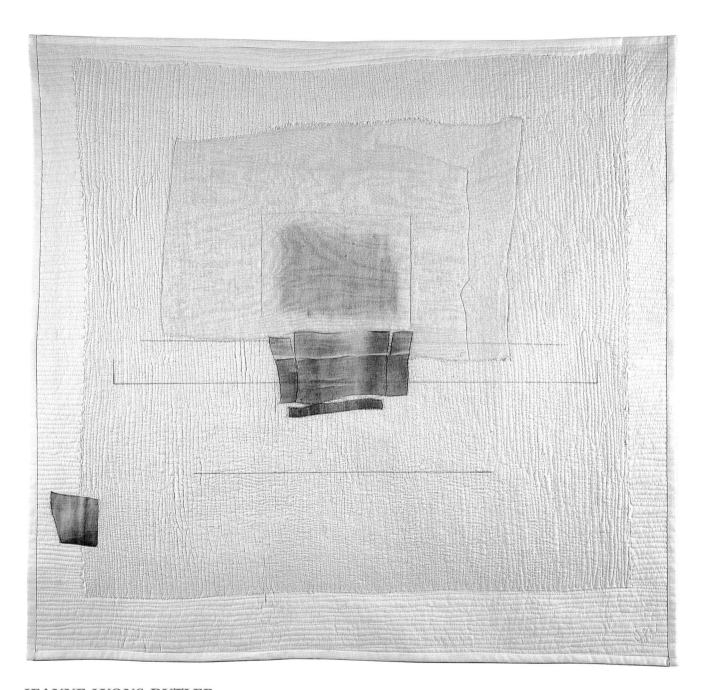

JEANNE LYONS BUTLER

HUNTINGTON, NEW YORK

White #2

Wool, silk, and cotton fabric;
cotton batting, rayon, cotton/
polyester, nylon threads; 42 x 42
inches (107 x 107 cm).

Stimulation comes from a desire for quiet and calm. Looking for peace, blurring the high energy of daily activity, allows me to take control.

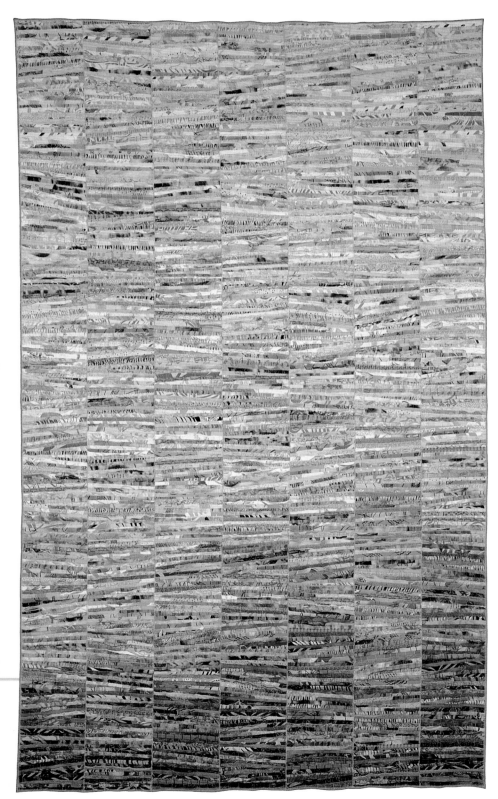

Condobolin is a small town in the center of New South Wales, and I have traveled the beautiful country road from Sydney on many occasions over the years to visit my favorite uncle and aunt. The last couple of trips were tinged with sadness as my uncle was in ill health and died before I could return. This quilt is about my memories of the landscape's colors, and my emotional response to the passing of an era.

JUDY HOOWORTH

TERREY HILLS, NEW SOUTH WALES, AUSTRALIA

Road to Condo #2

Torn and layered cottons stitched to cotton foundation; machine stitched and quilted; 50 x 86 inches (127 x 218 cm).

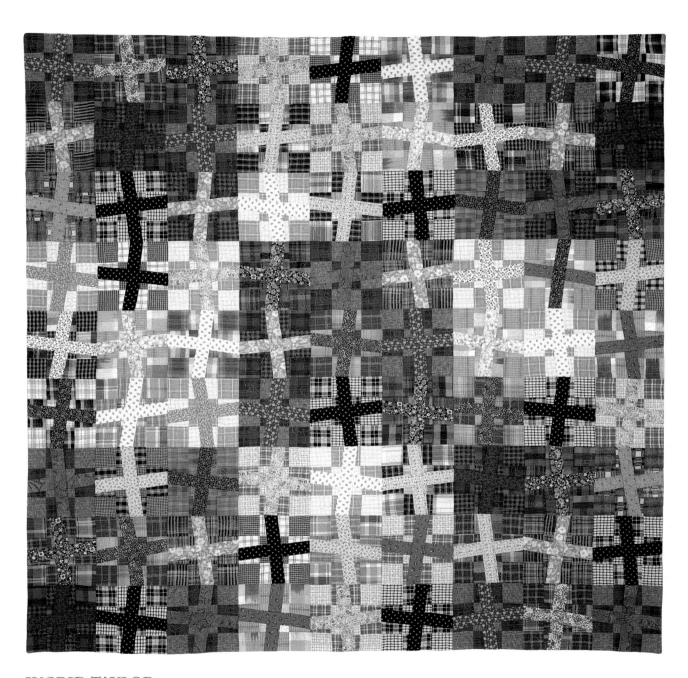

INGRID TAYLOR

FAIRBANKS, ALASKA

Dia de los Muertos

Cotton plaids and calicoes;
machine pieced and quilted;
60 x 60 inches (152 x 152 cm).

*A long-time idea of slicing nine patches and inserting other fabrics
finally came to fruition in this quilt. I was astounded that this simple
approach to piecing could result in such complexity: all colors, old/new,
small/large, traditional/innovative, simple/complex, static/dancing.
The more I looked at the quilt, the more it suggested the joyful approach
some cultures show towards death—the synthesis of life's experiences.*

2003

ANA LISA HEDSTROM

LAHONDA, CALIFORNIA

Riff II

Silk pique, shibori dyed and
discharged; pieced and hand
stitched; 47 x 69 inches
(119 x 175 cm).

*Indigenous American music—blues, bluegrass, folk, and
especially jazz—is often my working companion in the
studio. There is a correlation between the making of music
and the creation of pieced quilts. My dyeing and decision
making are improvisations of color, form and line rhythm,
pauses, repeats, and variations. Riff II is part of a series
dedicated to our inspiring legacy of jazz.*

This quilt series revolves around the family unit. The structure of the family is shaped and molded by life's circumstances, alternately strengthened or weakened by these events.

LORI LUPE PELISH

NISKAYUNA, NEW YORK

Injuries

Commercial cottons; machine appliquéd, embroidered, and quilted; 35 x 57 inches (89 x 145 cm).

493

2003

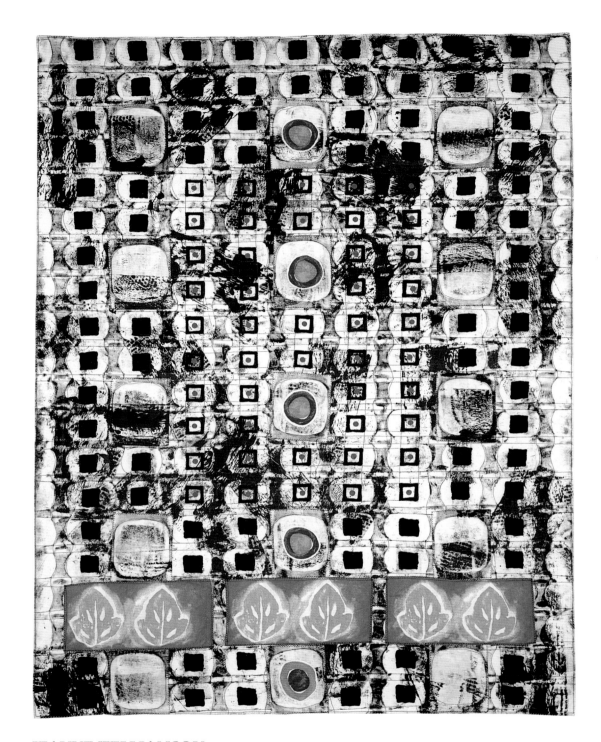

JEANNE WILLIAMSON

NATICK, MASSACHUSETTS

Orange Construction Fence Series #6

100 percent cotton fabric, fabric paint, monoprinted textures of construction fences, hand stamped with rubber erasers; machine appliquéd and quilted; 31 x 40 inches (79 x 102 cm).

My work incorporates scrap fabric, hand-stamped shapes used to form collages, and the hand-printed textures of the orange construction fences that seem to surround construction sites these days. I am working to combine the grids of the construction fence with other building textures and repeats, or with nature that grows around the construction.

NELDA WARKENTIN

ANCHORAGE, ALASKA

Tropical Dream

Multiple layers of painted silk
organza on a quilted cotton and
linen base; machine pieced and
quilted; 48 x 60 (122 x 152 cm).

*This quilt brings the viewer to the memory of a favorite time and
place, easily moving them into a dream of visiting warm, carefree,
tropical days that are waiting just beyond the horizon. Letting
your mind bring you to a sense of serenity can feel so good.*

ALISON F. WHITTEMORE

SAN ANTONIO, TEXAS

Funny Looking Kid (FLK)

100 percent cotton embellished with a gridded photograph drawn one square at a time; machine quilted; 37 x 52 inches (94 x 132 cm).

I was a very young child, having my yearly school physical, and I saw the doctor write the initials F.L.K. in the margin of my medical chart. Many years later, I discovered that F.L.K. stood for Funny Looking Kid, a term given to perfectly healthy, normal children who look and act—well—funny. The image on the quilt is from a first-grade picture, taken right before it dawned on me just how funny looking I was.

CAMILLA BRENT PEARCE

PITTSBURGH, PENNSYLVANIA

Lefferts Avenue Kuba I

Found fabrics; 9 x 12 inches (23 x 30 cm).

In making Lefferts Avenue Kuba I, *I was influenced by the African textiles that I saw frequently in my Brooklyn neighborhood. I wanted the formal challenge of juxtaposing the graphic quality of Kuba cloth with traditional American quilt patterns.*

NANCY N. ERICKSON

MISSOULA, MONTANA

Felis Forever (1)

Velvet, satin, cotton, felt (filler)
fabric paints, oil paintsticks;
machine stitched and appliquéd;
69 x 39 inches (175 x 99 cm).

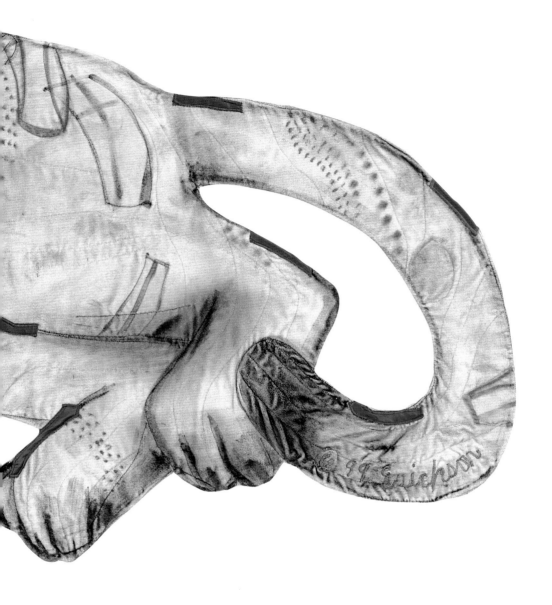

In the mid 1990s I worked on quilted pieces that showed bears in caverns or in rooms formerly occupied by humans and covered with cave drawings of early animals. The bears wander through these environments, teaching their cubs about history. In this new series, Felis..., the ancient history is imprinted on the cougars; the cougars are freed of caves and rooms, and they move freely on the wall.

ELLEN OPPENHEIMER

OAKLAND, CALIFORNIA

PW Block 4

Silk-screened dyes and inks
on cotton; machine sewn,
machine quilted; 66 x 66
inches (168 x 168 cm).

I have been working on this Block series for several years. They are composed of a series of 7 3/4-inch (19.7 cm) square blocks that are created by printing different patterns in both dyes and inks on fabric. I first draw the patterns on the computer, and then use the computer drawings to make photo emulsion silk-screens. There are many inconsistencies in the process and I am always surprised by the results.

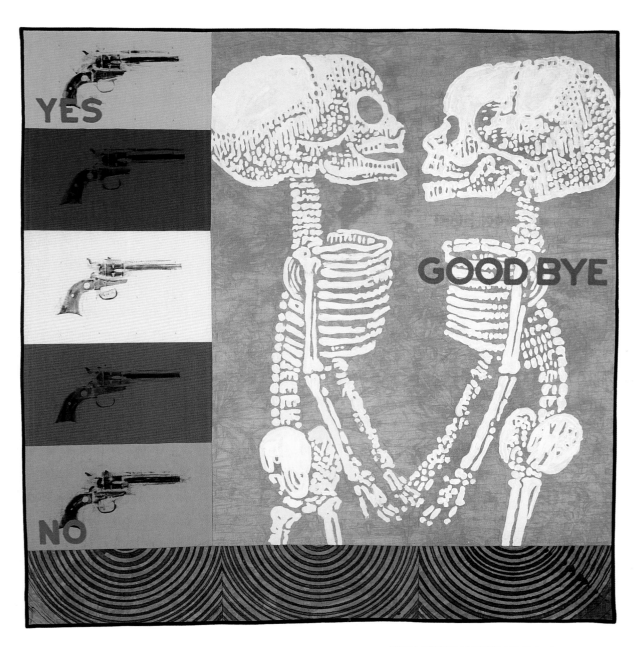

CREAM (CATHY RASMUSSEN EMERGING ARTIST MEMORIAL) AWARD
SPONSORED BY STUDIO ART QUILT ASSOCIATES

2003

BEAN GILSDORF

PORTLAND, OREGON

Ouija #1

Hand-dyed and commercial cotton fabrics, dyed, monoprinted, painted, and relief printed by the artist; machine pieced, appliquéd, quilted, and tied; 47 x 50 inches (119 x 127 cm).

Skeletons typically signify death, but for me they represent the essence of humanity. The visual elements in this quilt evolved from my fear and rage about violent events in my personal history and in American culture. While working on this quilt, I explored ideas about fate and precognition, using text from a Ouija board to evoke the indiscriminate nature of violence. This quilt is a warning, an amulet, and a private memorial.

about the
DAIRY BARN

THE DAIRY BARN Southeastern Ohio Cultural Arts Center is a unique arts facility in the Appalachian foothills. Its year-round calendar of events features both juried and curated exhibitions of work by regional, national, and international artists. In addition, the facility is the venue for festivals, performances, and a full range of classes for children and adults.

The history of the Dairy Barn is as colorful as its exhibits. Built in 1913, the structure housed an active dairy herd until the late 1960s. After sitting idle about 10 years, the building was scheduled for demolition. Fortunately, local artist Harriet Anderson and her husband, Ora, recognized the building's potential as a much-needed regional arts center. They worked tirelessly to rally community support to save the dilapidated structure. With only nine days to spare, the demolition order was reversed, and the building was placed on the National Register of Historic Places. The Dairy Barn Southeastern Ohio Cultural Arts Center, a nonprofit organization, was born.

The architects retained the original character of the building through several renovation projects as it evolved from a seasonal, makeshift exhibit space into a first-class, fully accessible arts facility. Early 2001 saw the completion of a one million dollar renovation project. The ground level now houses a 6,600-square-foot exhibition space and a 400-square-foot retail gift shop that features work by regional and exhibiting artists. The formerly unused 7,000-square-foot upper-level haymow now includes two large classroom spaces; three large multipurpose rooms suitable for classes, performances, and special events; offices for the staff; and storage space.

The Dairy Barn is supported by admissions, memberships, corporate sponsorships, grants, and donations. The staff is assisted by a large corps of volunteers who annually donate thousands of hours of time and talent. For a calendar of events and information about other Dairy Barn programs, contact the Dairy Barn Cultural Arts Center, P.O. Box 747, Athens, Ohio 45701, USA; phone, 740-592-4981; or visit the Internet at www.dairybarn.org.

artist's INDEX